EMBARRASS MY DOG

Borgo Press Books by DAMIEN BRODERICK

Chained to the Alien: The Best of ASFR: Australian SF Review (Second Series) [Editor]

Climbing Mount Implausible: The Evolution of a Science Fiction Writer

Embarrass My Dog: The Way We Were, the Things We Thought

Ferocious Minds: Polymathy and the New Enlightenment

Human's Burden (with Rory Barnes)

I'm Dying Here (with Rory Barnes)

Skiffy and Mimesis: More Best of ASFR: Australian SF Review (Second Series) [Editor]

Unleashing the Strange: Twenty-First Century Science Fiction Literature

Warriors of the Tao [Editor with Van Ikin]

x, y, z, t: Dimensions of Science Fiction

EMBARRASS MY DOG

THE WAY WE WERE, THE THINGS WE THOUGHT

DAMIEN BRODERICK

THE BORGO PRESS

MMXI

EMBARRASS MY DOG

FIRST EDITION

Published by Wildside Press LLC

www.wildsidebooks.com

DEDICATION

To the memory of *MAN* editor, **Fred C. Folkard**,
who bought my first paid story

And for his successor, **Ray Hall**,
who got me started in the magazine pundit business

"...they talk of hallowed things, aloud,
and *embarrass my dog*."

Emily Dickinson

CONTENTS

PART FOUR: POLITICS

PART FIVE: WEIRD SHIT

PART SIX: LIFE BEFORE WIKI

INTRODUCTION

"The past is a foreign country: they do things differently there." In grim postwar 1953, L. P. Hartley wrote that opening to *The Go-Between,* set in the golden summer dawn of the twentieth century. But the future, too, is a foreign country where they do things even more differently. Yet here's the weirdness: once you reach a certain age (after you turn thirty, perhaps), the present turns into the future, decade by decade growing ever stranger and more dislocating.

For many of us, at least in some moods, the true present is always those years when we were in our late teens or twenties. So this *now* we find ourselves stranded in cannot be, not completely, the vibrant, confident present. It really is already the future, where they take for granted some things we always imagined happening two or fifty or 100 years from today, way off in tomorrowland.

And yet the frustration of the thing is that quite often we find ourselves stuck in the *wrong* future. Wasn't that meant to be a time and place where <*fill in the blank*>?

Sometimes the tomorrowland <*blank*> contained images from old comic books or TV cartoons: flying cars or instantaneous matter transmitters, limitless cheap "atomic power," domes on the moon, invisible force fields that would protect vulnerable cities from H-bomb devastation, aliens from the stars.

Sometimes it stood for simpler dreams familiar to nearly everyone: a loving partner, a satisfying and remunerative job, the company of friends, perhaps children and the comfort of faith, all of it adding up to a blend of excitement and contentment—in a word, to happiness.

What the <blank> didn't contain, for most of us, even the science fiction dreamers, was a Moon abandoned 40 years in the past even as we harvested close-up pictures from the far reaches of the solar system, even as planets were found around hundreds of nearby stars. Computers not only on every desk but inside every portable telephone—a telephone that contacts other phones instantly almost anywhere in the world, and sends text, photos and videos (a feature of comic strip detective Dick Tracy's "2-Way Wrist TV" but now commonplace, as handy for thieves and drug dealers as for business execs and swarming fellatio-habituated schoolkids). Legal homosexual weddings, and a black US president, and new or resurgent infections, and seventy-year-old rock stars, and no Soviet Union, just an amorphous toxic cloud of international religious fundamentalist terrorists....

§

But first I need to insert a sort of heads-up alert for American readers about how these fragments from the time machine must be read: as a variant take on the familiar, a sort of not-quite-exact parallel universe (a charming one, I hope). I am an Australian now living in the USA, but most of these pieces were written in my home country where, of course, they have always done things slightly differently. And that means differently from the way they've been done (during any given period) in Britain as well as the USA, Canada, Japan, India, China, Russia, the nations of Africa.... Far more differently in the latter five cases, obviously, but significantly skewed from the great metropolitan centers of the West. It's complicated. Aussies play a different kind of football, and enjoy cricket (which endears them to Brits and Indians, but not to baseball-loving Americans) but listen to and perform rock and rap, and provide film actors of immense talent—who quickly switch their accents when they hit Hollywood…. So this world I'm reviving isn't just the past, it's not just *like* another country, it *is* another country. Yesterday Through the Looking Glass.

§

My mother's father (the grandfather I knew, and lived with on and off for some years) was twenty-four when the First World War broke out. An Australian from a country town, he enlisted in the mounted cavalry with his twin brother and fought in Europe, ending up as a machine gun instructor. My father was twenty-three at the start of the Second World War, and he engaged in hostilities from a distance, as a "reserved occupation" expert machinist making armament equipment. I was twenty when Australia introduced military conscription, against widespread protest, and twenty-one when the Prime Minister sent an infantry battalion into Vietnam. I was not called up, and most of my student friends were spared by the tumble of the conscription lottery. Of those conscripts who served, 1.3% were killed, and one in twelve was wounded.

This recurrence of deadly international violence during the early twenties of three generations of my family is a simple reflection of the history of the twentieth century. If I'd had a son in 1970, he'd have been twenty-one when the first Gulf War ("Operation Desert Storm") broke out, but the Australian troops who obediently trooped off to serve alongside American forces were spared combat roles. In 2003, when an Aussie contingent fought in the second invasion of Iraq, my hypothetical offspring would have been thirty-three, and perhaps by then himself the father of a young child—who would therefore be, as I write, just now entering adolescence. If the past repeats itself (a foreign country that does things differently while continuing to do the same thing at regular intervals), my imaginary grandchild is scheduled to enter his or her twenties just in time for the next big blow-up in, say, 2017.... A dismaying prospect.

§

Yet a key factor that we are almost unable to appreciate viscerally is how different the face of that recurrence will look. A friend who worked for many years as a spacecraft controls engineer for a major US military contractor commented to me recently: "Consider the great difference in the way your grandfather fought in WWI compared to today's soldiers and tomorrow's. These future (and present day) conflicts will likely mostly be fought by soldiers sitting in an office building in Nevada, controlling drones that will each drop exactly one super highly accurate guided bomb, which will carry only a very small explosive charge approximately equal to a single hand grenade, designed to destroy not personnel but rather the engine of war that is its mechanical target, making war far safer for both allies and enemies. We have really succeeded in tuning up our ability to fly unmanned into enemy airspace at night, drop one small bomb, have it penetrate a target building with a few hundred grams of pyrotechnics, then watch as that building explodes a few seconds later in a mysteriously violent blast."

So the future will be *foreign,* no matter how deeply embedded in our genes are the drives that manifest themselves century after century in human action. Maybe we can get a better grip on the Tweeting, Facebook'd, Googled, Palinized present and the uncanny future, with its mix of monkey antics and science fictional improbabilities, by vacationing for an hour or two in the not so long ago pre-Internet past, when today's elderly were fresh, naïve, hopeful, angry, curious, sexually adventurous amid the stifling fumes of Hays Office decorous pieties, out to remake the stuffy world of their own elders, fuming with piss and vinegar.

§

When does the shift of perspective happen? It's a subtle thing, and creeps up on you. I'm not talking about the clichéd "midlife crisis," if we take forty to be the fabled date for doubt and uncertainty and a frantic search for the last evidence of lost youth. This effect kicks in sooner than that. The change I'm tracking is more like the jolt when suddenly the music you love, the melodies and beat and lyrics that seized your attention at puberty and later teens, is gone, replaced by something alien and probably abominable to your ears. It could be the replacement by rocking Elvis of 1940s' and 1950s' jazz or soupy soapy romance ballads, or the appearance of the Beatles in the early '60s ("the fetal Beatles" as folk singers Peter, Paul and Mary called them contemptuously, and then vanished under their tidal wave, even as the Fab Four remade themselves again and again in a genius surge of innovation), or the sickening/fun move from heavy metal to 1970s' disco and bubblegum and Abba, or their evaporation under the onslaught of punk, and then the rise of hip hop rap with its discovery that you could get a lot of mileage out of just two notes, maybe three if your vocal range was ambitious, and a chanted frenetic angry street poetry of violence and misogyny (or so it seemed to those for whom the bell had just tolled)....

These jumps are mini-epochal cruxes when the flowing present abruptly stopped (for someone) and the future was arrested forever into an eternal watermarked "present" against which everything thereafter is measured, and usually found wanting.

So it's not just a matter of generations. These days the jolt comes very much faster than that. Still, the twenty-five-to-thirty-year ticking of the generational clock does seem to mark the biggest jumps, those moments when the present is glued shut and everyone younger, looking back at it a decade or two later from the outside, is struck into embarrassment and a kind of sickened grimace. "Eeewwww," as the kids were saying a few months or years ago, "gross! You liked *that?* You thought *that?* OMG!"

§

The great American poet Emily Dickinson caught it exactly, although in a rather different context, in a letter to a distant adviser:

"...they talk of hallowed things, aloud, and embarrass my dog."

She added: "He and I don't object to them, if they'll exist their side."

Exist their side, and leave her in peace, she meant. Well, that's not how generations operate now: their worlds interpenetrate, however compartmentalized by fashion and demographics and faith and race or ethnos, each marked by a different on-going present and future. And the composite pumped-up noise of the world trivializes all of these different hallowed things into blur and jump cuts and tweets, embarrassing the dog. The dog averts his gaze and growls. So this book is an attempt to soothe the dog even as we embarrass him with glimpses of a lost world, to display (and reflect upon, sometimes with rueful hindsight) several moments when the future became the present, and then the present left that future behind. But not without some torsion, not without a trace, not without regret and sometimes bitterness or, more often, I hope, simple disbelieving laughter.

§

Most of the essays and articles gathered here were published between 1967 and 1974, and written a little time earlier, so that their writer was aged twenty-two or twenty-three through thirty. A few come from later decades, and show how different times bring change to the same questing mind—but sometimes, admittedly, how markets ranging from men's magazines to literary journals focused that mind in a variety of directions. I hope it provides a glimpse of a Zeitgeist, as well as a time slice through the worldview of one rather eccentric traveler through the 1960s and 1970s, and beyond. I know it is sure to embarrass the dog, and probably the reader, but that's the price of admission to the past, where they did things differently.

You'll find that the pieces are bunched into those categories usually held to be beyond the bounds of polite conversation: Sex, Politics and Religion, of course, but also Drugs and a few items candidly declared to be (in a recycling of a series I wrote in the late 1970s for the Australian alternative newspaper *Nation Review*) Weird Shit. If you wonder how I can write about those turbulent times without mentioning that other partner of Sex and Drugs, namely Rock 'n' Roll, it's not because I wasn't there.

In February 1966, two Monash University friends started my nation's first pop music periodical, *Go-Set*, which beat the fabled US *Crawdaddy* into print by about five days. I chose not to get involved, fool that I was (the founding editors did rather well for themselves), but the following year I was enticed back from Sydney, where I was freelancing, to write about music and teen lifestyles. What I knew about these topics was scant (I fancied myself a young intellectual, not a clubber), and my weekly outpourings were usually cribbed from copies of *New Musical Express* and *Melody Maker,* airlifted from London. At the end of the Seventies, I condensed this borrowed wisdom into a rapture for a time that was already gone, as I observed with sardonic overkill. Later I recycled this paean and indictment into a novel, but here it is, in its mock-lyric brevity, to stand in for the absent section on Rock 'n' Roll:

DECEMBER ELEVENTH NINETEEN EIGHTY

The 1960s died on the 11th day of the twelfth month of 1980 when, outside his New York home, five bullets were pumped into the body of John Lennon by the music critic Ronald Reagan, who was later released after questioning by police.

The 1970s died much earlier, on the 19th day of the eighth month of 1969 when half a million children pitched their sad loony tents in a field outside

Woodstock, in upstate New York. A recorded interview was later released to the media.

It was the worst of times, it was the worst of times. Picture a skinhead bootboy with razorblades at his toes and safety pins through the flesh of his cheeks, stamping on his own face forever.

No. Picture four scrubbed and patched middleaged Swedes rampant on a field of armwaving eight year olds argent, droning the theme of the decade: "Money money money."

No no no. Picture Linda Ronstadt and Governor Jerry Brown on undecorated sheets in a single bed, Olivia Newton-John and John Travolta flicking and sliding in the mirror above their heads on squares of pure light.

No. Alice Cooper eating a live chicken. The Kiss in their six year old fantasy greasepaint and ten thousand decibels. Sid Vicious in spoiled brat psychopathic rage working out the punk dreams of his generation in the murdered flesh of a convenient woman.

The Seventies was waking into the hungover spoils of the party. Everyone had died during the night.

Jim Morrison was dead in whiskey, caught by the snake.

Hendrix was dead, all his flashing crying chords jangled.

Joplin was dead, swallowed up and chewed into lard and blood.

Presley was dead, fat and banal, in alcohol and spangled spansules.

Marc Bolan was dead, gnawed by Tyrannosaur's jaws.

The Beatles were dead, John by an assassin's gun, Paul (to all intents and purposes) by his own hand.

Abba were born dead.

Disco was a corpse plugged into a defibrillator.

Like old pre-industrial gods, the remnants of the pantheon took themselves into eclipse and changed their wigs, were reborn, shook it again in the video clips: David Bowie falling in endless rebirth, Lou Reed transformed, Carly Simon, Bruce Springsteen, Jackson Brown; Heavy Metal clashing by night, Tangerine Dreaming their remote electronic buzz; and Dylan was Born Again.

Robert Zimmerman was Born Again.

The music of the Seventies was a pike gaffed into the belly of the Eighties.

Man, I had *no* idea what was burning toward us in the next thirty years....

§

Here's how these pieces came to be written: on-the-fly, mostly for desperately needed immediate money—but I didn't regard them as mere hack work. I put my back into these articles, so it is not entirely implausible that they captured and retain some concentrate of their time. That epoch is now long past, and nothing like it will ever return, not exactly, anyway. When we were in our twenties, long hair blowing in the breeze, we laughed at the inevitable prospect of the future. Our children, we told each other ruefully, would wear business suits and brutal haircuts, carry executive briefcases, and work as lawyers or accountants. Strange visions! But for all our laidback utopianism, we knew at least that time brings change. As it happens, I now find myself married to an intelligent, self-directed woman who is both a tax lawyer and accountant—and a permaculture farmer, when she has the time. So that element of the counterculture persists, as does her kickass attitude (and mine) to the viciousness and stupidity of wrongfully directed authority.

In a rational world, at around the time I started writing these pieces I would've been immersed in a philosophy doctorate.

By now, I assume, I'd be an emeritus professor, although probably not at any of the grander universities. (In fact, I have the privilege of being a Senior Fellow in the School of Culture & Communication at the University of Melbourne, although I reside half a planet away from Australia, in Texas, the republic I dreamed of as a child devoted to cowboy movies.) In a more malign world than this, I would instead have recently retired from some dire factory, or perhaps be working in the fields, scrambling along half-starved behind a gaunt animal. Another reality that never happened would have seen me a priest in the Catholic Church, a prospect I embraced when I entered a seminary at the age of 15, and put behind me, thank God, two years later.

A series of unfortunate events turned me into an eclectic gadfly excessively interested in almost everything except my scholarship-funded studies. So at nineteen and twenty, I started to eke out a frugal living writing for popular magazines of a kind that don't exist any longer—intended for family reading— or the limpest of soft porn tits&ass men's monthlies. Some years later, I briefly served as editor of one of these, *MAN*, a periodical aimed at working men and boys, sometimes found in doctor's waiting rooms, more often in a metal locker. I kept the job for a little over five months. Prior to that, though, I had been dashing off unambitious short stories for *MAN* and its competitors; during an upgrade meant to combat more sophisticated, explicit product from the USA (*Playboy, Penthouse*, in the 1960s frequently banned in Australia), I was invited to adopt the role of a kind of youthful pundit, providing fodder for a new feature, "Men at Arms."

My first foray was the article that opens this book, "The Moral Revolution," which took the deliberately confrontational line that sex—or at least slavering and anxiety about sex—was overrated. This piece of one man think-tankery was followed by others on numerous topics: environmental degradation and the impending greenhouse effect (not yet something widely discussed in the late 1960s), the rise of the drug culture, the war in Vietnam that even then was hotting up. Eventually, to my great surprise, I managed to smuggle in thoughtful accounts of the radical thinkers Herbert Marcuse and Arthur Koester, although my attempt to insinuate a piece on the scarifying anti-psychiatrist R. D. Laing met a scowl and the rejection notice.

Later, I wrote for more serious journals, and a few of those later pieces are here as well (including one from an important recent anthology on atheism). At the same time, I was selling novels in Australia and the United States. I went back to university in my early forties (a sort of midlife crisis choice, no doubt, but shaped by the wish to delve into the mysteries of Derridean deconstruction and the social studies of science, in a delayed PhD dissertation). Those early articles embarrass not only my dog but me as well. They are desperately naïve in many ways, the work of a young man in a world swept by drastic change. But now they are a kind of time capsule, a means by which older readers may revisit their youth and wonder where it went and how we got here from there, while younger readers (I hope) can regard with astonishment the way we were, and the things we thought, back there in that foreign country with borders that have been closed and locked for decades.

PART ONE: SEX

THE MORAL REVOLUTION
(1967)

Let's stop getting hung up about sex.

It's really all very simple. Really. That's why it's so amazing and curious and bizarre and ultimately heart-breaking to find so many people so worked up about the whole thing.

And let us also forget the Sexual Revolution. There hasn't been one, neither are we in the midst of one. There probably will be a Sexual Revolution—that is, a major and radical dislocation in patterns of society's sexual behavior—in, say, twenty or thirty years time.

If it comes, it'll be a humdinger.

Have you heard the term "host mother"? That's a woman who, for a fee, carries another woman's fetus to term and gives birth to the child. A boon to the career-woman, the artist, the frail, the lazy.... It isn't possible yet, but only because of certain relatively minor immunological unknowns. At a rough guess, scientists will have the techniques before man sets foot on the cratered face of Mars.

Sexual Revolution? Have you read yet of ecto-uterine parthenogenesis? Clumsy words, but the concept they represent is supremely clear to medical researchers. Take a sperm, or an ovum; carefully divide the cell you have chosen. Under certain specific conditions, reunite the halves and place in an artificial womb. The doctored germ plasm will grow: sperm will produce a boy-baby, ova a girl.... No fantasy this. It has already been done with rabbits and dogs. Try this: half of one man's sperm plus half that of another man equals a son or daughter. Two married homosexuals could mutually produce and raise, in a household of the future, a family of their very own...

Revolution in sexual behavior? Do the words "genetic engineering" mean anything to you? They surely will before this millennium has run its course. Pick and choose the characteristics you desire in a human being. Design, according to the rigid specifications governing nucleic acid formation, a DNA molecule that will produce the living being of your choice. Nurture with love and care for nine months and you have: a superman; or a fabulous beauty; or a mindless, competent, endlessly happy drudge... Utterly impossible at the moment. But in the year 2000?

These are the stark bones of a possible tomorrow. They spell Sexual Revolution. And they need not concern us here.

What is of contemporary interest is nothing so strange, so frightening as that. And yet, the revolution of the moment is in its own way as fantastic as anything I have yet mentioned.

It is a revolution of ease, of security, and ultimately of moral attitudes.

If we must give it a name, let us call it the Moral Revolution.

§

"That moral attitudes may be changing is a fair observation," says Dr. Alex Comfort in his excellent study *Sex in Society,* "though in all such cases the change in behavior is probably far less than the change in pretensions. Much of the 'immorality' which convulses the traditionalists is in fact a gain in candor and an increased willingness to speak up for our real standards."

Enormous difficulty faces even dispassionate observers in measuring accurately what is changing and to what degree. Clearly, the last several decades have been notable for a growing frankness concerning the realities of sexual behavior. The West's incredible sexual inconsistencies—with widespread avowal of strict repressive morality and almost equally widespread disregard of that morality in practice—are gradually breaking up. (The rather breathtaking oversimplification of that last remark, of course, glosses over one hell of a lot. It much too neatly dishes together millions of human beings divided by money, social class, religious background, race, education, continental and local history... But it's the generalization closest to the facts.)

Roughly speaking, the vast majority of people are probably doing what their class (inherited or adopted) has always done—except that they're being less dishonest about it.

There has always been a percentage of the population anxious to boast of lurid, improbable (and generally imaginary) sexual adventures. I am not here concerned with that kind of neurotic bombast. Despite our culture's unfortunate super-sensitivity to sex, exploited in advertising and sermons both, that percentage is unlikely to have increased. If there is more candid admission of "sexual immorality," this is because fewer people feel any great urgency to hide the truth about their sexual behavior.

Undeniably, this new outspokenness is more a matter of indifference than a response to some noble spirit of honesty. Equally, it doesn't herald in an era of joyous, bouncy, anything goes, slap-n-tickle-in-the-street libertarianism. The bounds of decency are ominous as ever, even if they've shifted a little. Bluntly, doing it at a drive-in may require more ingenuity than doing it under a lemon tree, and there's less social pressure to deny doing it, but what's done remains pretty much the same. The sexual repertoire of most in the West is still astonishingly meager—even though bookshops sell, quite legally, volumes of Hindu temple art which demonstrate something closer to the full range of erotic possibilities.

The line, in other words, has been redrawn; but we must still toe it. It is now widely permissible to discuss illegitimacy, or the fact that Kinsey forcefully indicates that thirty-seven percent of males have adult homosexual experiences. But seriously suggest that a man may be a bastard or that he may belong to that one-third, and you're as likely as ever to get punched up the throat.

What has happened, on the whole, seems plain. All the factors of social change issuing from fifty years of World Wars, Cold War and technological explosion—adolescent prosperity and autonomy, female emancipation, decline of religion, and so on—have had their effect on sex. But the effect has not been a change in practice, except on the verbal level. Rather, the sturdy hypocrisy embedded in our traditional (and unworkable) morality seems slowly to be flaking away. It has by no means gone completely—we still suffer the absurdity of a flock of coy newspapers that provide a *potpourri* of inferior pornography, inflated rape-and-violence reporting, and pious mid-Victorian warnings about the fate worse than death. Absurdities always linger in the wake of defunct doctrines: nobody, thank God, believes any more that masturbation causes pimples, insanity and early death, and the same 99.9 percent who have always engaged in the practice can do so now with only residual terror or guilt; yet how many would publicly admit to masturbating?

As the wit said, the reason why sex-scenes on the silver screen are wicked is not because they excite the audience—but because the actors have to do it with the light on.

The major negative achievement of Western civilization, then, to paraphrase Dr. Comfort, has been to make a *problem* out of sex. "Our real need," he suggests, "is for a mentality in which the word 'problem' is banished permanently in favor of 'enjoyment'." Christianity, for so long the accepted formulator of Western moral principles, is manifestly ill-fitted to the task of producing a sane code of conduct in a field as dynamic and *earthy* as sexuality.

It might be argued that this baldly avoids those Christian writers who have tackled sexual morality in an intelligent and liberal fashion. But the sad and painful fact is that such teachers until very recently have had small influence indeed. We are concerned with the *dominant* Christian sexual ethic, and that has been (as recent Christian theologians have realized) appallingly and insistently disordered.

§

The sour tradition of Western sexual morality stems from St. Paul and St. Augustine. I could quote instances of Augustine's writings on sex that would make your hair stand on end. However, lest anyone complain that this frightening orthodoxy is long dead, I will present instead a recent illustration. Last year, the Reverend Gordon Powell published an address titled "The Case for Chastity" in an official Methodist magazine.

"The so-called 'New Morality'," he wrote, "...is ardently promoted by those who have abandoned Christian standards.... They are all too willing to drag others down to their so-called 'sophisticated' level. Similar motives lie behind some of those who fight so hard in these days against censorship. They say, 'It's bad to suppress sex. You only force it underground and make things so much worse. We should be adult and face the facts of life.' Yes, a decomposed dead dog in a back alley is a fact of life but you don't haul it into the sitting room. The other day some cement broke away from the top of a main sewer near our home. The stench was appalling and I imagine the threat to life was considerable. We don't say 'Take the lid off sewage and bring it to light. It doesn't matter if some children fall into it or a few people contract disease.' No, we keep it in its proper place. We cover it up and get rid of it as soon as we can."

Very many people, unfortunately, do cover it up and get rid of it as soon as possible. A great many others, though, are more prepared to uncover the whole supposedly dirty business and actually enjoy it, even if the rejection of Powell type attitudes is more often from indifference than disgust, more often from sheer healthy reflex than rational repudiation.

One cannot, of course, fix upon a mythical ogre "Christianity" and blame it for the underground status of a major part of Western sexual behavior. Religion is and has been as much a product of the total culture as culture has of religion. Surprisingly enough, the long medieval period of Church domination in Europe was astonishingly well sexually-integrated. Even a cursory examination of Chaucer, Boccaccio or a score of others shows how well the medieval Church accommodated the wide variety of human sexual needs.

For those people lived a Christianity which sanely and pragmatically understood the drives and requirements of sexual creatures. The ribaldry of their writers—to us pornography which is barely saved by its "literary merit," and that only recently—was for them a condiment (to borrow a famous analogy) rather than, as for so many of us, a diet.

Contemporary Christianity is gradually finding a sane moral voice, or at least one which does not preach unequivocal nonsense. The controversial publication of Bishop John A. T. Robinson's *Honest to God* (1963) was at least a step away from blatantly legalistic morality. Throwing aside metaphysical simplifications that have historically paralyzed Christian morality in the face of the rich complexities of humankind, he cautiously supported the New Morality.

"Nothing can of itself always be labeled as 'wrong'," he asserted. "One cannot, for instance, start from the position 'sex relations before marriage' or 'divorce' are wrong or sinful in themselves." Robinson seemed to lose his nerve momentarily, continuing: "They may be in 99 cases or even 100 cases out of 100." Nevertheless, he concluded importantly: "But they are not intrinsically so, for the only intrinsic evil is lack of love."

More outspoken, an Episcopal minister in the US, Frederic Wood, in his sermon of October, 1964, told the all-women student body at Goucher College: "There are no laws attached to sex. I repeat: *absolutely no laws*. There is nothing which you ought to do, or ought not to do. There are no rules of the game, so to speak... Premarital intercourse can be very beautiful." Closing his sermon, he added, "Well, I have not told you whether you should or you shouldn't—or even how far you should. And the reason is that I cannot. To do so would be to give you a new law, or some kind of new code of behavior."

This, indeed, is the cornerstone of the new evolving Christian doctrine of sexual morality—as, for that matter, it must be in any viable realistic morality. People differ from one another, situations of inter-personal relationship are almost infinitely variegated. As Dr. David Mace, an internationally known marriage expert, said in January this year on ABC radio, the idea that everyone should conform to a uniform standard of sexual behavior must be abandoned. A Christian himself, he accused the Church of mistakenly imposing "its unrealistic concept of sex on entire communities."

"Sexual intercourse," wrote Joseph Fletcher, a noted professor at the Episcopal Theological School in Cambridge, Massachusetts, "is not right or good just because it is legal (by civil or canonical law), nor is it wrong just because it is outside the law... In (the new) kind of Christian ethic the essential ingredients are caring and commitment. Given these factors, the only reason for disapproving sexual relations would be situational, not legal or principled.... There is nothing against extramarital sex as such, in this ethic...."

Situational ethics throws the burden of conduct right back where it belongs—to the people engaged in that conduct. It provides no child-like adherence to Authority; it demands responsible evaluation and responsible decision within a flexible matrix of possible choices. As Dr. Mace said in his radio talk: "Given certain safeguards, people in the future are going to have much more freedom to choose their sexual patterns— and they will make their choices on the basis of how mature they are as persons."

Even Christianity, then, as represented by these spokesmen, is doing something to heal the rupture it has itself done so much to promote between practice and principle. It is, if clumsily, working to forge a morality that is workable, humane and realistic. For the fact is that *traditional "morality" was no morality at all!* Morality is the concern of free, open, responsible human beings. A "morality" which seeks to program people according to a computer-like system of do's and don'ts serves only to morally castrate them.

That is why I call the sexual disruption of our time a "Moral

Revolution." Perhaps for the first time in the history of Western civilization, it is becoming possible to be truly moral sexual beings.

It remains plain enough that these new breed Christian moralists, despite their emancipation from the SEX = CORRUPTION equation, still hesitate. Sex is no longer a disaster, but it is still a "problem."

Equally, despite the refreshing candor typical of contemporary adolescents, the need to maintain a double standard is still urgently felt. In a recent issue of *RAVE*, a British pop-monthly, an article by the drolly-named "Virginia Ironside" began: "Funnily enough, the most dangerous line to use when a boy pounces on you is the traditional method. 'But I'm a *nice* girl,' you are supposed to say, 'I don't *do* that sort of thing.'

"Men's arguments are horribly convincing these days, so if you want to avoid the worst, it's as well to practice some subtler methods...."

Clearly, mass-markets still find it expedient to promote the view about the fate worse than death. In such a climate, as we have seen, sexual conduct remains as rampantly randy as ever. The likelihood of that conduct being integrated into a healthy approach to life, however, is shelled to the ground. In a society sick with frustration and discouragement, boredom and self-contempt, one of our basic paths to mutual enjoyment and growth has been barred and locked.

"Why," asked a doctor, in a recent *Nova* article, "ultimately, do we teach fear so readily, learn it so easily, cling to it so rigidly, yield to it so tragically...why? Why do we fear sex?

"Perhaps because we also fear life and death. Really to love is to be ready for anything: really to be ready for anything is to be finally free of fear."

That's being a bit cute about it, but the core of the matter is there. Fear builds fear—and saps the last deep vestiges of that pool of vitality in us that has not yet been polluted by our poisoned time. Fear convinces people that sex is nasty and revolting—because they find themselves and other people, in their fear, nasty and revolting. (It's no accident that the British, joshing or not, call sex "doing the nasty.") Or it assures them that sex is sacred and sacramental because that is a righteous way of avoiding the boiling multitudinous reality of themselves and the others whom they fear. Or it sends them in feverish and belling pursuit of sex—because that is the easiest method of all (apart from joining a mob and anonymously beating anonymous victims into bloody rags) to disguise and evade the fearful humanity of human persons.

Sexuality, in short, is one of those monumental basic capacities of human experience which our culture, after its abject fashion, has rejected, inflated, deified, demeaned, exploited and distorted. The Moral Revolution, as exemplified in its more sensible and perceptive representatives, is a sign that those wellsprings of vitality can never be entirely drained or contaminated.

The basic tenet of the Moral Revolution, in stark opposition to the prevailing orthodoxy of behavior, is best expressed in the words of its able exponent, Dr. Alex Comfort: That one should not exploit another person's feelings and wantonly expose them to an experience of rejection. In the specifically sexual sphere, it has an urgent corollary: that one should not under any circumstances negligently risk producing an unwanted child. These fundamental propositions require of the people involved the moral consciousness of civilized human beings. For as Dr. Comfort has said (speaking of the results of an American survey of male adolescent sexual behavior), "the depressing thing...is not (the boys') willingness to sleep with school and college friends, or the complete absence of parental supervision or counsel which we sense in the background, *but the aggression, egocentricity, and general lack of concern for the girl as a person which often went with it.*"

The recent development of an oral contraceptive that can be taken *after* intercourse; medical hygiene and control of venereal disease; candor in communication—none of these elements of a stunning and unprecedented sexual liberation will make us freer unless we possess the self-esteem and moral largeness of honest adulthood. James Baldwin has written with a fine contempt of those who have "opted for the one commodity which is absolutely beyond human reach: safety." And he continues, "This is one of the reasons, as it seems to me, that we are so badly educated, for to become educated (as all tyrants have always known) is to become inaccessibly independent, it is to acquire a dangerous way of assessing danger, and it is to hold in one's hands a means of changing reality."

So let's quit talking about sex. It's really all very simple. As simple as growing up and knowing that the world is people, and that sex is just another kind of intercourse between us.

THE Y FACTOR (1973)

"Look," I told her, "enough's enough." I rolled over and gave my impression of a man sleeping the dead-log sleep of the righteous. It was a mistake. My lover instantly cuddled up into the middle of the bed, which left me uncomfortably close to the edge. I may be unusually thin but I'm also over six feet tall, and I like to hang my legs across the bed. Besides, the damned woman refused to keep her hands to herself.

"It's like eating rum cake," I explained patiently. "Too much too quickly ruins the appetite."

"I can't hear you," she said.

I took my face out of the pillow.

"It's been a groovy day," I told her, and meant it, but a yawn muffled the ringing tone of truth. "For God's sake, woman, we've been up for twenty hours. We've done it on the carpet, we've done it on the grass with the sun and the birds and the insects and probably the neighbors, and we've done it standing up in the shower. Go to sleep."

She gave me a hug and said nothing.

But she still wouldn't keep her hands to herself; "It's getting longer," she observed.

"I know."

"It's beautiful," she said, stroking. "It's longer than any other man's I've ever seen."

"Oh, come on," I said. "There must be at least one or two—"

"Well, maybe, but it's in better shape."

"You don't wish it was more sort of, uh, the *usual* length?"

"Christ no!" she cried, and gave it a sharp tug. "I know there are a lot of envious bastards try to say girls like it shorter but they're up themselves." She's a liberated woman, my friend, and doesn't mince words.

"Frankly," I told her, "it's a damned nuisance at times. I mean, it must be a foot and half long and—"

"Longer!" she said, stroking.

"Hell, what's a couple of inches between friends? The point is, you keep leaning on it when I'm asleep. Frankly, I'm thinking of having a foot of it off if I can find anyone who can do it without making a botch of it."

She was horrified by the idea so I didn't press the matter. But by that time I wasn't tired any more, and we fell to with lusty cries.

Now since this is a candid, truthful article, I have to admit that I haven't taken the big step yet. You might think it's a fairly clear-cut situation, but there's more involved than you'd suppose. Think of it at one level as a matter of principle—which is not as absurd as it sounds. There's the fact that I *like* it the way it is. I'm accustomed to it being that long, and I think it suits me.

And my friend is dead right—it turns women on. It makes them look again, I can tell you, and it brings out the old stroking instinct.. You tend to take it for granted and then some beautiful girl at a party starts fondling it, and you tell yourself it's a better hook-and-sinker than the Alfas the other poor bastards are slaving their guts out to pay off.

On the other hand, in the face of all these manifest heterosexual advantages, there's always the hysterical clown in the crowd who decides long hair means you're a fairy—and if there's one thing in this world he wants to beat the bejesus out of, it's a bloody long-hair poofter.

Maybe a few guys reading this feel the same way themselves—in which cases they've probably already thrown the magazine down with an oath of disgust. It's pretty strange. On the other hand, it's fairly understandable and, despite a number of paranoid moments when it looked as though a few extra inches of cornified epidermal cells were going to earn me a belting, I don't really believe they're all neurotic bigots.

Basically, of course, the antipathy for longhairs has to do with sex and identity, and the defensive aggression we all display towards anyone conspicuously different from ourselves. By deliberately wearing my hair outrageously long, I'm bringing that reaction down, so to speak, on my own head. I'm not blind to the risk, so any consequences are my own responsibility.

Still; it's worth wondering why hair in particular should arouse so much belligerence... Why it has become the most flagrant symbol of the generation gap, over and above the slow cycles of fashion in all areas of personal presentation.

Other distinctions can have the same effect, of course—skin color, accent, choice of clothes. I've been roasted in pubs for wearing brightly striped trousers, bought off the rack at a city store, and that's essentially no different from the reaction a bloke in pin stripes and bowler would get stepping into a Kalgoorlie pub—or a guy in greasy overalls fronting an Opera House first night.

But any guy as shaggy as I am quickly discovers—and is reminded with tedious, infuriating regularity—that long hair is one of the few single physical distinctions that provoke apoplectic wrath in, say, passing truck drivers.

Not all of them, of course—I've covered too many miles hitchhiking not to know the majority of that tough, earthy breed is more tolerant and downright generous than most people. But I've also been startled more than once by a scream of pure rage over the thunder of a passing semi, and looked up to see the driver hanging out of a half-opened door, face purple, howling back at me that well-known, witty, incisive advice: "GETCHA FUCKIN HAIR CUT!"

§

How come? Part of it's to do with the illegal use by some truckers of amphetamines, gobbled like candy by the end of a grueling run, to keep them going when they're whipped out by fatigue. *Speed* is notoriously paranoia-inducing if taken for long enough, and when you're locked in the cabin of a roaring 40 ton semi with a deadline to beat and the outside world reduced to a welter of cutoff impressions, with the amphetamine poison churning up aimless hostility in your guts, you'll vent it all in a half-crazed outburst on the first target that passes. Like that bloody longhair walking along the road.

Even so, why should *long hair* on a guy serve as a stimulus to unleash all that locked-in anger? Like I say...sex and identity. The other common brilliantly original remark says it all: "Is it a male or a female?"

Maybe it's no accident that in historical eras distinguished by the male use of ornaments, lace and long hair, the codpiece was a prominent item of apparel. Like the contemporary pop star who offsets his flowing locks with several handkerchiefs stuffed behind his fly, the bulging codpiece proclaimed blatantly that the male was indeed a male and not a female.

The fact that anyone thought it necessary to go to such lengths, as it were, to reinforce the obvious, leads us to the basic explanation for all the present-day hullabaloo over long hair.

The sad truth is, sexual identity is often a fragile, vulnerable acquisition. For men and women both. Particularly when clothing conceals the unmistakable biological signature of gender.

Once you cover up breasts and genitals, the recognition of sex has to shift to garb, posture, beard or lack of it...and hair style.

Within that basic dichotomy, there is a multitude of further subtleties marking an individual, in a rough and ready sense at least, according to social class, occupation, mood, and even whether the person is working, relaxing or celebrating. Anyone who chooses to blur those distinctions, step outside the orthodox and intelligible set of signals, is going to generate confusion, uncertainty and, in the end, hostility.

He or she may merely be employing a striking form of identification to contact others of a similar uncommon disposition, but the corollary message goes out to everybody else: *I am not one of you, I reject you, you are alien to me.* That message may not be intended—but it's the other side of the coin.

Long hair and unusual modes of dress represent an assault on the conventions marking off male and female. But the attack is on conventions only. It would be the grossest sort of stupidity to suppose that males with long hair (or women with short cropped hair) are rejecting heterosexuality.

Indeed, much of the animosity towards young longhairs is precisely because of their undisguised, insouciant virility. Like I said at the start, girls like guys with long hair. That's because women know those guys like *them*...like making it with them, like them because a woman is a man's sexual complement, not because they're looking for a mother-substitute or a house-keeper.

They've rejected the ethos of contempt for women, the ethos of the 90-second quickie that leaves the woman cold and used and resentful. Because they like women, it turns them on to turn their lovers on.

I don't mean to suggest that they're alone in this. Plenty of young short-haired executives have also got the message passed along by Kinsey and Ellis, and Masters and Johnson, and plenty of middle-aged fathers have always known it. But long-haired hedonists are the very apostles of the sexual revolution, and a lot of guys resent them for it. Dog in the manger.

One of the most ludicrous sights I have ever seen was a mixed group of uptight late-twenties householders snorting and nudging as a well-heeled longhair passed them. "Are you," one of them cried with a righteous, trembling scorn, "a boy or a girl?" The hairy guy just smiled. The girl strolling with her arm in his was the most beautiful, sexiest chick I've ever seen. They both wore the languorous, lecherous, satisfied smiles of two people who've just torn off the most incredible three hour fuck of their lives.

§

Underlying all these factors, though, is the profound issue of why sexual dimorphism should be considered the most fundamental dividing line between one human being and another. It's the issue at the heart of the women's movement. It may well be *the* central human issue, more interwoven into the unfolding dynamism of the future than any other, including the gaps between rich and poor, intelligent and dull, young and old.

Yet, to some, it may not even seem a genuine question, for so deeply seated in us is the conviction that beyond all else a clear, distinct sexual identity is the primary human requirement.

Still, at the end of an exhaustive study, one might conceivably be driven to the conclusion that there is, apart from cultural overlays, no intrinsic difference between the sexes. Such an extreme conclusion would fly in the face of everything we accept as axiomatic, but it is not impossible. It is obviously tenable to inquire why the male/female distinction has such an overwhelming importance that every fiber of our language and thought is structured around that polarity.

What, in fact, *are* the differences between men and women?

Well, yes, little boys stick out there, and little girls fold in. Big girls bulge here, and big boys don't. Males produce spermatozoa and females receive it, sometimes conceive as a result, give birth and offer milk. But why should all that be such a big deal?

In fact, by itself, it isn't. It's relevant, but far from central, to the differences we consider really significant. What we mean by masculine is tough, unemotional, logical, aggressive, driven by a burning urge to conquer the outside world. By feminine we mean soft, yielding, intuitive, dedicated, protective.

Crap, say the women's libbers. It's a cultural conspiracy to enslave half the population, to castrate women psychically and rob them of their initiative. Back to the kitchen, retort the outraged males and many of their wives, you're no more than half-women, crippled by a perverse desire to be men.

There are two ways to find out which view is less distorted. You can investigate whether men and women are invariably, in every culture and age, differentiated in the same way. And you can study the genetics, biochemistry and neurology of the sexes, see if you can uncover any basic variation at that level. Let's try both approaches.

The classic model of the first approach, and still a shocker 25 years after it was written, is anthropologist, Margaret Mead's extraordinary study *Male and Female*. Drawing from an immense wealth of data about primitive societies, including her own field trips to seven cultures in New Guinea and the South Pacific, Mead weaves a startling tapestry of human possibilities. Many of the societies she describes have since been irretrievably altered by the impact of western civilization; in that sense, her book is timeless.

Despite insistence that TV has turned the world into a single global village, with its window displaying to each of us the intimate truth about every other society, Mead makes us realize how censored the pictures are we get through that window. The tingling sense of alien shock only slowly warms into a fuller, wider empathy with ways of life weirdly at odds to our own, yet at least comprehensible and enriching.

Her panoply of cultures is astoundingly diverse. She cites the Samoans, where male and female, young and old orchestrated their lives in a formal, stately pattern of planting, reaping, fishing and building. "The boy who would flee from too much pressure on his young manhood hardly exists in Samoa; the girl who is ambitious and managing has plenty of outlets in the bustling, equally organized life of the women's groups."

In contrast, the cannibal has "developed a form of social organization in which every man's hand is against every other man. The women are as assertive and vigorous as the men; they detest bearing and rearing children, and provide most of the food, leaving the men free to plot and fight."

Hard-pressed by scarcity, the mountain Arapesh had a gentle, co-operative society, so gentle that they were unable to compete with warlike neighbors. The Sepik River Iatmul, on the other hand, were totally polarized in sex roles, with brutal initiation rites inducting the young males into an outlandish form of over-compensated masculinity. The women were viragos, the adult men fierce and brittle in their pride, dedicating themselves to building superbly carved war canoes and enormous ceremonial houses from which the women were excluded.

Clearly, masculinity and femininity are variables—forms of identity and self-image far more mutable than the basic facts of gender.

In his controversial book *The Great Australian Stupor*, conservative Catholic psychologist Ronald Conway observes, "Many writers on Australia have noted our brasher reactions from psychosexual anxiety, but have rarely understood them for what they are. Donald Horne was getting close when he wrote, 'Men stand around bars asserting their masculinity with such intensity that you half expect them to unzip their flies.' Men who find it necessary to assert the obvious with such stridency are usually insecure about what they assert."

The reluctance to appear passive, weak and "sissy" hampers a man's natural expressions of tenderness, sensitivity to beauty and ultimately his chances of relating fully to a woman. The escalating polarization between masculinity and femininity prohibits each sex from large areas of possible experience. Each is crucially impoverished, and a child must learn to conceal and eventually to extinguish any element that has come to be thought the exclusive signature of the opposite sex.

A society like that of the Samoans accepts that both men and women share most interests, in varying degrees, in common. We are loath to accept that, and the dealings between the sexes become attenuated and predatory. It is extraordinarily revealing that though the super-male ethos encourages seduction as a principal pastime, and bombastic boasting of it over a beer, a man whose sexual success comes from his genuine liking of women is caustically dismissed as a "ladies' man." There's more than a hint that, like the vigorously virile longhair, he must really be a homosexual—after all, he gets on well with the enemy.

But even if we accept that our prevailing view of the distinctions between male and female is over-stated, we must still consider the deep underlying demarcations between the sexes.

§

Psychological and physiological studies over the last fifty years have accrued vast quantities of pertinent information, but the findings have often been ambiguous or contradictory. The best summary of available data is Dr. Corinne Hutt's 1972 Penguin, *Males and Females*. Starting with chromosomal differences, Hutt proceeds through the latest work on hormones, brain structures, mental capacities and non-learned behavioral responses.

Not surprisingly, she concludes that science has plentiful evidence that males and females have acquired, in a million years of evolution, drastic genetic variations in a range of characteristics. There are more differences, in short, than the mere anatomical contrasts. "The evidence strongly suggests that at the outset males and females are 'wired-up' differently. Social factors thus operate on already well differentiated organisms— predisposed towards masculinity or femininity."

We now know that the basic blueprint of the human is the female. Maleness is, in the first instance, a genetic adaptation of this basic template. The shrunken Y chromosome causes the primitive undifferentiated sex organ to alter into testes in the seventh week after conception, and thereafter hormones produced in the body further the process. In the absence of a Y chromosome, the fetal sex organs develop on their own into the ovaries of a female.

Yet the Y chromosome itself carries little or no genetic information. What this means is that the sexes are much more similar than is commonly supposed. The Y chromosome is a switch that instigates enormous long-range effects, but in essence each organ and hormone in the male has its exact equivalent in the female. The separate ways in which they develop, however, have important effects even in the structure of the brain.

This is because the hormones from the sex glands quickly come under the control of other hormones secreted from centers in the brain. The most important of these centers is the hypothalamus, which is also crucially involved in regulating emotions and motivation.

Hormonally, the female is more complicated than the male, and her hypothalamus functions differently. Women are cyclical in their hormone outputs, because their reproductive function is based on periodic menstruation. Male control hormones, however, are produced in a fairly constant flow.

"The single fact," says Hutt, "that *some part of the brain* is *characteristically different in males and females,* is one of the most significant findings in neuroendocrinology. "

Neuroendocrinological studies provide a key to differences found in every human culture between any large group of men and any equally large group of women. In IQ scores, for example, men collectively have a higher average score in tests of arithmetic and visual-spatial discrimination—aptitudes that make for proficiency in mechanical tasks and linear, logical thinking. Women score on the average higher on verbal, deftness and short-term memory tests.

Overall, as well, there is evidence that male scores are distributed more widely than those of females; that is, there is a greater percentage of men with very high *and* very low scores. This accords well with the greater variability of males in other characteristics—weight, height, susceptibility to illness. It seems plausible that the "wired-in" differences that occur in the prenatal stage account for many of these phenomena.

What it is essential to stress, however, is that "sexual dimorphism does not mean that certain characteristics or behaviors are *exclusively* the property of one sex, but simply that they are more *typical* of one sex than the other." There are no "male" or "female" capacities, other than the brute facts of reproduction.

§

Our society is far from comprehending this fact. A tradition of debasing women scars our history. Evelyne Sullerot, in *Woman, Society and Change*, cites the Catholic Council of Macon, where "women were granted a soul by a majority of only one vote." And, she adds, in the interests of balance, that "the Protestants at the Wittenberg Conference even tried to prove that women were not human beings."

With those attitudes looming behind us, it is little wonder that men generally rebel against the new insurgent life-styles that question the gulf. Little wonder, either, at the terror women at large feel for the abrupt demands of radical feminists.

It's time to take stock of what we know, recognize that males and females are indisputably made of the same clay and just as indisputably formed in different molds. But those molds are themselves remarkably alike in shape, in every essential we call human.

We are not aliens dwelling together in uneasy truce, or ought not to be. The intimations of change in our society, insofar as they reflect this fact—from women's lib to guys with long hair—are not the threats they seem, but may, in truth, be the forerunners of a time of greater joy than we have known.

CYBORGASM: THE SHAPE
OF SEX TO COME (1974)

If you were a James Bond freak in the 1960s, when a fondness for super-agents was *de rigueur*, you're probably a fan of his '70s television counterpart. Steve Austin, the Six Million Dollar Man, is literally half machine: a latter-day Frankenstein's creation known as a "cyborg."

Austin parted company, during an experimental lifting-body crash, with an eye, an arm and both legs. Wily CIA types salvaged what was left and turned him—with the/help of computerized prosthetics—into a souped-up one-man blitz. It's all rather boring, to tell the truth, once you're past that mind-boggling opener. But one thing keeps me watching. I'm not convinced that Steve Austin's replacements were fully itemized. It's a family show, so they have to be discreet—but his women friends always look *amazingly* satisfied. Could his secret be... *cyborgasm*?

If so, it's a pale imitation of what tomorrow's sex might really be like. There are more delights awaiting us in the curious world of computers than your accountant will tell you.

Back in the days before she chopped off her hair with a mattock and hurled herself into the significant issues of our time, Jane Fonda starred in a soft, billowy confection of, uh, science friction. Depending on your current sexual politics, *Barbarella* is now either passé or reprehensibly sexist. As a glimpse into the erotic possibilities of the Space Age, I must confess it left me fairly unmoved. But I do have fond memories of the French comic strip from which director Roger Vadim, Fonda's then-husband, adapted the script.

Devised by Jean-Claude Forest, the cartoon was the first adult essay into future sex—and hung its racy plots on some marvelous, astringent gags. At a time when most thrillers still depended for their horror on such threats as a laser beam ravening towards the hero's shrinking, unprotected testicles, *Barbarella* offered new paradoxes of dread. Notable was the ingenious punishment inflicted on our permissive heroine by a mad scientist. Rejecting as jejune such devices as the whip, the Iron Maiden and the dentist's drill, he strapped Barbarella into the phallic focus of the dread Excessive Machine, and beat her into submission with jolt after electric jolt of...unendurable pleasure.

But Barbarella had compensations, of sorts. No chauvinist, she ranged far beyond her own species for delight, opening her loins to winged angels and green monsters. Most charming, perhaps, was the panel in which, languorous in a vast sunken bed, she murmurs to her robot companion, "Diktor, you have real style!" Her lover, one segmented arm resting on silk-draped metal knees, photo-electric eyes masked in self-doubt, replied humbly: "Oh! Madame is too kind...I know my shortcomings... There's something a bit mechanical about my movements."

Screwing a robot (and I use that verb with all due tact) may not be your idea of the Joy of Sex. But the erotic games of 2001 and beyond will surely be no less strange. The enlightened humanism that enables me, at last, to regard with equanimity my warm, tender feelings for—let us say—my rubber galoshes, will hardly be fazed by a meaningful relationship with a computer.

The true Sexual Revolution will not stop at unconditional tolerance for your own and other people's quirks and preferences. Our society has known generous moods in the past, and certain societies have known nothing else. But an open-hearted reappraisal of values is only part of the epochal syndrome we call the Sexual Revolution. For today's erotic liberation is being catalyzed by science, and tomorrow's sexual possibilities will be enhanced by the startling products of scientific enquiry.

§

Consider the following extract from a science fiction fairy tale for adults by Fred Pohl, titled "Day Million" (1966):

> "On this day I want to tell you about, which will be about ten thousand years from now, there were a boy, a girl and a love story.
> "Now, although I haven't said much so far, none of it is true. The boy was not what you and I would normally think of as a boy because he was 187 years old... The reason the girl was not a girl was that she was a boy."

And the love story? Well, they met, fell in love, went to the encoding room and had their identities taped,

> "exchanged their mathematical analogues and went away... It was an idyll, really.
> "They lived happily ever after...
> "Of course, they never set eyes on each other again."

Pohl intended you to be puzzled, thrown off balance, confronted by a situation that's *almost* recognizable, but still thoroughly alien. He's saying that the future will be *different*: not just the standard spaceships and folk with green skin. Sex and love will be different, and the lovers will not be like the people we know now.

So why waste time thinking about it? Why did Pohl bother to write such a fantasy in the first place? Alvin Toffler, in the bestseller *Future Shock*, gave one answer: at the rate the future is coming at us, it'll be here before we've had time to adjust. Something as weird as Fred Pohl's love story might not be

10,000 years off; some of it might come true by 2001.

Let's take a closer look at his imaginary couple. The fact that the boy is 187 suggests not only that medicine will find a cure for death, but that it will slow the process of maturation at any desired point. Not really so unlikely; biologists have already approached that goal with rats. Indeed, if the key to aging is found before you die, it may also unlock for you the secret of rejuvenation. It could be that in 2001 you will be young again, retaining the wisdom of many years but physically hearty and sexually vigorous as only an adolescent can be. That'd really make your retirement something to look forward to.

The girl who was really a boy is an example of genetic engineering, a technology that is already off the drawing boards, if only just. Pohl was writing from the assumption that some homosexuality is biologically, not culturally, based, and that surgeons of the future might be capable of altering a male fetus's gender "if his aptitudes were for being a woman." Perhaps this was a sexist assumption, but the follow-through from it is valid and important. Generations to come will be able to shape the genetic material as they please. The implications of that notion alone are breathtaking, and we'll come back to them.

But the most riveting element, and probably the most unacceptable, is the idea of a love affair between two people who never again see each other...in the flesh. Don and Dora, the lovers of Pohl's future, are much too busy actually to live together. So they obtain immensely subtle and detailed recordings of each another's personalities. After all, if the brain is a computer built of cells instead of solid-state circuitry, there is no obstacle in principle to copying its contents in all their staggering complexity on a recording device. The ultimate home-movie— a total replica, in electronic form, of your loved ones.

Absurd? Listen to Pohl's explanation. Bizarre, but not absurd. "Genital organs feel nothing. Neither do hands, nor lips, nor breasts; they are only receptors, accepting and transmitting impulses. It is the brain that feels; it is the interpretation of those impulses that makes agony or orgasm, and Don's symbol manipulator gives him the analogue of...wild, ardent hours with the eternal, exquisite and incorruptible analogue of Dora." And for Dora, of course, her analogue device of Don is no less convenient.

Pohl does not specify what you do if you fall out of love, have a vicious spat with your electronic lover. Presumably you wipe the memory. It's cheaper than divorce, and there's no murder rap.

For many—me included—that image of a self-indulgent, totally depersonalized "relationship" is horrifying. It seems the ultimate brutalized prostitution. Yet, on reflection, is it really anything more than an enhanced form of masturbation, the supreme way to enjoy in solitude your own sexual feelings— and, incidentally, perhaps less narcissistic than masturbating to images from the solitary, self-referring prison of your own head? Reflecting on future sexual possibilities always brings us around in a great circle to an examination of our own practices, responses and secret fantasies.

Certainly, some rudimentary form of that process will take its place in tomorrow's sexual repertoire. From as far back as Huxley's *Brave New World*, imaginative thinkers have seen that electronic and film recording can have only one final outcome: "feelies" or "sensies," entertainments appealing convincingly to at least the five commonplace senses. The much heralded "smellovision" is only the first step in that direction.

And Pohl was right: it is the brain, ultimately, that sees, sniffs, touches, registers changes of balance and temperature. Brain neurologists today have a detailed and sophisticated under-standing of which parts of the brain relate to which sensory experiences. It has been known since the 1950s that an elec-trode applied to a suitable region of the brain can trigger real-istic sensations and memories. Once the bugs are worked out, it will be possible to record an actor's entire subjective experi-ence, if not his thoughts, and play them back to a "wired-up" audience.

Such an entertainment might have the full-blown character

of an exceptionally vivid dream, tempered by the never-quite-submerged knowledge that you were actually semi-conscious in a theater. Actors employing The Method will come back into vogue; a pretty face and torso will not compensate for any deficiency in perception.

Censorship, if it hasn't vanished by that time, will float belly-up in the shock-wave; it will quite evidently be safer to "feel" a torrid love scene than to experience the thug's shock as a bullet smashes into his body. For those "wire-heads" with weak hearts, in either case, it will be necessary to turn the gain down during the most tumultuous scenes.

More central, perhaps, to the true heart of the human condition, such technologies will allow us truly to appreciate, for the first time in history, what sexuality means for our partners. If your alarmed mental image is of bodies clinging sadly together amidst a spaghetti-tangle of wires and flashing dials, forget it. The technology of genuine cyborgasm will have done away with wires. Electromagnetic fields, subtle and impalpable, will pulse in an invisible aura around the lovers, monitoring their responses, comparing them through a computer, and feeding back to each information about the other's needs and joys.

If sex can be above all the attempt to reach and comprehend another person in every dimension, cyborgasm will be one of the profoundest achievements of the human race. For we shall no longer experience merely the behavior of others, no matter how sensitively; we shall share their experience directly, in an electronic conduit opened from soul to soul, as the twin lobes of your own brain are linked by nature.

The computer will be no obscene, mechanical voyeur, prying pitilessly into the bedroom. It will be genuinely an extension of ourselves, calming the too-hasty, amplifying and assisting the uncertain, mediating in a communion of flesh and thought and emotion which even Tantric mystics have never dreamed of.

§

Other technologies will doubtless assist. Specific drugs— sensory enhancers, aphrodisiacs, erotic hallucinogens—may become popular. Ancient semi-sciences like acupuncture and yoga will be codified, simplified and taught routinely, so that our insight into the strengths and limitations of our bodies will be considerably enriched.

Already, biofeedback devices are on sale that enable people to obtain voluntary control over certain brain states. It is thought that states of relaxation and harmony achieved by yogis only during many arduous years of practice can thus be attained in weeks or months. Sophisticated teaching machines, they do not affect the brain directly, but bring to our conscious attention and control aspects of the mind's functioning which previously have been inaccessible.

Naturally, there are dangers in such technologies. Leaving aside Yippie-style fantasies of turning whole cities into day-long ecstatic orgies by dumping authentic aphrodisiacs in the water-supply, there are several indisputably gruesome possibilities. Consider a drug that obliterated the last hour's memory. Such drugs are indeed under development. A rapist might go on an endless spree, secure in the knowledge that his victims would never be able to identify him. Indeed, armed as well with an aerosol of Rand-E, he might find himself pursued by a victim eager for more.

And of course an unscrupulous government, or consortium of advertising agencies, would find such substances a boon more gratifying than anything since Nero discovered Bread and Circuses.

I recognize, of course, that for many people today "science" is the only dirty word left in the lexicon. It's true that Big Science—funded by greedy conglomerates and power-hungry military—has produced nuclear terror and denuded, unstable ecologies, while leaving most of the world starving and miserable. In medicine, warped by sexism, it has produced contraceptives that can endanger the health of women but not men, failed to conquer venereal disease, and hindered the average person's self-knowledge by encouraging doctors in the belief that they are sole custodians of secret, sacred mysteries.

But for all that, we now *do* possess extremely reliable contraception with fairly few side-effects. Our enjoyment of heterosexual coitus is no longer overshadowed by the risk of unwanted pregnancy. Indeed, at a profounder level, one of the gifts of scientific analysis is finally to purge us of those ancient fertility-cult obsessions which once made all non-reproductive sexuality suspect, even wicked. Our insights into the mechanics and strategies of both social and biological evolution illuminate that old hang-up: why, for all its painful psychic consequences, it was once useful, and why it is now, thankfully, redundant.

§

Ours is a species remarkably ill-equipped in tooth and claw, superior to all others only—if superlatively—in flexibility of thought. For our ancient forebears, overwhelming pressures constantly reinforced the link between sexual gratification, fecundity, and nurturing roles. Too many babies and small children perished in an environment generally hostile to their fragility. Too many of the surviving adults were worn out and dead by 30. The Agricultural Revolution of 8000 BC brought surpluses of food, and time for inventive reflection. But that breathing space was soon lost as cities bloomed, with their epidemics and wars.

A reconstruction of history even this sketchy is ample to show why evolution ensured that we are capable of producing far more children than a modern civilization needs (since most babies, for the first time consistently in history, survive and thrive), and that the link between sexual enjoyment and child-bearing is an evolutionary gambit we can now safely abandon in most erotic encounters. Human beings are, above all else, adaptable animals. Our hunter-gatherer talents of curiosity, acute perception, patience and loyalty to the group have found fresh, enlarged fields of play. These lie now in the quest for nature's limits, in the creation by superlative artists of new aesthetic worlds, and our appreciation of them, in humane impulses which extend beyond our own parochial group to the entire world of humanity. And our sexuality, as cultures less repressive than ours have long recognized, is just as fluent in the tongues of inventiveness and the songs of pleasure.

If our generations have rediscovered this truth, enlightened by the most humane practitioners of science, how much more exciting will be the lives of those generations to follow us? Assuming our worst impulses do not first misuse the potentials of technology and obliterate us.

A species as various as ours will not be satisfied with a modest return to that mythical Eden where man and woman, man and man, woman and woman, sport—in Freud's rather mealy-mouthed phrase—in "polymorphous perversity." We will use our minds and our bodies, and the instruments that Marshall McLuhan has called the "extensions of Man," as probes to plumb the limits of the possible. Which may include, as a minor *divertissement*, having it away with your family robot.

The farther ahead one looks in time, the more remarkable are the changes to be expected. Trivially, sex in weightless conditions is bound to be unusual. The closest approximation anyone has yet got to this is underwater, in scuba units—unless some of the astronauts are gay, and they're not telling. (Though there was at least one Russian woman cosmonaut in orbit...)

But sex in space is not likely to be enjoyed by any except the most exceptionally wealthy for centuries. Other innovations, far more fascinating, involve the partial or wholesale alteration of the human species itself: genetic engineering.

Molecular biology does not yet have a full map of the basic human hereditary material, nor the means to tamper with it. But knowledge in this field is exploding, and incredibly swift computers are doing much of the leg-work. It is not implausible that by the end of this millennium scientists will know how to effect a number of important alterations in the human template. Immediately, the mind cascades with images. Winged men and women with light, graceful bodies—and, like birds, hollow bones—soaring to their, uh, love-nests in the sky. Lithe, powerful beings fast as tigers (though, one must hope, decently slow as lovers), padding on prehensile paws. Aquatic folk, bubbles gliding in silver clouds from their gills, locked like dolphins (and maybe *with* dolphins, if those sea-going mammals turn out to be as intelligent as they seem) in finny rapture.

And more! True hermaphrodites, capable of fathering and mothering children, self-sufficient if they so desire. Vaginas like roses opening from the navel, the armpits, the palms of the hands... Penises and pseudo-organs in profusion, until the entire body quivers and flutters with erotic tendrils eager for the lover's caress...

But genetic engineering will not be applied to human beings before all its ramifications have been worked out on laboratory animals. And one line of research suggested by author and futurologist Arthur C. Clarke is the development, during such experiments, of "super-chimps." Modest increases in the brain size of the common or jungle chimp, along with minor changes for speech, could create a new breed of menials happy to do humanity's boring or dirty work. And if you follow that through, you may find a new meaning for "bestiality."

Like it or not, recorded history shows no dearth of people eager to fulfill fantasies of dominance at other people's expense. If some future cat fancier decides to flesh out his dreams of houris with a beautiful, humanoid slave shaped from the genes of his favorite Persian, for whom will the bell toll? Not for thee: you're human, and there are severe sanctions against enslaving people. But supercats—furry, compliant, imprinted with a desire to serve, not too intelligent—are *not people*. Cf. the decision of the Supreme Court of South Africa, April 22, 2044...

Most staggering of all these possibilities, though, booming with resonances from the darkest caverns explored by depth psychology, is the clone. Take a cell from your body, any cell except a sperm or ovum, jolt it with enzymes until it thinks it's a zygote, implant it in a real or artificial uterus, and it will develop into a fetus. When he or she grows up, leaving aside the small matter of personal history and experiences, the cloned person will be—you...or rather, your delayed twin.

A bit of simple genetic surgery at the egg stage will turn a cloned boy into a girl (Pohl's Dora, the girl who was really a boy). So the ultimate narcissist male can, in this future world, have a woman made in his own image—and seduce herself until he is both tired of themself.

With a clone group of 10 or 12, nurtured in identical circumstances, we may have the ideal commune. There's the question of incest, of course, but that will probably pass gently in any case from our *morés* when contraception is finally perfected. For the Pharaohs, remember, incest was not forbidden but mandatory...

The shape of sex to come? There's no single form, no simple prediction with any hope of validity. Will the winged men loathe the wire-heads, and the superchimps call for liberty? Or will the disease of racism and sexual discrimination seem, then, in that endless garden of variety, the incomprehensible shadow from the past which it already is?

SEX: LOOKING BACK FROM NOW

The Moral Revolution

The opening essay in this time machine of a book was published in August, 1967, in the dawn of the Summer of Love (according to Wikipedia, that indispensible, unreliable source of all knowledge). Except that it appeared in Australia, on the flipside of the planet from San Francisco ("Wear some flowers in your hair"), so it was in fact the Winter of Love, a cold, wet and thoughtful season in my neck of the woods. Hence, perhaps, the admonitory tone, less hippie bliss than coolly utopian in the mode of Aldous Huxley, whose novel *Island* (1962), his anti-*Brave New World,* I'd read in Penguin paperback a year or two earlier, as I'd read B. F. Skinner's behaviorist utopia *Walden II* (1948) earlier still, and been unnecessarily impressed.

Truth in advertising also mandates that I admit my small elision in the opening paragraph. When the essay appeared, launching an Antipodean equivalent to the OpEd items in US magazines aimed at horny guys (which is to say just about all guys) who wanted to be able to say they read it only for the articles, it began: "Let's stop talking about sex. Which is to say, let's stop getting hung up about it." That was a misleading way to broach the topic, which after all was the *raison d'être* of the entire magazine. But I was twenty-three, and world-weary in the way of young men, and I felt the need to make it really clear that I was being deliberately provocative, in this mild soft-core tits&ass magazine I would end up editing four years later. "Let's stop talking about sex" meant: Get over it, already. Do we sit around in a fever of anxiety wondering whether or not to eat or sleep or talk to each other or wash or listen to music? Well, as it happens, most people in most cultures *do* get wildly excited about what they may or may not eat, and when to bathe, and whom to talk to or what is permissible to read... It's human to stress out about this stuff. I figured the angst would go away pretty soon. *Lady Chatterley's Lover* had been banned in my country until, incredibly, 1965, but the tide had changed.

The most remarkable and shameful absence in that 1967 essay is any real awareness of the nascent or resurgent women's movement, still then somewhat derisively known as "Women's Lib," and the equivalent gay movements. I was aware of feminism, as were many of us by the mid-1960s, but Germaine Greer's bombshell *The Female Eunuch* didn't arrive until 1970, and I was sufficiently arrogant that I dismissed it, at first flip through, when I found Greer carelessly informing her readers that humans possess forty-eight (rather than forty-six) chromosomes. Actually this had been the general medical belief until a couple of decades previously, and it was hardly a key to her case, but this is the way males tend, even today, to respond to statements by women (and often, it's true, by other men): pounce on the weakness, ignore everything profound and revelatory and confrontational.

So my model of sexual bliss in the new redeemed age was a kind of male narcissism, a projection of an idealized male *laissez faire* of sex onto the whole species. I was a slow starter, sexually (having spent several formative years, alas, trapped inside a Catholic monastery) but by twenty-three I'd been in bed with a few young women, and in love with one. I thought the emerging doctrines of the Summer of Love were pretty right on. Sex was wildly exciting for men and women alike, done right. But people were more than their gonads. The real sex organ was the brain. And so on. I still think that's true, but my egalitarianism was a kind of projected male fantasy. I wanted to believe that, shorn of inhibiting conditioning, women were exactly the same as men, but with deliciously different decoration. That was an advance on the Victorian prudery that purported to find women an inferior species, to be used and disdained or placed on a pedestal and protected from anything that might harm them (like freedom). But as a couple of decades of feminists since then have shown, this was not much of an advance. It was basically the same controlling, penis-worshiping ideology that had throttled women for centuries, millennia, probably forever.

Gay sex was simply outside my comfort zone, as was surely the case for most men and many women in the 1960s. I only started to hear the demand for gay rights a decade later, when homosexuality was dubbed "camp" by its more daring defenders. It would have seemed entirely preposterous (or satirically science fictional) to assert that men might legally marry men, and women marry women, within three or four decades. Still an uphill battle in the USA, but a new generation pretty much takes gay equality for granted. The pendulum might swing back. It usually does.

Some of the points the essay does make were unfamiliar to most of my readers, and must have seemed equally absurd. Louise Brown, the first in vitro fertilized baby, was born in 1978. "Host mothers"? It was a medical term from the 1930s, and I had no way to know that the term of art, twenty years later, would be "surrogates." But my prediction was pretty close to the mark. (And we still aren't an inch closer to standing on "the cratered face of Mars," although we have mapped the whole planet with uncanny vivid precision.) A decade or more after 2000, reproductive science has not yet managed to create a child by joining a pair of ova or of spermatozoa (it turns out they are marked by chemical gadgets that prevent such a simple fusion), let alone growing a fetus to term in a tank. But in the meantime, cloning has become a reality for many species, and it is really politics and moral sensibilities that prevent human cloning (or its publication; I wouldn't be surprised to learn than it's been done in North Korea, say, or one of the other autocracies).

The Y Factor

Dark-haired Ilizane is angular of frame, tall and straight-backed, square-jawed and broadshouldered. Karate is her favourite sport. She has little time for make-up or fashion. Xenia, fair and blue-eyed, is, Ilizane concedes, much more "girlie." She loves Barbie dolls and wants beads, bangles and fairytales.... What they do share, however, is a condition called CAIS (Complete Androgen Insensitivity Syndrome). It means they are hermaphrodites, possessing both male and female genitalia. Although they have vaginas, they have testes where their ovaries should be, and no uterus. Neither has a penis. Outwardly they look like girls: in truth they are half and half..."What is interesting," says [foster father] Neil, "is that theoretically it may one day be possible for Ilizane to father a child"—another reason, he says, why she should think long and hard about surgery to remove her testes.

Olga Craig, "We are not what we seem," *Sunday Telegraph,* 29 Feb 2004.

"Is it a boy or a girl?" That is still the first question asked when the baby is born (or after the first echo scans). Forty years ago, as I noted above, enraged thugs screamed it at any long-haired youth. A couple of decades later, they howled it at shaven-headed girls instead. Today, allegedly, desire makes no crass distinction between male and female bodies, Straight Guys benefit from the Queer Eye of fashion advisers, emerging as stylish metrosexuals. Cultural theory insists that gender is a social construction, ultimately a choice. Gender bending went from pop shock to cool custom. Still, although we are now in an era of fluidity and choice, sex and gender remain a source of endless fascination—and anxiety.

Is sex really so adaptable, a fashion statement, or an ideological option? For decades we were told it is upbringing and preference. Margaret Mead's evidence about gender roles, cited approvingly in the 1960s, above, has been shown to be based on brief contact with her jesting informants, hopelessly contaminated and unreliable. For a long time, one of the strongest arguments against biology's dominion was the Canadian case of John/Joan. A twin boy, Bruce Reimer, lost his penis at seven months during a botched circumcision in Winnipeg in 1966, was then castrated, surgically sex-reassigned and raised as Brenda. For years, his/her Johns Hopkins University sponsor, Dr. John Money, claimed the case as a triumph of adaptation, snails and puppy dog tails gracefully morphed into sugar and spice. It grew into the classic instance cited endlessly in feminist and poststructural "social construction" texts and courses.

In fact, as we learned a decade ago, the poor child was a psychological mess, rough and tomboyish to a fault, even standing to urinate, and finally came out in adolescence as a male. He changed his name to David, a biblical memento of his battle with Money, had painful and somewhat successful phalloplasty to create a working penis, toiled with the other men in a slaughterhouse, and married, with adopted children. And in 2004, aged thirty-eight, deep in angry depression and following a separation, tragic end to a tragic life, he killed himself.

In the uterus and then during infancy, the brain starts down specialized male or female developmental cascades. Once hormonally launched, nurture cannot reset all the implicit behavioral templates, or many of the physiological ones, even in the absence of testicles or ovaries. The motive for surgically sex-reassigning babies born with ambiguous or damaged genitalia was surely kindly, if misguided. These children, it was thought, would be tormented by their peers, grow up with damaged self-esteem and probably become psychotic or self-destructive. In Reimer's case, this proved true of the treatment rather than the "disease."

The past eighty years have witnessed a slow gavotte in psychological fashion, aligned with crude and hideously cruel geopolitical struggles. Nazis taught that all was blood, and killed millions in that cause. Communists claimed all was learned culture, and killed those polluted by wrong opinions. Racism and, more recently, sexism were countered in the West by nurturists, making genetic models appear the ideology of bigots.

For a decade, this consensus has seemed to crumble under the impact of new science and evolutionary insight. Money's case was almost certainly wrong, based on misleading evidence from intersex people whose brains were likely cross-wired during fetal development. But what of those many transgender people who choose to switch later in life, after years of hetero-sexuality—must they always have been pre-wired to make the move? This is perhaps as dangerous a preconception as the purely socially constructed version. Queer theorists are surely right that some people can choose either to expand or specialize their sexual desires, at least to some extent. Urologist and child psychologist William Reiner, also at Johns Hopkins, has reported that despite hormone treatment and surgery, 25 baby boys born with no penis but normal testicles (like Reimer), then castrated and raised as girls, all retained strong male character-istics and most switched back to male. We are male or female because our brains are our key sex organs, and they become set in their ways, due to complex chemical feedback loops, long before our more visible genitalia allow happy parents to cry: "It's a girl!"

What of normative male and female brains? After a couple of decades of Women's Studies courses claiming that (A) both are basically identical, with constructed differences imposed by patriarchal hegemony, and (not-A) they are very different indeed, with the special or essential gifts of women denied and suppressed by patriarchal hegemony, it's difficult to decide. Louann Brizendine, M.D., a neuropsychiatrist, has lately published *The Female Brain* (2007) and *The Male Brain* (2010), which argue a large common ground—we are all humans, after all, with male DNA a tweak on the basic female recipe—but detail many distinctions that combine to make an overwhelming difference.

A sharp rebuttal comes from a cognitive neuroscientist, Dr. Cordelia Fine, whose *Delusions of Gender* (2010) claims, for example, that "Nonexistent sex differences in language lateralization, mediated by nonexistent sex differences in corpus callosum structure, are widely believed to explain nonexistent sex differences in language skills." Positing such neuroanatomical differences is, according to Fine, no more than neurosexism. In a special issue on the topic in *Scientific American Mind* (May/June 2010), Dr. Lise Eliot, Associate Professor in the Department of Neuroscience at the Chicago Medical School, looked into the surprising "Truth about Boys and Girls": that "researchers have found very few large-scale differences between boys and girls in brain structure or function." Eliot's book about brain plasticity in the sexes is *Pink Brain, Blue Brain: How Small Differences Grow into Troublesome Gaps and What We Can Do About It*.

Perhaps we shall have to await even more subtle instruments and theories, or maybe it all comes down to sexual politics, just as enraged disputes over human-caused global climate change usually turn out to be a reflection of prior political convictions and prejudice that warp the way we receive and weigh evidence. Come back in fifty or 100 years and see if much has changed.

Cyborgasm

I was incredibly right about all this, but incredibly wrong. Men did not turn to cyborged vaginas but to Viagra, while women found new routes to pleasure (often solitary pleasure) with clitoral vibrators. (I read that Tupperware gatherings have made way for suburban sex toy parties.) Gay liberation allowed many to emerge from closets and find long-denied dignity and surprising new possibilities, although the US military still insist on the absurdly mealy-mouthed "don't ask, don't tell" doctrine. Bisexuals and the transgendered dare finally to speak their name, as do tops and bottoms and perhaps sideways. Metro-sexuals blur the boundaries, while retrosexuals try to reinscribe them. Men and women and children tease themselves with on-line porn of every imaginable variety, and some beyond any given human's imagination, and into the emerging realm of cyberspace, from sex chats ("What is the sound of one hand typing?") and naughty self-portraits emailed around the planet at the speed of light or posted on Flickr, to immersive romps in imaginary worlds where your avatar acts out your wishes and dreads. (Virtual rape, for disturbing example: search on "Ra-peLay video game goes viral amid outrage," by Kyung Lah, CNN.) Meanwhile, though, the first steps have already been taken toward building and marketing mechanical brides. The Japanese seem to be the world specialists in this kind of randy (or sentimentally romantic) robotry (see, for example, David Levy's *Love and Sex With Robots: The Evolution of Human-Robot Relationships*). Until humans are uploaded or inloaded into cyberspace, though, I suspect the archetypal vanilla templates will continue to rule the roost, with technology providing only occasional boosts and modest enhancements.

PART TWO: DRUGS

ACID (1967)

It is related (but Allah knows all), begins Schehe-
razade on the 826th evening of her three-year filibus-
ter in the *Arabian Nights,* that roguish collection of
Oriental folk-lore—*that there were three friends in a
certain city of Arabia.*

*These good fellows were all endowed with admi-
rable subtlety and wit, their manners were excellent
and their faces pleasing. They kept common purse of
their takings, great and small, and spent an equal sum
each day on food for the body and hashish for the soul.*

*When they sat at night before the lighted candles to
take their drug, its course was to expand and elevate
their humor; and they never fell to brawling or bad
words. Their intelligence mounted as the hashish diminished and it was in those delightful moments that
they hit upon the most inspired of their drolleries.*

Let us, then, get this firmly established right from the start:
the use of mind-expanding substances is part of an ancient,
enduring human tradition. The explosive intrusion into social
awareness of marijuana, hashish, mescaline and LSD-25 has
obscured, momentarily, the age-old continuity in the use of
such substances. For if other cultures, more intuitive, exuberant
and social than ours, have maintained that tradition, Western
culture had pretty successfully snubbed it out of existence. The

West's old-maiden-ignoring-sex-type stance virtually obliterated public knowledge of mind-liberating specifics.

Yet our civilization—be it strident, overbearing, sexually-repressed, often ugly, rarely sensitive, hung up on a thousand self-inflicted paradoxes and disorders—still remains inventive, rich, physically healthy and astonishingly flexible. Inevitably, escapist misfits and creative artists preserved the tradition of what are now called "psychedelic" or "mind-manifesting" agents. Just as inevitably, in the backhanded fashion typical of our violent-and-timid culture, unsentimental science independently unearthed new nectars of nirvana unbelievably more potent than the Arabian trio's hashish.

The fact that psychedelics have been enthusiastically received in many quarters for millennia, let me hasten to stress, does not constitute an automatic argument in their favor. There has been, of course, wider and no less zealous approval of bloody war, racial hatred and sexual exploitation.

It is my intention to feel out some of the major threads in the currently raging psychedelic controversy, try to make a sane and open-eyed evaluation of where we stand and where we're heading. For our time is spawning three revolutions which, when their cycles are run to completion, may alter the very warp and woof of human existence beyond recognition.

The Cybernetic revolution, with automation and computers, will change people's relation to the world. It will relieve us of work and war and could (frighteningly) snatch from us the joys of discovery and creation.

Our relations with our fellow humans may find richness and depth: the Moral Revolution finds paths of tolerance, respect and sexual freedom.

The Psychedelic Revolution could lead us, as Aldous Huxley has suggested, into the heaven and hell of our own scarcely-explored consciousness. And because the Psychedelic Revolution may directly affect our personalities, it may ultimately be of the largest significance.

II.

Start here: "Marijuana, which induces a feeling of blissful tranquility, is not intrinsically dangerous, and certainly less harmful than alcohol. It serves, however, as a stepping stone to the deadly drugs of addiction and particularly, in Sydney, to heroin." Journalist Guy Morrison told readers of the *Sydney Morning Herald* this on March 18, 1967.

Consider further: "The chemical that opens the door to a sensory awareness untainted by flags, dollar signs, job titles, brand names has been well known for centuries to cultures that stress delicate, sensitive registration of sensory stimulation: the Arab cultures, the Indian cultures, the Mogul cultures. It is marijuana. There is no question that marijuana is a sensual stimulator—and this explains not only why it's favored by young people, but why it arouses fear and panic among the middle-aged, middle-class, whisky-drinking, blue-nosed bureaucrats...." That, from clinical psychologist and LSD *guru* Dr. Timothy Leary, in a now-famous September, 1966, *Playboy* interview.

Consider: "Marijuana smoking does not lead to physical or mental deterioration, it does not cause addiction... The habitual smoker knows when to stop because excessive doses of the weed usually reverses the pleasant high he is trying to get. In most instances the behavior of the smoker is of a friendly, sociable character. Aggressiveness and belligerency are not commonly seen." So reported the New York Academy Medicine to Mayor Fiorello LaGuardia in 1944. The report did not prevent legal prohibition of pot (marijuana), but it ensured that the law was formulated and administered liberally.

Consider: The latest official report of the Sydney Drug Squad, dealing with arrests during 1964, reports the conviction of a man charged with being found in possession of marijuana. He was sentenced to six months imprisonment with hard labor.

III.

But marijuana, though illegal, was not the *agent provocateur* in the Psychedelic Revolution. Of all the hallucinogens—or mind-altering, reality-changing agents—pot remains the most clearly defensible in terms of legalization and general distribution. While it *can* interfere with the split-second decisions demanded, for example, by driving (analogous with the effects of alcohol and tranquillizers, both legal), it lacks the antisocial payoff of the former and the poisoning deterioration of both. However, pot has really only come into the limelight tagging on the coattails of the true harbingers of the Expanding-Consciousness Revolution.

By now, everybody who has read the Sunday Press can recite with an air of casual accomplishment the esoteric tongue-twister, "d-lysergic acid diethylamide tartarate." LSD-25 is the fabulously potent hallucinogen first created nearly thirty years ago but brought into prominence only seven years ago by Dr. Tim Leary. Dismissed from Harvard after three years of tremendously provocative research into psychedelics (the reason: his unconventional approaches, plus the underground campus cult that surged into being around him, met with the displeasure of the circumspect university), Leary has become a charismatic hero martyr to an international psychedelic movement.

Others, before Leary, had written favorably of psychedelics. Aldous Huxley, who wrestled all his life with the conflicting yet complementary concepts of control and freedom, had predicted, decades before in *Brave New World,* a decadent "scientific" dystopia. His satirical, savagely delineated world was lulled into ugly stability by *Soma*, an imaginary tranquillizing drug. In later years, Huxley investigated mysticism and brought to the attention of the world the drug mescaline, an hallucinogen which stimulated mystical states. In 1962, shortly before his death, Huxley published a Utopian novel, *Island,* virtually a reply to his earlier satire, and as entrancingly beautiful as the other was horrific. His answer to *Soma* was an hallucinogenic drug that assisted self-awareness and mystical transcendence.

Leary, however, was to be the prophet. He walked out from a laboratory rather than a wilderness, but he offered more than the mystic's incoherent account of self-discovery and religious experience. He brought with him LSD—"acid" to the initiate— and with it he carried the Psychedelic Revolution out from academia into the market place.

The hurricane that has hurled itself out from that decision of Leary's, spiraling across learned pharmacological journals, theological debates, bills in the legislature, has scattered a debris of febrile hostility, raging curiosity, fanaticism and perplexity. It has created a chic subculture of thrill-seekers. It has become a focal point of pervasive American undergraduate dissatis- faction. It has also thrown Leary into the can on a thirty-year sentence of imprisonment.

§

I think that the sensory intensification typical of acid trips is well-enough known now that I won't bore you with another repetition. The jeweled, brilliant colors seen in everyday objects; the rich, subtle scents; the panoply of taste, sound and touch; these are the promised pleasures that draw in the psychedelic adventurers. More significant, and much less publicized, is the vivid playback of early memories and the amplified awareness of self which the voyager often experiences in an eight to twelve hour acid trip. The combined expansion of consciousness and self-consciousness make up the significance of hallucinogens. If the outside universe you contact is larger, more rhythmic, more exciting or terrifying than normal, so is the inner universe you travel through.

The human brain and central nervous system, after all, are not only physiological media where we receive and store infor- mation from within and outside our skins. They are also, and very importantly, organs that control and censor our percep- tions, memories and thoughts. Psychedelics interrupt the sorting process so that, in a sense, we have larger amounts of reality to chew on. Moreover, the hallucinogens characteristically elicit material that our memories have stored but blocked off from ordinary consciousness. They may be memories which, unpleasant and repressed, still trigger emotional responses without our being aware of the source. It is possible for the "mind-changing" drugs to bring us into confrontation with such stuff. This, it is claimed by opponents of LSD, may well be an insanely reckless thing to do, though success can be therapeutic.

As well, acid or the other psychedelic agents often link together in serene tranquility and loving unity the many disparate features of the world we usually live in. Objects or events we have never associated with one another are experienced as parts of a Whole. On the other hand a bad trip can evoke another sense of Wholeness, rank and terrifying in its monolithic evil. Psychedelics, in short, can indeed be Heaven and Hell.

One inference that has been driven from this, naturally enough, is that "genuine" mystical experience is just this process—without drugs. Huxley has convincingly collated many of the classic writings of religious visionaries, and demonstrated how endocrinal changes brought on by fasting, privation and self-flagellation mimic those produced by chemical hallucinogens. Perhaps the mystical encounter with transcendence and desolation, divine grace and its withdrawal, Beatific Vision and the Dark Night of the Soul, are basically identical with the psychedelic inner voyage.

For the humbling truth is that what each of us construes as Reality, the fixed immutable Way Things Are, has very little relation to what is outside of our local human habits of thought. The earth is *not* flat, the Sun does *not* spin about our world; but for more than 100,000 years humans did not know it. The table is *not* solid (except to our clumsy senses); yet we still cannot really appreciate emotionally what we're told about electrons and force-fields. In other words, our grossly limited capacities cannot begin to grasp the subtle reality of the universe. We must simplify as a child does when representing friends by drawing stick-figures. Only, unlike the child, we generally have no yardstick by which to measure our limitations.

Oddly enough, those restrictions are tremendously important. Our senses, both those that interpret the world outside the skin and those that unobtrusively watch the internal machinery, are vastly more sensitive than even an acute hunter-gatherer would realize. If we were tuned-in to peak performance all the time, we'd be literally inundated by sharp, clear and totally unmanageable swarms of information. From before we're born, and particularly in the months following birth, we are learning how to pick the relevancies out of (in William James' expressive words) "the blooming, buzzing confusion of pure sensation." Even the tiny spectrum of reality we are equipped to take in must be ruthlessly chopped, edited and tied together so we can handle it.

And different cultures have their own characteristic "frames of reality."

Western and Oriental constructions of reality differ rather severely. While Western minds learn from the cradle to treat matters as if the world worked by strict, separate chains of cause-and-effect, the East sees events as huge knotted skeins where each cause has many effects and each event has many causes. The driving impulse in the West was seen as Law; in the East as Tao, or a spontaneity principle that creates order of such complexity as to defy analysis. The Oriental view is closer to the truth, and Western science has eventually arrived at it. Yet our traditional, erroneously simplified view was needed to get scientific technology started. The East would never have made it alone: that view of reality was just too daunting.

The psychedelic experience cuts at the roots of these pruned-down "realities." Suddenly we are hurled into a world even more complex than that of Oriental philosophy, where richness and texture flood beyond control, where the Wholeness is wonderfully rewarding or frighteningly uncontrollable. It is a world new to us, exhilarating if we are secure, adaptive and strong, but disruptive and terrifying if we are inflexible, emotionally estranged from others.

IV.

Why, if the hallucinogenic high is a valid if novel view of the real world, is there so much legal opposition to it? "The laws," charges Leary, "are hysterical, because the men who passed them have allowed their ignorance of LSD to escalate into irrationality. Instinctively, they put LSD into the same bag with heroin. They think of drug-taking as a criminal activity practiced by stuporous escapists and crazy, deranged minds. The daily diatribes of police officials and many legislators to that effect completely ignore the fact that the use of LSD is a white-collar, upper-middle-class, college educated phenomenon. The LSD type is not a criminal type. He's not an underground character or a junkie."

I suspect, actually, that Leary was not telling the whole truth in describing his acid-heads. At that time, true, acid was a campus phenomenon because campus kids were the only ones in a position to get this new, rare drug. Since then, college-educated people probably still stand a better chance of obtaining or synthesizing it. However, with a growing black-market, this aristocratic elite will not retain their exclusive status.

Even so, the basic point remains. Psychedelics, hallucinogens, consciousness-expanders—call them what you will—are qualitatively different from addictive junk. Hunter J. Thompson's friend, journalist Lionel Olay, remarked pungently of the junkie breed: "Ironically, the hallucinogens are exactly what these cats do *not* want, since the kind of self-awareness it induces becomes unbearably painful, for the deluded especially, operating precisely in the opposite direction from the opiates—morphine, heroin—which is their nirvana." If you wish to become stupefied, if consciousness is so unpalatable that you're anxious for the zombie, vegetable life William Burroughs describes in his novels, psychedelic agents will not take you there.

§

They can, however, drive such a person insane. The occasional precipitation into psychosis of an acid voyager is a cogent argument for the restriction and careful control of these powerful drugs. The *British Medical Journal* said in its leading article for June 16, 1966: "In Britain LSD became front-page news as a result of reports of the use among teenagers of morning glory seeds, which contain LSD. Since statements about teenagers and pleasure-giving drugs are often overweighted with emotion and prejudice, it is unsafe to conclude out of hand that there is a manifest social danger here which would justify repressive legislation..." However, the journal instanced persistent psychotic disturbances reported of people on LSD, and went on, "This indictment seems enough to warrant the proscription of so dangerous a drug."

Yet, the article warned, the cases were all from psychiatric situations and it was surmised that most patients who developed adverse reactions should not have been given the drug anyway "since they were manifestly unstable or pre-psychotic." The *Journal* suggested legal and administrative handling of LSD on the lines used in controlling, though not prohibiting, amphetamine stimulant drugs.

This cautious, responsible position is very similar to the stance adopted by Dr. Leary, though he sees further to a desirable day when "marijuana and LSD are put under some form of licensing." Licenses for "mild psychedelics like marijuana should be similar to those for the automobile license. The applicant would demonstrate his seriousness by studying manuals, passing written tests and getting a doctor's certificate for psychological and physical soundness. The licensing for use of powerful psychedelic drugs like LSD should be along the lines of the airplane pilot's license: intensive study and preparation, plus very stringent testing for fitness and competence."

At the moment, simply not enough is known about the strong psychedelics for anyone to feel easy about their casual use.

When something like LSD becomes a fad, a status-symbol, those first afflicted by the urgency to partake might very probably be individuals more responsive than their more staid, more contented neighbors to its disruptive effects. Danger is certainly present, as two psychiatrists from the UCLA Center for the Health Sciences stressed in an angry letter, replying to Dr. Leary's optimistic interview. Many of their research subjects (patients who had presented themselves after trips with "hallucinations, anxiety to the point of panic, depression with suicidal tendencies") had suffered in their first trip. More significantly, "others had had up to sixty previous 'trips' on LSD. Often they took it with a 'guide.'

"Contrary to what Leary implies," they stated, "many such patients do *not* respond promptly to tranquillizer medication; some remain hospitalized for many months. Many such patients functioned *well* before their LSD adventures and under no circumstances could have been classified as even borderline cases of emotional illness." There is, they claim, *no* way to predict—"not from psychological testing, from psychiatric interviews, from being in the right setting with friends and a guide, from being tension free nor even from having had a number of previous trips"—who will be safe.

Many psychiatrists, in fact, refuse to use the emotionally-favorable term "psychedelics" for the substances, preferring "hallucinogen" or more often "psychotomimetic." This, it seems, is going beyond scientific detachment to the other extreme. While the drugs do indeed frequently elicit hallucinations—the patient mistaking one object for another, or vividly imagining a sensory stimulus which is not present—this may be largely the kind of error expected of someone re-structuring his view of reality. Equally, "psychotomimetic" implies that the subject's behavior indicates a temporary and artificial psychotic derangement, that is, a complete slip from reality. But since "reality" is a contentious word, this is begging the question.

The drugs are used, in fact, in psychotherapy to break down a neurotic patient's defenses and allow him to experience emotionally the normally well-guarded mental conflicts which are producing his sickness. If he is strong enough to sustain the guilt and tensions thus released, LSD therapy can bring him in hours or weeks, rather than years, to a new and better balance. On the other hand, with his defenses down a patient lacking the stamina to sustain savage internal clashes can easily take refuge in real psychosis.

One man, for example, being treated at Powick Hospital in the west of England for despondency, intense disturbing aggressive impulses and sexual shame, developed a manifest schizophrenic psychosis under LSD. After treatment was discontinued there was no remission, and he was subjected to a lobotomy.

By the same token, a highly successful and fascinating case occurred in the same hospital. A fifty-five-year-old university educated man, good in his responsible post, suffered a breakdown with acute anxiety, neurotic depression and sleeplessness. He was not a self-confident man, and he had become trapped in a human chess game when several superiors tried to use him against one another, involving him in serious conflicts of loyalty. Before treatment began, he had been sick for some months and unable to work.

During the first ten of fifteen LSD treatments, he had many vividly experienced memories of childhood, reaching back to his earliest years. "I came to understand myself better," he reported. His condition improved and he returned to work.

A state of increasing anxiety attended his next four LSD treatments, "terror," as he expressed it, "in the absolute—connected with nothing." A climax came during the fifteenth trip, a feeling of terrible compression. He felt himself collapse, curl into fetal position, felt something being done to his navel. Abruptly, he realized that he had re-lived the experience of being born. A pink light suffused around him. "Mind you," he told the doctor, "not light coming in through the eyes, but like something I was in, like water, perhaps, and then I saw all in connection—I felt my mother, her fear, her sexual fear of my father."

Whether this overly-Freudian and unlikely experience was

really reconstructed from true partial memory, or whether it was purely fantasy, the client found that sustained improvement followed. He was no longer irritable over small everyday matters, so much so that for a long time his wife was convinced he was keeping strict control over himself all the time. His previous habitual disposition to perfectionism and easily aroused guilt was considerably diminished, and in general the experience of LSD therapy left him more understanding and tolerant.

Experiments conducted in 1964 with normal subjects, and reported in the *Journal of Nervous and Mental Disease,* found that the favorable experience of that man—rather than the terrifying fate of the lobotomized schizophrenic—was the general case with LSD therapy.

The rapid lowering of defense mechanisms in a secure and supportive environment provided an initial shock and some anxiety. But this was frequently followed by the realization that the subject was not overwhelmed and defeated: rather, he or she felt liberated from the burden of protecting against symbolic threats.

Tests to detect any increase in fluency, flexibility and originality were negative, but as Leary has pointed out, psychedelics "enhance the creative perspective, but the ability to convert your new perspective...into a communication form still requires the technical skill."

§

Thus we have, perhaps, the defining limits of what advances a Psychedelic Revolution will make. The lives of some will be destroyed, tragically, the mirrors of their minds scarred and splintered in their own reflection. Others will find themselves and those they love in a new dimension of ease, openness—an honesty of self possible to people whose symbolic hang-ups have been unsnarled and stacked in order.

For most, a fine, enhanced creative responsiveness and appreciative participation in a turned-on mode of unity which complements the fragmented mode of cause and effect. And for some, the creative members of the species, the Psychedelic Revolution may offer the scintillating universes of multiple realities—to breathe, to learn, to capture, to portray, to bind and orchestrate the human and cosmic realities into a rich weft that is not a rat-race, but a dance.

And yet, though it is possible, I doubt that anything so sane and lyrical will ever make it. The Psychedelic Revolution is on, and it can't be easily stopped (unless in some unforeseeable catastrophe the drugs are a psychic equivalent of Thalidomide, building to some critical point of mental burn-out for Leary and his energetic seers); it won't be easily stopped, but its main channel may be diverted and perverted.

For I read in *The New York Times* the other day a report of gentle, altruistic horror:

> Dr. Edward C. Taylor said the United States Army was interested in synthesis of the marijuana chemical because it had potential use as an agent to incapacitate the enemy without doing permanent harm... Through another modification, the drug may also be used to help the allied forces, Dr. Taylor explained. He noted that Baluba tribesmen in the Congo use marijuana before they go to battle because it makes them fearless in the face of gunfire.

HOPE FIEND (1973)

You fold open the morning paper over a bowl of cereal, putting off that first smoke because your mouth still tastes foul from last night, and you read how a fourteen-year-old girl has killed herself accidentally with car sickness tablets.

The girl had skipped school with a girlfriend and taken a handful of her mother's tablets. The word was out that ten or so would give you a trip. The coroner found that she'd died after taking the pills for the purposes of "youthful experimentation."

You grimace, push the paper aside.

Why do the silly little buggers do it? But then you remember a friend telling you last night about her twenty-year-old cousin, due to be married on the weekend. His mates had insisted on the traditional stag's night, though he wasn't all that eager. They'd all got roaring drunk, good old tradition, and somewhere along the line he found himself in a car. He was scared, drunk, wanted out. His mates had tried to keep him in the car.

Struggling to get out, he'd had the car door slammed on his wrist. Right hand, of course; he's a clerk. Artery and tendon were severed.

Booze and pills. You reach for the packet and light up, coughing.

Booze and pills. That's one of the reasons why the fourteen-year-old girl died. We're a drug-dependent nation. The sunburned war hero, if he ever existed, is half-stoned most of the time on one euphoric substance or another, and his kids are simply forging ahead down the same Kokodeine trail. "Youthful experimentation." Terrific.

A man with forthright views on the subject is Dr. Bob Webb, Director of the New South Wales Mental Health and Drug Education Program. One of his department's publications, "Informed Opinion," has some crisp comments on the problems of drug abuse.

"The more one learns about drugs, and the people who abuse them," states this document, "the more one becomes aware that the drug problem is a problem of living that will not be solved by any single set of programs. Well-intentioned energies currently devoted to the drug problem are simply being distracted from the more basic social maladies that cause and promote drug abuse.

"For these reasons, the emphasis of the program has shifted from the 'drug' to...the 'quality of life' theme."

Bob Webb is a short, powerfully built man of fifty, with a grey-black beard and a sun-tanned dome. He has a deep, resonant voice: a fluent instrument, but he's also prepared to listen. With inevitable, unpremeditated irony, the first thing you ask this drug educator is whether it's okay to smoke in his office.

There's a hunt for an ashtray. He hasn't got one; he stopped smoking a couple of years ago. You settle for a metal waste-paper basket, crushing out the butts on the smooth grey paint, smelling the fumes of scorched acrylic.

Dr. Webb admits that he's given up smoking more than once. He'd thought that after a two-year break it might be possible to enjoy cigarettes instead of being hooked on them: a couple of cigarettes a day, perhaps. But...he laughs sardonically.

Broderick: Is this an example of the physiological changes which seem to be involved in all the drugs of addiction or habituation?

Webb: Yes. Cigarettes are genuinely addictive.

Broderick: You can't break the habit even after two years' abstinence?

Webb: Right. The evidence seems clear. I understand there's a physiological change in our cells. More important, there's a psychological dependence which can get you back after years off them. This is the factor which frightens alcoholics. AA's attendance is pretty bloody good; alcoholics continue to attend because they're terrified if they don't they'll argue themselves into having just one for the pleasure—and then *zoom.*

Broderick: How did you get into this field?

Webb: Well, I'm a psychiatrist, employed in the State Psychiatric Services. I published a paper on teachers and mental health and how teachers can be trained to discern which kids need help and refer them. So I was asked about four years ago to look at preventive psychiatry opportunities, using education methods. Then, three years ago, the Commonwealth funded half a million dollars to drug education, to be shared among the States. I was then mental health consultant; drug education was added.

New South Wales was lucky; we already had this Division of Health Education. The other States had no skeleton to flesh out. We recruited a team of 16: since the 21C was a psychologist and I was a psychiatrist, our approach was one of community psychiatry rather than education. Most people equate education and information. We didn't fall into the trap, luckily.

Broderick: What method do you use instead?

Webb: We settled on group discussion and debate. Schools was only one of four areas we tackled—and *not* because we thought drug abuse was primarily a youth problem. But it seemed a logical place to begin. We needed to get kids fairly young if we were to prevent it starting.

The major effort was with kids, but also with their parents, who have quite different needs. Parents are scared, uptight. People will ring us here, saying they've found some tobacco-like substance, and they'll be crying, feeling that this is the end of the world. So they need factual information on drugs, and reassurance. Kids, on the other hand, need to be confronted with the likely consequences of their behavior.

Broderick: You mean kids who are not yet using drugs?

Webb: We don't know. We prefer to make contact with them either pre-experimentation or during the experimental period.

Broderick: You specified four programs. You've mentioned children and parents. What are the others?

Webb: We have a program for communities—villages, towns, armed service centers—who come to us wanting a program; we offer aid. Perhaps such a group approaches us seeking a one night lecture. Since we reject the straight information format, we encourage them to set up a committee which runs debate groups. Our funds make it possible to support them with small sums for mailing and so on.

In these groups, as with parent oriented programs, we put up for consideration the normal person's use of socially accepted drugs such as alcohol and tranquilizers. We try to foster better communications, particular between parents and the children.

Our fourth program contacts "key persons"—doctors, lawyers, school teachers, medic students and so on. These are people who, because of their social roles, should know what the issues are, and though their key positions can influence behavior.

For example, we've had nurses discussing to what extent legal drugs are over-prescribed. It's been customary in hospitals to give all patients sedatives at night. The nursing staff concluded that it's feasible to cut down on many of these drugs. The problem they were faced with is that if a patient has been in hospital for six weeks, receiving barbiturates every night, he might go out with a habit.

At Sydney's Prince Henry hospital, our program slashed night sedation by a third. In conjunction with the staff, we changed the system slightly. Patients no longer had to go to bed at ten—they could watch TV until they grew tired naturally. The automatic administration of night sedation was abolished. Four months later, this approach was still proving to be effective.

The nursing staff later admitted that they'd never liked the old system, but that individually they'd felt powerless to change it. Same with the doctors. Our seminar was a catalyst transforming individual concern into collective decisions.

Another "key person" program aims at kids in, to date, twenty Sydney schools. In high school, we suspect that some kids miss the special attention they're accustomed to getting in primary school by having a single teacher for the whole year. We're trying to make up for that loss by a program called "Senior-Junior Discussion."

Certain Sydney schools gave us permission to train 5th Formers as discussion leaders and mentors for 1st Formers, with each senior pupil responsible for six juniors. They meet at least once a fortnight, and discuss whatever comes up. Backup resources were either teachers or us. Most of this was done in North Shore schools, both State and private.

Spinoffs from this program are vastly improved communication between the younger and older kids, weekend activities like bushwalking, coffee shops in local areas—the Students' Association of the Pittwater Area has a coffee shop run by themselves in Avalon. The program's been going for three years.

Broderick: What age group is experimenting with drugs?

Webb: When we started, we thought around sixteen. Now, we're thinking we should have these programs for late primary children. I'd guess—and it is a guess, aided by such survey material as we have—experimentation happens somewhere between first year and third year at high school.

First-year kids are often very antidrugs. Ask them what they'd do to a pusher, they'd re-introduce the death penalty. Ask the same question of a Third Former, he's likely to sing his praises.

Broderick: Is this just adolescent revolt against authority?

Webb: Not that alone. They're going through an immense

upheaval: puberty, the transition from protection in primary to freedom in secondary school. They're being asked to think for themselves, encouraged to seek information and experience. And in this mad turmoil drug experimentation is likely to start. There's evidence indicating that drug use is higher at school than it is at university, that the experimentation phase is generally over by the end of school.

Broderick: What drugs are the kids experimenting with?

Webb: Basically grass (marijuana).

Broderick: There was a flap in Britain a few years ago about abuse of amphetamines and barbiturates—pills of every shape and color, rather than just grass.

Webb: That seemed to be a peculiarly English scene. I don't think it happened here the same way. Australian authorities banned amphetamines rather early, a piece of legislation that appears to have worked.

Broderick: How does the New South Wales approach to drug education compare with approaches in other countries?

Webb: Drug education has adopted a number of different models. One is the legislative model. Laws are made, enforcement bodies try to ensure that the prohibitions are carried out, and it's assumed that the problems will then vanish. Typical of this approach is the United States. An adequately policed law on, say, heroin, is supposed to result in no addicts, no pushers, no market because they will all be locked up. We now know, from the evidence, that in the States that didn't work.

Another model is taken from medicine: the English model. The addict, in this view, is a sick guy whom we're most unlikely to be able to treat successfully. So, to de-criminalize his illness, we'll *give* him his heroin if he comes forward. He's treated like the diabetic needing his daily shot of insulin. In general, although it sounds highly risky, that approach seems to work better than the law enforcement model.

Australia uses a sort of mixture of both approaches. We

give methadone, an addictive drug which allows for improvement, but we don't give heroin, which doesn't.

Broderick: William Burroughs and other articulate ex-junkies overseas claim that some addicts with high-level jobs—typically, doctors—can use heroin for many years while still functioning normally. If a doctor can write his own script for the drug he's out of the pernicious circle of pushers, criminals and ever-rising prices, and can thus handle the habit. Is this true?

Webb: I wish I knew. I, too, hear these stories, particularly of doctors, but I've never met such an addict. I really am in doubt about how possible that is.

Broderick: Wouldn't the English clinics have information on this?

Webb: I haven't seen any reports on that. But now we're talking about methods of treatment, which is not really my sphere of interest.

What we want to do is allow people the opportunity to debate many taboo issues associated with drug abuse, including authority, parents, education and so on. Our job is to see that the facts which go into the debate are as accurate and up-to-date as possible.

If, at the end of an exhaustive debate, people decide either to take drugs or not to take them, we're content. Provided the person is making a discriminating choice about his future actions, that's as much as we can do.

Broderick: But as an official of a government which prohibits marijuana, say, as a narcotic—which, pharmacologically, it's not—aren't you obliged to give people scientifically false information? Or do you simply say: "These are the medical facts we have at the moment, but you'd be wise not to use grass because you risk jail."

Webb: One of our publications states that the greatest danger of marijuana smoking is the loss of your personal liberties, restrictions on your future travel, and so on.

Broderick: This, I fear, reminds me of the dangers of opposing the State in the Soviet Union. Your greatest risk is that they'll put you in a psychiatric institution and throw away the key. Are you in such a moral dilemma?

Webb: We've escaped that problem by refusing to pursue drugs as such. We say that use of drugs for social or non-medical purposes is a type of behavior—a behavior that could be dangerous, in this case—and our debates examine the whys and wherefores of different behaviors, rather than drugs. While the Great Marijuana Debate was raging, with everyone getting nowhere, we were saying that it didn't matter. Nor does it matter that alcohol is allowed by society, and grass isn't. Cigarette smoking gives you a carcinogen mixed with an addictive chemical. It would be criminal if someone had just invented cigarettes and said: "Look, I want to mix something which will kill with something that will keep people smoking it." We'd say, of course: "You're mad even to think of it."

But we didn't get caught in all this, because we said we weren't terribly interested in those social paradoxes. Our concern was the behavior. Why do people choose one thing rather than another? How much is the result of peer pressure? How much is impulse? Do you know the dangers and the pleasures? Have you decided if it's worth the risk or are you just going to do what your neighbor does?

Broderick: These are the issues you put forward in your debates?

Webb: We allow them to come up. Very often, nowadays, young people for instance are not all that interested in drugs. Environment issues come up a hell of a lot. Sometimes drugs gets a mention as an issue, but we've always treated it as a behavior.

Broderick: It sounds as though you're running a civics course, a program in becoming a "good citizen."

Webb: That could be. I know you're implying a criticism. You may wish to argue that a certain locality has high drug use because, socially and environmentally, it's a lousy area.

We don't let you get away with that. We ask: "Are you going to do anything about those conditions? If you are, we'll help you."

For instance, very often young people say there's no place for them to go, nothing to do, so what else is there except to turn on or shoot up? Okay, we bring aldermen along to the group, if they ask, and tell them how to go about setting up coffee shops, how to present their arguments to the local council and so on. They've got no money, so we bring in someone who's successfully raised money, someone their own age usually, who can show them how to do it. How to get around the law that specifies that you can't have a club unless someone's in charge who is over twenty-one. In all of these areas we restrict ourselves to aid and advice.

Is all of this drug education? I guess that if alternative activities is anything to do with prevention of drug abuse then these kids are going, at least, to be too busy to get stoned. (laughs.)

In this State we never paid much attention to disseminating straight information, straight lectures. We've always believed information, as such, had nothing to do with attitudes or behavior. That was slightly misleading, as we'll see in a moment. We also vetoed one-night stands as being nothing more than PR exercises. And we don't use fear; it's counterproductive, a boomerang effect.

How many people have been turned on to sex by clergymen raving and ranting against it in Victoriana fashion? I'm sure I would have been. So these are the approaches we've abandoned: long films, didacticism. And that left little else but group discussion.

I've just come back from a conference in Switzerland where they found a correlation between amount of knowledge about drugs and behavior. People who use drugs know more about them than those who don't. Whether this is because the users have had a drug information program, or whether their previous decision to use drugs has led them to check out the pros and cons, I don't know.

In fact, if you go to a school and tell the kids all about drugs, honestly and factually, you'll probably leave having turned on that school. But we don't know which is the horse and which is the cart. Being a cautious guy, I would view information services as risky. Telling things to captive audiences has always been unappealing to me; now it seems positively dangerous.

Broderick: Is this a "forbidden fruit" effect, where people do something simply because an authority has warned them off? Or is it that they find, when you give them reliable information, that many drugs are not as horrendous as they'd been led to believe?

Webb: That's possible. Studies in the States show clearly that when drug information programs have been given to schools, knowledge about drugs has increased—and so has the use of drugs.

Broderick: Use of heroin?

Webb: That wasn't specified in the reports.

Broderick: Maybe if you tell people the truth about marijuana, a lot of them will smoke it, but if you tell the facts about heroin they will be deterred.

Webb: We're doing a before-and-after study in New South Wales right now, and should be in a better position to answer that question.

I believe our approach of allowing people to ventilate about any causes they think might make them use or not use drugs, rather than us telling them, is the right one. We haven't yet got figures to prove that contention, but it's coming into favor all over the world. Certainly the US is doing quite amazing things.

Last year, starting in October, they tore up all their old drug program literature. They've destroyed $10 million worth of printed information. They admit that their concept of drug information has failed. The two reasons for the "scene" over there, they say, are the failure of drug education based on scares, ex-addict testimonials, straight information—within the context of a punitive law enforcement model. They're going to adopt a rather amazing program based, uh, on, er... love.

Broderick: Love?

Webb: One of the TV shorts they're going to use shows a young man wandering about, telling how he got busted, had to leave his home town, the hard life. An older man appears at the door of a house; it's his Dad. They run toward one another, embrace. Then there's a hairy guy playing a guitar, saying: "There's a whole new language for it—it's love."

I think the Australian isn't quite emotional enough to buy a program like that—

Broderick: Yeah.

Webb: —but the States might.

Obviously they feel it's safer because they feel that their previous program, plus the law enforcement model, is responsible for the bad scene they've got over there.

Broderick: Maybe the strongest effect of such an ad would be on the parents, encouraging them to be less punitive in their attitude.

Webb: Perhaps. Art Linkletter, who went on TV to call for stiffer penalties after his daughter died as a result of a bad acid trip, is now saying he made a mistake then.

Broderick: But this new program retains the law enforcement context?

Webb: Yes. I just heard that New York has stiffened its laws regarding pushers. But in my view, and that of many people at the congress, the law enforcement model is a retrograde step. It's looked upon with approval by authorities, seen by them as effective, but they're wrong.

In fact, one of the messages of this congress was that if we don't get ourselves sorted out, develop a policy that recommends and uses methods which are safe and don't create a scene, are not a gross imposition on people, many societies in desperation are going to do the only thing that seems available: make a law.

Broderick: Many counter-culture philosophers argue that punitive, authoritarian drug laws are not adopted out of desperation but are an integral part of authority's techniques for
dominating antagonistic or alternative elements.

Webb: I think that when drug education programs have palpably
failed, there's a sort of lash-back. "We'll have to get tough"
sort of thing. And it's far cheaper to make a law than to drop
half-a-million dollars into a novel education program. It's far
quicker, too, to say "Let's make it illegal." And in the case
of marijuana it's fair enough, while the researchers get on
with their studies and tell us the long-term effects, to ban it
anyway until new evidence turns up.

Broderick: But there have been large groups smoking grass for
hundreds, if not thousands, of years. There must be as much
information available on the physical and psychological
properties of grass as there is on the vast number of accepted
medical drugs.

Webb: Medical drugs are having a tough time being accepted
now. Thalidomide did that, at least, for us.

Broderick: In the psychiatric realm, though, there are many
drugs in common use which have only been known since
the '50s.

Webb: True, but they've been properly researched. What
evidence there is on cultures which have used marijuana for
hundreds of years—Egyptian medical reports, for example—
is all very harsh toward grass. They blame grass for *every*
admission to their psychiatric hospitals.

Most of those studies have been rejected by the West
as not taking into account factors like starvation, disease,
poverty and so on. But still, the papers from those countries are negative toward grass. We've just got to let modern
research methods run their course. Most of the old evidence
is based on no more than interviews and expert guesses.

Broderick: Can you see a time when an acceptable, definitive
statement on the properties of marijuana will be available?

Webb: I hope so. It's bad for us not to know. I hope sometime soon someone will tell us.

Broderick: Why, in general, do people use or abuse drugs?

Webb: There are two answers. One is the list of answers people give when asked: boredom, curiosity, as a gesture against authority, for pleasure. All of these are relevant. But people abuse drugs, I believe, because of their specific personality makeup, needs, personal resources, capacity to handle stresses from outside. We need drugs when our internal resources cannot keep us reasonably happy. If we use the wrong drug—one of the addicting substances—we get hooked. Tobacco is an example. It's an anti-stress drug. When I was smoking, I would often reach for a cigarette in a stressful moment. Then the nicotine got me habituated.

Broderick: Does this mean there are only so many people at risk, that if the worst happened and the entire at-risk group became part of the drug market, that's where it would stop?

Webb: No. Remember what took place in Europe and the States when opium was freely available. There were literally millions of opium addicts, mainly people taking it as laudanum. The idea that the type of person who's likely to be an addict is pretty much in the minority would be true only for a drug which didn't have a huge potential, as heroin does, of addicting people.

Broderick: Imagine a drug with all the effects of heroin except addictiveness. Would you reject the use of that drug?

Webb: I'd favor its use in treatment of current heroin addicts.

Broderick: But should it be legalized and sold freely on the market? Is heroin banned for its psychological effects, or because—like syphilis, say—it causes physical deterioration and finally death?

Webb: It's banned, like all addictive substances, because a human being becomes quite literally a slave of an inanimate thing.

Broderick: As we're slaves of oxygen and food?

Webb: I think your argument is a good one for adopting, with this hypothetical drug, a medical rather than a law-enforcement model. I can't really see a panacea drug which instantly transported us away from our troubles—and if it existed, I'm sure I for one would be addicted to it.

Broderick: Suppose this drug worked directly on the pleasure center in the brain. Would or should society ban it? If, like the hypothetical junkie doctor who can work while shooting up, you could achieve bliss on demand, many would argue that this would corrode social relationships and perhaps destroy society—without physically harming the individuals using it.

Webb: It wouldn't be the education or medical people who'd have any voice on that; quite certainly it'd be a political decision. It would depend on whether a country wanted millions of "happy" citizens, or wanted working citizens.

Or maybe it might be restricted to once-a-month ceremonies. But you might well debate the issue and find that though this drug seems to be physically harmless, it's bad for us as thinking, creative human beings to have such easy access to nirvana. That would be a logical decision, and you'd have reached it through honest education, debate, and, hopefully, with the correct facts.

Broderick: What's the extent of the "drug problem" in Australia?

Webb: I don't know. There are surveys and police reports. It isn't a desperate scene, it can be coped with at the moment; it's under control.

It's impossible to say how many heroin addicts there are. Some say for every narcotic addict you know there's another seven busily on the scene. At Brisbane Street clinic in Sydney, there were 140 patients on the methadone program as of September, 1972.

Broderick: Is the use of the "soft" drugs increasing?

Webb: I expect a drop in the use of grass, provided enough people experiment with it, paradoxically. The younger people I know are turning off grass. They're turning off grass parties, because they're so dull. If you go along sober, looking from the door, there seems to be a lot of communication going on. But there isn't. It's repetitive—"Far out, man," over and over—and unless you're stoned yourself, it's a bloody bore.

Broderick: Some feel that way about going to church, yet you find the devout returning to church services year in and year out. Further, some argue that this reaction you cite is a proof of how we've lost "inwardness," that we too-readily seek immediate kicks rather than being prepared to sit for years, perhaps aided by these drugs, to help us get into a quieter, more meditative mood.

Webb: The word these days is "alternatives," and one of the things which people are looking at as an alternative to drugs—indeed as a treatment—is transcendental meditation. At the Swiss conference it was claimed that one can get the pleasures which drugs are alleged to give by such non-drug methods. Apparently these methods are regarded as acceptable, which has a bearing on our discussion earlier about a non-addictive drug.

Broderick: But if these meditators in turn also drop out of industrial society, how long will it be before their practices become an offence under the law?

Webb: Yes, this is what we don't know, do we? Or perhaps we go the way of the Polynesians—someone else comes along...

Broderick: Many drug education programs are attacked for failing to come to terms with the underlying social problems. You seem to spend most of your efforts on just this area.

Webb: Yes, we're largely concerned with social issues. We could almost be called activists in provoking change. I believe that the New South Wales program, based on human behavior, attitudes, using techniques of discussion and debate—which has been largely criticized by many bodies for not being "tough enough"—has been endorsed by the 1973 world conference.

What we've been doing for three years, the rest of the world has just got around to recommending. So we've avoided the disastrous experiences of other countries, because we've adopted a psychological approach rather than a didactic one.

DRUGS: LOOKING BACK FROM NOW

Acid Hope Fiend

What we didn't know about in 1967 and 1973:

The illegal future of ecstasy (MDMA, popular only since the late 1970s and early 1980s), or crack cocaine, or crystal meth, or ketamine, or glue- and gasoline-sniffing... Or illegal anabolic steroids to make manly men even burlier (while, apparently, shrinking their balls and stoking their rage), and date-rape roofies. Some old hippies and their devotees still talk raptly about "entheogens," natural or synthesized stuff like peyote, 'shrooms, ayahuasca or indeed LSD that purportedly puts the seeker after truth into contact with transnatural states and entities; some of these were known four decades ago, but not widely.

Or the legal, indeed heavily marketed, selective serotonin reuptake inhibitors such as Prozac and Zoloft. The routine treatment of bipolar depression-mania with Lithium was not widely known (approved by the FDA only in 1970). Children were not being widely treated with amphetamines for attention deficit disorders. Today, legal pharmaceutical industries are immensely large and wealthy, with considerable lobbying and other influence over elected governments. Meanwhile, illegal mind- and mood-altering substances form the basis of extraordinarily vicious criminal distribution systems that have almost brought Mexico to collapse and fund the fundamentalist foes of the West in Afghanistan and elsewhere.

Marijuana (California's largest crop, despite its illegality) is ever so slowly becoming decriminalized in some US states and elsewhere, mainly for the benefit of desperately ill cancer patients undergoing nauseating and debilitating treatment by radiation and vastly more toxic chemotherapy drugs. Physicians are permitted to prescribe and administer opiates to ease the agony of the dying or badly injured, but these uses are held under tight control. Meanwhile, ecstasy and other euphoriants are simply part of the twenty-first-century landscape for the young, like the cellphones thumbed day and night by a new breed of placid herd animals who can't abide separation, while their elders largely keep hitting the liquor and the pill bottle to get down or up.

What more can one say about drugs, finally, except that our mad hunger for them, for their exciting or soothing or enraging effects, is out of control and, like petroleum, is one of those wonderful imports whereby western communities simultaneously soothe and smooth our moods, fuck ourselves up, and fund our enemies?

In March, 2010, the *Guardian* reported that in Mexico, with "more than 2,000 people killed since the new year, 2010 is shaping up to overtake the record 6,500 drug-related murders last year, which exceeded the toll of more than 5,000 in 2008. The killings have happened despite an offensive against the cartels involving tens of thousands of soldiers and federal police launched in December 2006 by the president, Felipe Calderón." By August, with some 28,000 dead, Calderón and other officials were beginning to admit the merit in legalization as a way to break the cartels.

Is the answer, simply or simplistically, depending on your stance, Just Say Yes? Recalling the barbarities and corruption of alcohol Prohibition from 1920 to 1933, and the failure of society to collapse after the Eighteenth Amendment was repealed, we might surmise that relaxation of drug laws would solve most of the horrid problems entailed by proscription. Or would "the floodgates be opened" (that perennial metaphor), with heavy duty drugs exploding into general usage, neither Huxley's pacifying *soma* nor elevating *moksha* but slow brain death to great swathes of an increasingly out of work community?

Legalizing casinos and other forms of easy, sometimes ruinous, gambling has destroyed some lives, but certainly put a crimp in the income stream of organized crime. The same seems to be the case with legalized prostitution, in places where sex work is regarded as mildly odious but inevitable, and the better for being scrutinized for disease and violence. Could open access to marijuana and perhaps ecstasy possibly be worse than nicotine cigarettes and booze? If some desperadoes are fated to a life of heroin addiction, isn't it more sensible and humane to make the drug available as a prescription medication, maybe even providing it free of charge? (Declaration to the Thought Police: I do not use *any* of these drugs; I prefer my own brain's neurotransmitters. But I dutifully purchase and ingest every day prescribed drugs to deal with gastritis, hypertension, asthma, prostate troubles, and cholesterol, some of which have quite unpleasant side effects.)

Nearly fifty years after the Summer of Love and Dope, legalization is still a radical notion, curdling the blood of conservatives tormented by fear of excess, the unruly, stoned lunatics charging down the road in stolen cars for the sheer deranged hell of it. It could happen that way. Those millions routinely texting and emailing and blathering on cellphones as they drive are not all imbeciles, but commonplace temptations can make most of us into fools. In the meantime, though, the costs of Just Saying No mount and mount: costs in billions of dollars pouring into the coffers of drug syndicates, murders by the thousands, international wars, and threats of wars, to rival the bloodiness of the wealthy world's hunger for oil. It seems like time to try a different way.

PART THREE: RELIGION

IF THERE'S NO GOD, WHO PULLS UP THE NEXT KLEENEX? (1967)

I.

Friend, when the raw meat and bunched muscle is finally pared back from the bone, when—under the cool scrutiny of historians not yet in the womb—today's frenzied, furious, quietly desperate, sunburst paradox of anger and complacency is harmonized into a profile of our age, perhaps our children will see this culture as betrayed by its own brash energy. Perhaps they will discern, with surprise, a flaw in our time so obvious that we ignore it, mistake its cancer for whole flesh, leave its reckoning to the maunderings of hacks.

In the midst of our achievements and triumphs, beyond the growing pains and the agony of our stumbling exploratory steps, there *is* a flaw. I hold no brief for the smug, sad, balding gentlemen flapping their dreary mouths about the depravity of our age. Civilization does not leap fully-armored and resplendent into existence. It's two million years since our ancestors dragged their knuckles on the ground, eight thousand since they invented agriculture: we're getting there, brother, but it's taken a couple of mega-years so far. Give it time, we've still got that monkey on our back.

Yet in large degree the malaise, the central wound of our culture, *is* singular and peculiar to this century. Men have known it before but never, I think, so widely nor so intensely. The widening ripples of its shockfront are snatching us all, democratically and pell-mell, into a turbulence we hardly recognize.

I am talking about the need for direction, for a compass-reading, and our common failure to find one. I am talking about people whose fears and aspirations, forged in thousands of years of starvation and illness and ignorance and oppression, have spun into irrelevance. In its most general expression, I am talking about the critical confrontation of Science and Religion.

§

For a couple of generations, of course, we have been loudly and frequently assured that religion and science do not conflict, have nothing to fear in one another. It is all quite clear, the man in the street is told: science concerns itself with experiments, observations and theories about the material universe, while the realm of ultimate explanations, human values and the reality beyond scientific investigation is religion's domain. The facts science reveals go only so far; beyond that, faith carries us surely into truths of the final nature and purpose of creation.

Nevertheless, science appears to creep beyond the limits marked out for it. Many of the basic questions about the origins of universe, life and the nature of human experience seem to many people more satisfactorily answered by science than by religion. Traditional religions, of course, find that their unpopular views on sexual morality empty more churches than does the rather rarefied intellectual challenge of science. Yet even here behavioral studies in psychology and sociology provide popular support for non-traditional morality, and medical research, through prevention of disease and pregnancy, offers the opportunity.

In actuality, sophisticated views of both science and religion differ enormously from their popular equivalents, and the confrontation at this deeper level is rather unlike what we have just seen. Importantly, churchmen themselves reject a great deal of previous religious thought. Many theologians jettison as unscientific and primitive the orthodox picture of God; strikingly, a contemporary religious movement teaches that "God is dead." At the same time, renowned agnostic scientists such as Sir Julian Huxley are presenting concepts of religion and divinity that, they argue, have immense relevance to an enlightened humanity.

Unlike Americans, Australians, on the whole, do not find the conception of God and the supernatural vital or meaningful. Church attendance is social and, though religion (with sex and politics) is one of the three topics one avoids arguing about, it is hard to grasp that only a few hundred years ago nations were torn apart in bloody religious wars. As a recent study noted of today's Australian, it's not so much that he is actively opposed to religion, as that religious faith is irrelevant to his life. "He can conduct everything from his domestic life to his scientific experiments without ever bringing God into consideration; nothing he does seems to have any connection with the God he began to learn about in Sunday School. And in the churches on Sunday, the existence is preached of a God who is nowhere visible in his life."

Given such a climate of opinion—or the significant lack of it—is there any value in pursuing the matter? Contemporary man, even when he sends his children to Sunday instruction, is letting religion slip quietly out of his life. Need any other than fervent believers and professional philosophers concern themselves whether or not science and religion are in conflict?

My unfashionable guess is that twentieth-century Western man, caught on the lip of the technological revolution, bereft of any goal larger than the satisfaction of his desire for comfort and security, dedicated to consumption rather than achievement, may yet find the confrontation to be of seminal consequence.

For our ethos is scored deep with the imprints of both science and faith. Though the methods of experimental inquiry have hurled human knowledge forward in huge exponential arcs, and though these procedures are now beginning to be applied successfully to rigorous study of the human species itself, religion remains a vast if questionable repository of human encounters with fear and hope.

Exciting and dynamic as it is, unparalleled as is its available energy, Western culture lacks a core. This is our flaw. Too wise, perhaps, for the old religious structures that held firm the awe and terror which threaten at times to overwhelm us, we find ourselves thrown without purpose into war and invention. Our specialty is becoming the point-by-point flow program, the rigorous application of techniques for production and consumption. Hell has, in a very real psychological sense, been replaced by the twin fears of social failure and the fusion bomb. Heaven loses its urgency when the standard of living is high, and we feel ourselves free of immediate oppression. Thus, though the practice of science calls forth our best qualities, its technological products often crucify imagination in the name of utility.

Poignantly, the deflation of the currency of our idealism is shown most completely in our wars. We fought to *defeat* Nazism, we burn Vietnam to *prevent* Communism. Finally we are not sufficiently courageous to adopt any real stance except in opposition to another's philosophy. We are less capitalist than anti-Communist. We are less democratic than anti-totalitarian. Rarely do we battle for what humankind might become: we are happy to maintain a status quo. (I simplify, of course, by presenting matters in a light as idealistic as possible, leaving out of account greed and power lust.) Our aspiration, detached from traditional religious goals and fears, has largely sunk back to a mere (if mightily implemented) posture of protectiveness where we and our fellows may consume without achievement.

Is this tendency of our culture, to whirl in splendid neon-flashing undirected extravagance, a necessary consequence of a world dominated by science and technology? Is this the bizarre result of the clash between science and religion? It does, admittedly, seem less brutally ugly than a world of religious wars. But one suspects that the sizable enterprise humanity finds itself engaged in—of fashioning a world of adult, open civilizations—may ultimately suffer greater wounds from its defensive, random violence. Has religion, then, something yet to offer our flawed society?

The sentiment of our time suggests that the religious impulse is antiquated, at least in its Christian manifestation. It is not without significance that Eastern religious modes derived from Vedantic rather than biblical roots are, in bastardized form, finding acceptance here. Nonetheless, though acid-heads pursue enlightenment under the direction of the *I Ching* and the *Book of the Dead,* and housewives turn to Yoga, it would be difficult to argue a religious orientation in most western nations.

Let us look more closely at this failure of religion, see if we can locate the virus of our existential sickness in a crucial collision between faith and science.

II.

When you awaken in fever, your bed steaming with your sickness and your nerves shrilling with dread, dark bulking shadows stalk over you. Your courage rots to water. You know voices beyond the ear's threshold, ancient voices that shred all but the last vestiges of your manhood. You crawl from your sickbed, stiffen your shaking legs against fear, and snap on the light.

And you are safe. Ill, weak, you are safe from that dread because, once again, you face the world on your own terms. Light places shadows in ordered perspective, makes of them shelves and tables and fabric. The voices are exorcised because you are no longer a naked vulnerable creature at the mercy of dark unknown forces: you are a man, in the context of man's created world. The light has banished disruption. This pocket of the universe is recognized and under your control.

In that moment of fright, you have experienced something of the world inhabited by primitive humans. For two million years our forebears spent their short lives in the fluid, ghost-haunted land you have visited and escaped. All the forces of nature—the thunder, the heat, the wind, the wild burgeoning of plant and beast—stood beyond the grasp of a man's understanding. He was hunter and hunted in a game played by the living and the dead, and it was very terrible.

Being man, the creature with mind as well as passion, he sought explanation, or invented it. By naming the unknown he made it less terrifying. His dread and his wonder found their object, eventually, in spirits and demons and gods. Let it be quite clear: the dread was there before the gods. Man did not invent idols and fall in sudden fear before them. He knew awe—he howled for control and security—he splintered that awe into fragments less likely to overwhelm him; from huge forces beyond his command he fashioned gods and restrained them. Worship and propitiate them he did, with vigor and ingenuity, but whether he knew it or not the victory was his.

That, curiously, was the historical genesis not only of religion, but of science also. After our fashion we each respond to the unknown with both fear and curiosity. The urge to flee or destroy vies with the desire to investigate and comprehend. By degrees, the magical systems of early men transmuted themselves, polarized by reverence or inquisitiveness, into religion and non-sacred learning.

Equally curious, man's long and brilliant development of tools, commerce and weaponry did not generate science. We tend, today, to equate faith with metaphysical conservatism, and science with hard-headed practical experiment. It seems odd that magic rather than craft should hatch scientific enquiry and its fabulously successful pragmatic results. Yet it is this common ancestry of science and religion that today makes their confrontation so important.

For science, above all, is a symbolic and intellectual manipulation of the reality we experience. It is a method and an edifice: a framework and a means of modifying that framework. Hunting, building, seafaring—these are piecemeal enterprises, done by guess and by damn. Science is unifying, moving from hypothesis to experiment and back again. Like religion, it seeks to integrate and explain vastly disparate fields of human experience. It throws off a bewildering Christmas-box of useful inventions—light, warmth, transport, drugs—yet beyond and before these applications it creates a series of world-pictures. It places the universe in unified equations. It enables us to manipulate reality not by trial and error but out of our increasingly profound understanding of what constitutes the workings of reality.

The primary difference between science and religion is one of method. If both, to some extent, are trying to do roughly the same thing—achieve accurate knowledge and a valid overview of humankind and the universe in which we exist—then it is the method they each use that we must scrutinize.

Amusingly, the past half-century has seen antagonistic partisans of each method undergo a reversal of theoretical position while continuing to maintain righteous indignation at the folly of their opponents. It used to be held by many scientists that religion, depending upon faith rather than test, was a slippery fraud. Science, they claimed, was a mighty edifice grounded on repeatable experiments; some of its rooms (indeed whole wings) might not be built yet, but the foundations of truth were solidly laid. On the contrary, it was argued, religion slowly but clearly shifted its basic claims as scientific facts forced theologians to modify their beliefs. In short, religion misrepresented itself by presenting "truths"; these "truths" were spur-of-the-moment adjustments, as likely as not to be totally abandoned under the pressure of newly discovered facts.

Today quite another position is maintained. Science, it is claimed. is a flexible method dealing not with facts but with observations and hypotheses. Religion, however, is based upon revealed truths that must be absolute and unshakable or the whole fabric falls to the ground. Yesterday, the scientist was unhappy with religion because it lacked the basis-in-fact of science; today he argues with it because it claims such a basis.

Underlying these adroit and confusing philosophical games, however, there does seem to be a fundamental problem. Whether we talk of facts or observations, theories or truths, the dispute involves an important issue. Simply, it's this: when different views of the world are proposed, how are we to judge them? A multitude of religions offer claims of various kinds and provide advice to us about the management of our lives. Ideologies from every corner present their credentials and demand our allegiance. It is possible to confirm or falsify their allegations, or at least try to. The impact of science on religion has very largely lain precisely here. Strictly speaking, it is improper to say that science offers a seductive alternative to religious belief. What science has offered is a rational critique of religions and ideologies.

"We cannot and must not allow ourselves to believe exactly what we like," urges Oxford philosopher of religion John Wilson. "If we did we should be able to make no distinction between ourselves and madmen who believe that they are pursued by Martians or that there are invisible little men swinging on the lampshade. We must have *some* way of disqualifying those whose religion demands human sacrifice or whose morality insists on putting Jews in gas chambers. In other words, we must be able to produce *some* kind of reasons, some publicly acceptable defense, for our beliefs. Our own feelings, intuitions, hunches, faith, consciences, or whatever are not good enough."

There is the nub of it. It is an unhappy fact that religions have a long and bloody record of intolerance. After all, religions and sociopolitical ideologies receive their charter as human institutions because they claim some knowledge about good and evil which is superior to that of other creeds. And, if you feel certain that you *know* the truth, it is highly likely that you will indoctrinate your children in the same belief, thereby seriously impairing their chances of human and intellectual openness in later life. It is even possible, as the annals of slaughter in the name of religion demonstrate, to burn unbelievers for the sake of their souls. As somebody has pointedly remarked: objecting on humanitarian grounds to the torture of people performed by religious zealots is rather silly if torturing them really *does* save their immortal souls from eternal torment in hell. The objection, rather, must be that as rational people we *cannot* really be sure that it does.

"We cannot abdicate from rationality," agrees Wilson, "if we wish to remain sane and human. We must go through some rational process of assessment, weighing evidence, discussion, and considered judgment... For there are some rules which must surely apply to any rational consideration: one rule must be that we should start by regarding the question as an open question, that we must not think that we already know the answer; and another rule must be that to justify a belief we must give some kind of publicly acceptable evidence for it."

This approach is a scientific one, in the sense that science is the rigorous application of rational methods of inquiry. It does not, we should note, deny the truth-claims of any religious belief, nor does it affirm some "scientific morality." Why, then, has the rise of a scientific culture gradually edged religion out of our lives?

§

As we have seen (and the observation is now a commonplace), much of the motivation and support for traditional religions has been the poverty and uncertainty of human life. Industrial society mitigates or abolishes many of these natural depredations. Men and women today, enjoying the plentiful wealth and health so abundant in our community, increasingly find less need for supernatural compensations in a future life. It can be argued, of course, that such an understanding of religion is shallow and trite; nevertheless, that is the way it has been presented to most people and it has consequently lost its audience. Equally, the easy permissiveness of affluent communities finds unpalatable the strict legalistic morality of traditional Christianity.

At the same time, the rational approach of scientifically-educated people finds the religious world-view unsatisfactory or unnecessary. Anthropology has traced the psychological genesis of religion; as Dr. Alan Isaacs has said in *The Survival of God in the Scientific Age,* "the fact is that almost every human culture has had its own form of supernatural agency... All one can safely assume is that every conceivable arrangement has been tried at one time or another. Even today, after 3000 years of carefully recorded history, we have five major religions each with its own concept of God."

Such a vista of opinion, with the adherents of each system intuitively convinced of its absolute rightness, leads many people to throw out the lot. "This proliferation of opinion," in Dr. Isaacs' words, "permits only two conclusions: either man created God or, if God created man he must have done so in such a way that man himself has had to re-create God." Pressed to a decision, many people today would find the first choice the more plausible.

In other ways, the use of the God concept is failing in explanatory power. Traditional arguments for the existence of God, using the observable universe as part of the proof, are revealed in the light of what we know today to be not only wrong but meaningless. Although cosmology and mathematical physics are still far from providing satisfactory theories on the nature and creation of the universe, they find no evidence of a supernatural agency.

One might go further. A traditional argument for God's existence is that the universe must have a cause outside itself. Yet experimental evidence reveals that our normal, everyday concepts of cause and effect cannot be extended much beyond our own limited range of sensory experience. Says Isaacs, "In view of the apparent indeterminacy of the behavior of elementary particles, it would not be inconsistent if the universe itself were to be an effect for which there is no specific cause." If such a suggestion outrages our credulity and commonsense, it is worth remembering that commonsense assures us that the Sun circles around a motionless flat Earth.

The most damaging blows wrought by scientific rigor to

standard religious thinking have been dealt by the philosophy of language. This analytic approach to our beliefs and the way we express them has, in the opinion of many philosophers, completely demolished our idea of God by showing it to be literally meaningless. That is, linguistic philosophers have advanced the view that the term "God" is as empty as the term "round square." And if the believer retorts that the experience of God transcends our rational limitations and analyses, the philosopher will concede the possibility—except that then, he points out, there is absolutely no way to choose between the convictions of two people holding intuitive but variant, even mutually contrary, beliefs.

III.

Out of this drastic encounter face-to-face of science and religion, is it possible for belief to retain any moral integrity? Is there any place left for religion, other than as a well-worn stick for beating morals into children and finally as a comforting myth for the senile aged to ease the pain of their passing? Or can faith become purely a cultural art form, a manifestation of our historical identity with two million years of suffering, fearful, hopeful, exultant humanity?

The concept of Christianity as a mythology is not new, was given by indirection a contemporary boost in the works of the German theologian Rudolf Bultmann. His thesis involved a rejection, a purging, of supernatural "mythological" language from the Bible.

A score of influential modern writers has proposed views that agree mainly in their insistence that "god-language" is out-dated, that it hinders any vital participation of religion in the plight of mid-century man. Some of their names—Tillich, Bonhoeffer, Bishop Robinson, Harvey Cox—are widely known, though their influence outside formal religious circles is dubious.

Loosely linked in the public mind with the challenging phrase "God is dead," they seek to draw from the ashes of discredited religion a faith less concerned with God than with humans, less with worship than with existential courage in the face of alienation and estrangement. "They have taken Nietzsche's *God is dead,*" an Australian scientist wrote recently, "to mean that the *idea* of God, congealed into the traditional image held by the Church, is hopelessly anachronistic, but that God is still a living active influence in the world, a reality to be experienced in human lives, be he acknowledged there or not. Religion is not, for them, something apart from life or something added to life—as Tillich has said somewhere, *There is more religion in the leg of a chair by Cezanne than in most religious paintings.* God is *in* the secular world."

In its extreme expression, radical theology seems to cut its ties finally with religion as it is generally understood, and enters the ambit of humanism. "When we say that God is dead," explained Thomas J. J. Altizer, an American exponent of religion without God, "we are in fact intending to make a Christian affirmation that God has died in his transcendent form and reality, and is now fully incarnate in every human hand and face. It is a way of saying that Christ lives more fully and more comprehensively now than He has ever lived before."

§

One detects in this comfortable revolution a failure of nerve. One feels uneasy, more than a little distrustful, on hearing this flutter of convenient Welfare-humanitarianism. The suspicion grows that, underneath the radical shock-treatment, nothing fresh quickens that might be capable of healing the blank desolation in the core of our time.

Biblical religion, I think, simply is not hooked into the dynamo of our age. It is too firmly entrenched in patterns of thought and emotional response long superannuated; it has a weight of centuries on it. Stripped to fighting weight, it comes out punchy, dazzled and blind in the light, its jab is short and feeble and directed at shadows painted on its own eyes.

Yet there remains that brooding violence in our culture's belly, the large reality which magic and religion, before our day, handled not unsuccessfully. Perhaps, with Julian Huxley, we can call it *the divine,* the latent potency that is not supernatural but *transnatural.* It is, I suggest, the same coiled spring which drove primitive man, in a fury of invention, to build gods as its representation. It is the subterranean torrent of dread and exultation that is the twin realization of our blurred insignificance before the towering presence of the universe and our inevitable personal extinction, and the full, rich, scarcely-glimpsed flowering of human possibilities.

Here, perhaps, is a central existential reality we must neither propitiate nor ignore, but embrace. It finds a statement in Huxley's scientific panorama: "This new vision is both comprehensive and unitary. It integrates the fantastic diversity of the world into a single framework, the pattern of all-embracing evolutionary process.... There is no supernatural realm: All phenomena are part of one natural process of evolution. There is no basic cleavage between science and religion; they are both organs of evolving humanity."

There seems, as I mentioned, to be something ludicrous in the assertion that our having relinquished religion might be the betrayal of our civilization to vast undirected energies. Yet it is not implausible. In casting off a belief in God which "has ceased to be scientifically tenable, has lost its explanatory value, and is becoming an intellectual and moral burden to our thought," we have carelessly lost sight of the divine that antedated gods.

Norman Mailer has spoken of the plight of our time, that our world "reduces one's sense of reality by reducing to the leaden formulations of jargon such emotions as awe, dread, beauty, pity, terror, calm, horror and harmony," that it "leaves us further isolated in the empty landscapes of psychosis, precisely that inner landscape of void and dread which we flee."

And yet it may not have to be that way. "Maybe we are in a

sense the seed, the seed-carriers, the voyagers, the explorers...;
maybe we are engaged in a heroic activity, and not a mean one."

EFFING THE INEFFABLE
(1990)

Deconstruction has become an intellectual buzz word more often used to frighten the innocent than to clarify debates. Which is no reason to dismiss its claims in advance, especially those by the philosopher Jacques Derrida. It reminds us (always a valuable service) that the words we use to think and communicate are sedimented with inconsistent meanings, that our discourse is invariably seized in pernicious metaphysical traps.

But its practice is not dedicated, as one might expect, to opening those traps and setting our poor bruised words free of their jaws (on its own analysis, a hopeless ambition). Rather, it aims to demonstrate, as Kevin Hart puts it in *The Trespass of the Sign: Deconstruction, Theology and Philosophy*, that "no text can be totalized from within or without, and this is so by dint of the conditions of possibility of textuality." Yet "the condition of possibility of interpretation is also and at the same time its condition of impossibility for totalizing a text." *Totalized* is another buzz word, but Hart's case can be simplified thus: something always escapes any trap, but it is that something, so to speak, from which the trap is built...

John M. Ellis, in a recent counterblast *Against Deconstruction*, notes how trite or absurd the outcome of these deep thoughts usually turns out to be:

> What is gained is not sophistication of logic but instead the appearance of sophistication and

complexity... But more important still, the character of the performance is most unoriginal: for the rhetorical device used here is simply the standard formula of many branches of religious mysticism.

This might seem a surprising suggestion, since deconstruction has been taken widely as a godless assault on ancient verities (or what are trumpeted as such), not least those of ethics and theology. How accurate Ellis was can be seen in Dr. Hart's limpid, nuanced attempt to situate upon a deconstructive nonground a mystical theology beyond the positive, the negative and the metaphysical. His extraordinary book draws on an intimate and learned acquaintance not only with Derrida's difficult writing (Hart calls it "tangled and somewhat frenzied") but with his equally rebarbative ancestors, from Kant and Nietzsche to Heidegger, with theology old and new, and with mystical writers in the Jewish and Christian traditions, especially the Pseudo-Dionysius. (And yet it remains strikingly sectarian: theology, deconstructed or otherwise, is equated sans argument with its Christian varieties, ignoring all other pretenders.)

Transcendental Meditators and Moonies try something similar with quantum theory, turning "quantum weirdness" to advantage in claiming scientific support for levitation and the production of massed good vibes to heal the world's ills. Creation Scientists borrow elements of advanced relativity to argue that the speed of light has been slowing down since the chap with the big white beard created the universe only six thousand years ago. Dr. Hart's deconstructive judo throws are vastly more supple and sophisticated, but no less comical. A "God of aporia" takes over from the once fashionable upper-class Anglican "God of the (scientific) gaps." In a very nice touch, this Catholic convert's study is dedicated *ad majorem Dei gloriam*, a slogan that generations of dazed parochial schoolkids have penned in abbreviated form at the top of each page of inky homework. Thus is the premier skepticism of the day co-opted for the true believers.

Perhaps this hilarious outcome should be no surprise, reminiscent of existentialism's hijack by religion in the 1950s. But more than any other philosophy of this century, deconstruction lends itself to a brand of silliness of the most exquisite kind.

The deconstructive intervention is often posed by its proponents as something like a new and more hygienic way to think (and "write"), rather as dialectical logic was advanced by Hegelians and Marxists. In many respects, the former seems merely to be the most recent incarnation of the latter. Happily, Sir Karl Popper showed long ago—denying the utility of "dialectical logic"—that abandoning the principle of non-contradiction allows any utterable premise p to yield any other q (no matter what q might be), rendering all discourse utterly vacuous. The proof is perfectly straightforward, devastating and unarguable. If we allow both p and its contradiction $not\text{-}p$, the logical step p or q obliges us to accept q—which might be any inane statement such as "the Moon is made of puce cheese."

But identity and "self-presence" (the stability that prevents any given p from slopping over into $not\text{-}p$ and thence into any q) are precisely the postulates against which Derrida directs his chiefest objections. Deconstruction vitiates identity in advance with the claim that every premise is fatally riven internally, not merely subject to contextual redefinition. The incoherence of such a claim is exemplified in Derrida's placement of key terms "under erasure" (a borrowing from Heidegger which supposedly allows one to have never had one's cake after eating it).

Thus Derrida, says his translator Spivak, asks us "to change certain habits of mind: ...contradicting logic, we must learn to use and erase our language at the same time." Spivak notes explicitly that such contradiction is "not acceptable within the logic of identity." In a nifty passage, Paisely Livingston has shown clearly why the result ruins all prospect of rational discussion. The abolition of identity on which deconstructive methods depend dooms those methods to saying, literally, everything and nothing—p, $not\text{-}p$ and q:

The full playing out of the undecidable requires saying that we can and that we cannot; it will not do to assert univocally that the "lack at the origin... is the condition of thought and experience." We must also add that the lack at the origin, which is a certain nonlack of the origin, is not the condition of thought and experience, which is also non-thought and non-experience. In this way we remain (and do not remain) profoundly faithful to Derrida, for in his terms (which are not his terms) the logical "habits of mind" are at once *necessary* and *under erasure*.

"The negative theologian," Hart tells us, "uses language under erasure, and this, I think, gives us a better account of what happens in mystical discourse than has been done under the familiar rubric of 'paradox'." No doubt. Hart's essay in effing the ineffable is superbly deft and undoubtedly a more appropriate use of deconstructive non-thought than its recent glitzy application to architecture. To the unbeliever, alas, it remains the deft in service of the daft.

In subverting complacencies and recovering attention to the marginal and despised, its specialty, deconstruction has been bracing and inventive. But it has the inevitable weaknesses of any radical subversion of reason: it is self-refuting, ultimately defeatist. When its complicity in the mystical is brought out as relentlessly as Dr. Hart contrives, it powerfully drives its own nails (which are also not-nails) into its own empty coffin.

A CHAOS OF DELIGHT
(2005)

It's very hard to get our heads around the stories ancient people told each other about the world, its origins and nature, the obligations that knowledge imposes upon us. Thousands of years ago, most people believed things so weird it's hard to grasp how they managed it without laughing. Then again, many of us continue to have ardent faith in a small set of those claims, while declining to accept most other traditional opinions or dogmas. It's possible that more people today have a working knowledge of astrology than they do of scientific astronomy. It's claimed by pollsters, to the horror of biologists, that a majority of Americans sturdily assert divine creation of humans within the last 10,000 years.

Is there any way for us to appreciate these deeply divisive explanations for the world, to reach back into history and prehistory, to reach outward ecumenically to cultures whose beliefs seem frankly crazy or offensive? Or is that ambition itself nothing better than a wishy-washy politically correct denial that some sources of knowledge actually are more equal than the rest?

Professor Geoffrey P. Dobson is a medical scientist at James Cook University in Townsville, as well as a founding director of biotech company Global Cardiac Solutions. In his spare time, he's been delving into the history of religion and myth in the Western tradition, trying to sort out the sources of today's ideas, trace the lineage of those always provisional truths he practices as a scientist. Unlike debunkers of the Richard Dawkins school (I'm one), in his book A Chaos of Delight: Science, Religion and Myth and the Shaping of Western Thought Dobson maintains an even tone as he makes his careful way from the mythologies of ancient Sumer and Egypt, with their practical and conservative political values, through the reasoned if bizarre analyses of the Greeks, their rediscovery by Islamic and eventually Christian theologians, and the slow demystification of the intellectual world by ever more effective sciences.

This might seem well-trodden ground, but Dobson's story is not triumphalist, not a "Whig history" determined to show that our current happy state (if it is that) is the predestined outcome of clueless and misguided ancestors. Nor does he wring his hands at the woeful state of a world in which runaway science and technology are stripping from us the consolations of mythology and religion.

Starting from "the changing roles that science, religion and myth have played in shaping the images of ourselves and our place in the wider universe," he seeks a deeper understanding of their intersections and divergences, in the belief that "diversity of opinion is healthy and essential; it is blind acceptance of dogma that impedes understanding and progress." At the heart of Dobson's search is his conviction that the most certain thing about human knowledge, its one unifying feature, "is its uncertainty."

This might seem an open and uncontroversially generous credo, unusual in a scientist, since we have been led to believe that practitioners see science as our premier path to truth, paving over the potholes of superstition and blind conviction. Many do, of course, even as they admit that half of what they learned in school is already obsolete if not frankly wrong. It's only natural to cling to the hope that your painfully uncovered research will stand the test of time.

Dobson takes his title from a phrase by Charles Darwin, observing a Brazilian rainforest: "The mind is a chaos of delight, out of which a world of future & more quiet pleasure will arise."

Science is the residue, so to speak, of sensuous delight, the distillate of analysis, the rich abundance of the world "recollected," as Wordsworth said of poetic emotion, "in tranquility." That's all very well, but the mournful sense I carried away with me from Dobson's relentless march across thousands of years of confusion, complete with tabulations and diagrams, was not so much a chaos of delight as a chaos of darkness. There's little sense here of the driving forces impelling these rather abstract shifts in opinion, although historians and sociologists are quick to pile them up for us.

Natural science, Dobson concludes, is "proof without certainty," while religion and myth are "certainty without proof." Himself an agnostic, disbelieving "in a personal god, heaven or hell, the afterlife or the notion that human beings are special creations of God," he predicts with optimism that "the world will never be totally demystified," that while religion is firmly bounded by accidents of history, nonetheless it remains "a system that is just as dynamic as science and other systems of human thought." This certainly seems the lesson, surprising to many materialists, of the last decade and a half since the collapse of Soviet oppression and the resurgence of evangelical Christianity and warrior Islam.

Yet these expressions of human hope in the face of disappointment and frustration, of mortal limits and death, themselves stand at an opposite pole from cautious and principled uncertainty. Meanwhile, epochs of belief and argument stretch behind us in cultures that Professor Dobson was unable to incorporate into his extensive overview: the ancient and complex worldviews of India and China, of the native peoples of the world. A chaos, a tangle, a minefield of stories about our origins and our destiny. It would be ungrateful to fault Dobson for not doing the impossible, but perhaps we of the Western tradition may find a kind of chilly reassurance in the knowledge that while people from other cultures differ tremendously in their myths and pieties, they agree to a marked extent when it comes to physics—and how to make really big bombs.

THE COMPREHENSIBLE
COSMOS (2007)

Do we live in an age of resurgent belief, as the rise of fundamentalist Christianity in the US and of Islam elsewhere suggests? Or is the "faith of our fathers" getting corroded, as many believers suspect with dismay, by an unholy blend of skeptical science and consumerist self-indulgence? The popularity of *The Da Vinci Code* and Philip Pullman's death-of-God trilogy for young readers, *His Dark Materials*, is certainly striking. Meanwhile, film stars enthusiastically endorse a cult claiming that a galactic overlord named Xenu stranded us here 75 million years ago. And defiantly atheistic books have been bestsellers: evolutionist Richard Dawkins's *The God Delusion*, philosopher Dan Dennett's *Breaking the Spell: Religion as a Natural Phenomenon* and Sam Harris's brilliantly incisive little tract, *Letter to a Christian Nation*. Then there are the claims by filmmaker James Cameron that the tomb of Jesus has been found. What in heaven's name is going on?

I have a sneaking suspicion that recent doubts about faiths are fuelled less by the shock of Darwinian insight, say, than by a deep, unconscious revulsion after ardent true believers murdered nearly 3,000 people on September 11, 2001.

Detesting militant Islam required no great courage on the part of Westerners, but a side effect has been a dawning sense that if one major faith could propel such brutality—could constitute, indeed, the new post-communist threat—then perhaps religious conviction in general might be questionable.

Traditionally, brand-name religion is instilled from infancy, often with ferocious warnings against heretics and infidels, making it hard to doubt the precepts with which one has grown up. When I was a child in a parochial school, I parroted a catechism that explained, vacuously, "We cannot see God because he is a Spirit, and cannot be seen by us in this life." Later, I learned classic proofs for God's existence, such as the argument from design (the world is complex and so must have a watchmaker), which the proven process of evolution had long ago dispelled.

Other arguments seemed, eventually, equally frail. The First Mover gambit was amusingly parodied by a journalist's phrase (one I used as a title elsewhere in this book): "If there's no God, who pulls up the next Kleenex?" One last-resort argument for the necessity of the divine was a real puzzler, though: Why is there Something, rather than Nothing? Who put the bang in the big bang? Veteran particle physicist Victor J. Stenger offers an answer to that deep question in *The Comprehensible Cosmos* and *God: The Failed Hypothesis*, arguing a materialist, God-free account of the cosmos, equally antagonistic to superstition, the paranormal and religions archetypal and newfangled alike. He refuses to accept the polite accommodation urged by agnostic Stephen Jay Gould that science and religion can never be in conflict as they are non-overlapping "magisteria."

Faith, for Gould, dealt with morals, science with testable fact. This bid for mutual tolerance gained little traction in either camp. Evolutionary psychology pressed hard against the territorial prerogatives of religion, showing how traditional ethical codes had developed on the basis of templates genetically selected— for good and ill—by a million years of human prehistory. But aren't the central dogmas of Christian civilization, indeed of all the Abrahamic societies including Judaism and Islam, derived from the infallible word of God delivered in Scripture? Stenger offers a familiar corrective: the moral guidance of the Bible is confused and often reprehensible, supporting slavery and other atrocities. We interpret its words according to today's superior moral insight and sensitivity, so the interpretations given by Christians "must depend on ideals that they have already developed from some other source." Unlike some critics of faith, Stenger takes the tough line that deity is not just an unnecessary hypothesis or one where an honest thinker can choose to accept or reject it. No, it is "the failed hypothesis."

This is a bold claim indeed and certain to meet scornful rejection from prelates and pious alike. Undaunted, Stenger trots briskly through all the obvious claims and his objections to them, concluding in each case that the evidence for the traditional God is too weak to accept or can be dismissed as mistaken.

For example, while human life is well-suited to this planet (inevitably, since we evolved here), the universe as a whole is an uncongenial place, vast, empty and hostile. Far from being carefully designed and calibrated for humankind, the cosmos looks precisely the sort of place one would expect had it emerged unplanned from the void. That assertion still seems to most non-scientists merely a conjuring trick. How can something burst into existence from nothing? Philosophers debated this for centuries but the question assumes that "nothing" has a clear meaning. Actually, we never see nothing, only the change of one thing into another, the slow dispersal of energy into exhaustion.

As Stenger points out in his remarkable book *The Comprehensible Cosmos,* all the matter and energy in the universe, including the newly discovered dark matter and dark energy that comprise most of the cosmos, balances out to zero. "Nothing," as physics Nobel laureate Frank Wilczek put it, "is unstable." The void cannot be conceived as ultimately empty.

The astonishing random event that led to an explosion of matter and energy and expanding spacetime—to the creation of a local universe—seems finally within our mental grasp.

Stenger does not stint in his treatment of these remarkable ideas. The first half of his book sets out for any reader with a basic scientific training the way in which symmetry gives rise to the laws of nature: conservation of energy and momentum, the quantum rules that rewrote physics in the twentieth century, special and general relativity. His lucid if demanding treatment offers a somewhat contentious account of the way in which everything we see about us takes the form it does because of one simple demand: that no standpoint is privileged over another.

This does not mean, as he takes pains to stress, that anything goes in the postmodern vein. Readers prepared to follow his argument into elementary calculus and quantum theory will find it spelled out in detail in the second half of the book. The tragedy of the twenty-first century is that so few people have been equipped by the education system to take that journey into hard-won insight. Which is probably one reason, when the pain and confusion of life become too great to bear, so many of us turn to Xenu or God and abandon the struggle to understand.

BEYOND FAITH AND
OPINION (2009)

Do I believe in a god? No, I don't. So far, that makes me a *nonbeliever*, rather than a *disbeliever*.

More specifically, do I believe in the deity of the Abrahamic tradition? (Or is this already a confusing way to put it, since the Jewish tradition insists on a unitary deity, its Christian offshoot asserts three divine and equal persons in one God, whatever that means, and the Muslim version is back to just one unified God, but with a new final prophet?) When it comes to God in any of the Abrahamic senses, I'm prepared to go further. I do *disbelieve* in these alleged deities. Indeed, I'm inclined to think that the existence of such a supernatural being is not just unsupported by any sound evidence, but is logically impossible and self-refuting.

On the other hand, my grip on logic and reasoning is no better than most people's, despite some formal training in philosophy. Can I have any *absolute* warrant in my confidence that deities are unbelievable? I might be wrong, after all, and so might you.

I do not mean to rehearse the well-known arguments for and against various gods of anyone's choice, but rather to make a sort of meta-argument about the vulnerability of all arguments. This might cut equally against disbelief and nonbelief as it does against the varieties of belief in the divine, but I think it's worth keeping in mind. Perhaps it urges a certain modesty about any utter conviction that what we know is true, let alone *obviously* true.

§

The Austrian philosopher Ludwig Wittgenstein, according to a perhaps unjust version of one famous anecdote, once asked a colleague, "Why did people believe the Sun went around the Earth?"

"Well," the colleague mused, "I imagine it was because it looks as if it does."

"Ah," said jesting Wittgenstein. "What would it look like if the Earth went round the Sun?"

This is startling and funny, because, of course, the Earth actually does go round the Sun, and always has, even when people of faith insisted otherwise. But as we laugh at his poor colleague, it is worth stopping for a moment to see that this is a rather misleading question.

I suspect almost everybody gets confused about this without ever thinking it through. Yes, the Sun does look as if it goes around the Earth, but that has absolutely nothing to do with the Copernican fact that the Earth orbits the Sun.

At some time deep in the remote future, tidal drag will slow the Earth's rotation until one hemisphere faces the Sun forever— at least until the Sun's expansion swallows the Earth or burns our ancestral planet to a crisp. From the nearside surface of the Moon, the Earth already hangs always in the same place; looking up at the terrifying face of the nearly dead Sun, our descendants (if they still exist, if they have forgotten all their science) would have no cause to speculate either that the motionless Sun circles the Earth or that the Earth circles the Sun.

If science had not long ago established that the Earth spins on its own axis once a day at an equatorial speed of 1,670 kilometers per hour, we'd have no way of estimating how the daylight sky should look if the Earth orbited the Sun (as, of course, it does).

The moral of this little story is that we think we know more than we do, or, at any rate, the way we phrase questions sometimes tangles up what we really *know* with what we have only been told, what we *believe* to be true although perhaps we have never for a moment thought it through.

There is ample evidence to show that we poor humans are readily bamboozled. I happen to think that religion is a prime example of the ways in which we easily get trapped in emotional and cognitive tangles. But my own *dis*belief could be due, of course, to just such pathologies of thinking and feeling. Many people disbelieve that smoking tobacco conduces to lung cancer. Having a healthy suspicion of my vulnerability to error, perhaps I ought to be cautious and step back from active disbelief to a more modest lack of positive belief.

I was raised in a pious Catholic household in the predominantly white Protestant mid-twentieth-century culture of Australia, where Catholics comprised about a quarter of the population but were mainly working class (like my family), comparatively poorly educated, and without much prospect of rising in the world. My generation, overlapping with the earliest of the baby-boomers, began to break free of those limitations, but the parish church and its parochial schools staffed by nuns and teaching brothers remained to a poignant extent the heart of a heartless world. Knowing down to the bone that the world of experience is finally a vale of tears, a place of testing and spiritual growth preparatory to a more glorious existence on the far side of death, made a life of privation and moral rigor at least acceptable and perhaps devoutly to be embraced as a kind of leg up to heavenly reward and destiny.

My childhood and adolescence were suffused with a hunger for grace and the knowledge of divine purpose in the world. I was lackluster at my lessons in all subjects except Religious Knowledge, which I aced effortlessly, carrying home pious volumes as my only scholastic award at the end of each school year. Urged on by my mother, who grimly awoke me in the dark hours of winter and pushed me out into the rain wearing a long heavy altar boy's soutane, I learned to mumble Latin Mass responses that meant nothing to me, privileged to kneel as the priest performed the miracle of transubstantiation, bringing

God physically into the room under the guise of a round rather tasteless wafer of bread.

I learned to work my way up and down the nave, pausing for several minutes in front of each of the fourteen Stations of the Cross flagellating my own guilt and shame for having contributed to the abominable suffering of my savior. Did I also experience raptures of sacred bliss, floods of the joy of faith? Now and then, I'm sure, in my jejune way. At any rate, I was sufficiently impressed by the priority of my faith over all other objectives in life that at fifteen I left home and entered a seminary 1,000 kilometers away, intending to become a priest.

Five years later, out of the monastery and at university, I left the church for what struck almost everybody as the most preposterous motive (or wicked pretext) they had ever heard. This was it: I did not *know* that the claims and doctrines of the faith in which I had been adventitiously raised were valid, had any support other than the assertion of local authority. What's worse, it was obvious to me that the psychological pressures of *practicing* the faith—mandatory weekly Mass, frequent guilt-inducing confession, familial solidarity in the profession of belief—made it almost impossible to evaluate the truth or otherwise of these doctrines.

And really, when you started to think about it from even the slightest distance, some of them were very, very weird indeed. As weird, perhaps, as the lunatic notions embraced by those other religions or sects that gave all good Catholics a comfortable laugh. And what if biblical scholars in the Protestant tradition, or outside the Christian faith entirely, were right? What if Mary had not remained a virgin when the Christ child exited her uterus (perhaps by kind of teleportation), but was just a "young childless woman" as the Aramaic word actually states, correctly translated? Fundamentalists argued for a cosmos just 6,000 years old, pointing to inerrant Scripture as their proof, but for educated Catholics of my stamp that was just a simple-minded mistake, a confusion of ancient metaphor for literal scientific proposition. Yet they clung vehemently to their error, appealing to the force and validity of personal faith. Might not my own equally contingent set of beliefs in my middle-of-the-road Catholic doctrine be no less due to indoctrination (and surely that word was no accident)?

And so I took a small step outside the complex, psychologically elaborate threats and appeals of "the faith of my fathers"— and, somewhat to my surprise, found that, month by month and year after year, what had seemed to me entirely self-evident, true, rewarding, uplifting, the very purpose and pith of life was, at best, irrelevant, a set of fairytales less interesting than the science fiction I loved to read, no more likely to be true, and, at worst, actively malign, manipulative, cruel, and vicious.

Was it any wonder (although it was years, despite scurrilous rumors, before I learned of this horror) that many deracinated lonely men, celibate by clerical imposition, regressing to a kind of awful endless replay of childhood sexuality, molested those in their care? It was a pathology precisely fitted to the peculiar craziness of the Catholic clergy. Other faiths had worse disorders; fundamentalist Muslims and Hindus did vile things to women, some sanctioned by their Scriptures, some incorporated from barbarous cultural traditions. Yet all claimed divine sanction, wrapping themselves in the Cross, the Scimitar, or some other symbol of unquestionable faith. What was missing, as I realized belatedly at the age of twenty, was testable public evidence. Not just testimony. Not just the thundering and minatory voice of authority, or the tender and sweetly tempting voice of Mother Church (or the bitterly betrayed voice of your own mother, for that matter).

§

It is very striking how often believers in God or gods assail disbelievers who express doubt about the truth of religious ideas regarded by the faithful as entirely sane and plausible (sticks turned into snakes, seas parted at command, rotation of the earth halted for a day, virgin births, magical revival from the dead, water turned into wine, bread turned into god, people turning into birds or vice versa, golden plates revealed by angels, gods with elephant heads, talking animals, demons possessing the psychotic, all that completely sensible stuff). Making this point to a believer once, I was reproached for my diatribe. But a diatribe is defined as either "a bitter and abusive speech or writing" or "ironic or satirical criticism." If listing the kinds of claims made by believers is held to constitute bitter abuse, something interesting about such claims is being revealed. And note that "satire" requires some element of preposterous exaggeration. If people of faith cling solemnly to laughable nonsense as their deepest truth, they ought not complain angrily that they are being mocked just because their favored nonsense is reported outside the kirk. (This is just what Scientologists do when Xenu, the extra-galactic tyrant who exiled "thetans" to Earth seventy-five million years ago, gets mentioned by scoffing disbelievers.)

Pointing to any book that asserts its own indubitable truth as sufficient evidence that its revelation is true (as many Jews, Christians, and Muslims do) is insufficient grounds for belief. In fact, it's ridiculous, even perverse—but saying so is likely to get nonbelievers into serious trouble. In practice, the knowledge available to most of us from science has much the same self-validating character; we read it in school books, or see it on television. The crucial difference is that the scientific claims can be put to the test by anyone who wishes to learn the appropriate techniques.

Those claims of science, whether empirical or theoretical, often have a surprisingly short shelf-life by the standards of scriptural doctrines. Yet the practitioners of science in every country in the world share a common understanding of how the world works, even if many of the details remain up for grabs. By the age of twenty, I had come to suspect of my own inculcated Catholic faith—despite its preferred title of universality, despite its periodic upgrades, despite my own religious experiences—that it was indeed a system of *belief* rather than remediable *knowledge*, of hardened opinion, of ancient guesswork caked over the surface of the world. Freeing myself from its choking embrace meant the loss of certainty, of comfort, of periodic emotional purgings, of a kind of surety in my conviction of the ultimate benignity of the universe. Was I right to take that step away from belief more than four decades ago? I can't be *absolutely* sure, but I believe so.

RELIGION: LOOKING BACK FROM NOW

This section's selection of essays starts in 1967 but tracks forward in roughly two-decade leaps to provide a kind of long perspective on the topic and the changing responses of at least one observer whose basic ideas were formed and reformed in the 1950s and 1960s. The most notable absences in my 1967 essay, I guess, are Islam, especially an emergent radical Islam, and the persistent power of fundamentalist and evangelical Christianity in the most technically advanced society in the world, the USA.

If There's No God, Who Pulls Up the Next Kleenex?

Certainly this is not the twenty-first-century many of us were looking for. A grotesquely large proportion of the population of the United States confesses its conviction that evolution is a hoax (51% of those polled in Texas in 2010), that humans and dinosaurs walked the earth together a few thousand years ago (30%). At the turn of this century, several crews of what we must suppose were convinced believers in Allah flew hijacked aircraft into American buildings and murdered thousands, plunging the nation into wildly disproportionate panic and dread. In the interests of profit and power, some of the richest nations of the West have been engaged since then in what is widely seen by Muslims as a far more murderous attack on their faith (or at the very least, on their fellow adherents), an assault against which their piety and anger compels them to respond in kind.

We were supposed to be heading into a non-sectarian, indeed secular, future, guided by the increasingly clear and persuasive light of science. I started out as a child of faith, fervent in my belief in the truths taught to me by nuns, priests, and my parents. At a certain point, I realized that this sense of conviction was shared by almost everyone else in the world, except that, mysteriously, the Hindus (I had never met any, but I was sure this is the case) believed ardently in the doctrines of their totally bizarre faith, just as the Salvation Army man living across the street was certain of the validity of his variant on Christian teachings, just as the Scientologists I had once visited to have my IQ and personality tested were entirely convinced that L. Ron Hubbard was correct about the thetans and going clear.

That last case was interesting, because back in the '60s most Scientologists were converts to their faith, unlike some kids today who are third-generation believers in that crackpot and ludicrous congeries of bad science fiction. I found a clue in the difference. It focused my attention, eventually, on a rather remarkable coincidence: how almost everybody knew, with a bristling certainty, that what their parents taught them in the way of religion was utterly and unchallengeably true.

I was twenty years old by the time this insight gelled, and I realized that if everyone else maintained faith in assertions that could be tested only by looking inside one's own soul (that murky place filled with confusion and sometimes delusion), shaped by translated words from an alien culture established in Neolithic times, mightn't the same be true with my own belief?

I determined to de-program myself, in the first place by abandoning built-in reinforcements such as weekly Mass on Sunday, to the absolute horror of my parents—because I was now clearly on the road to burning forever in hell, by my own prideful choice. Oddly enough, I found that without regular conditioning to drum my supposedly internal faith into my uncertain soul, the doctrines I had once taken as demonstrably true started to fall into tatters, or worse yet had taken on the sorry look of a crackpot standing on a box in a park, heckled by jeering passers-by.

For all that, it was obvious to me that religion (any religion) spoke to some profound human experience not easily accessible to the logical rationality of science or history. It was closer to music or painting or sculpture, and surely it was no accident that the great masterpieces of art sought the numinous. Yes, the subject matter was often explicitly religious exactly because those who funded it were wealthy and powerful shepherds of their shorn flock, but there was more to it than that.

You could look at a Cézanne and choke up with emotion somehow more transcendental than hunger, or lust, or the greed for power. I think that sentiment, that suspicion, was shared by many of us in the 1960s. In one direction it led to what has been called the spiritual supermarket—the panoply of New Age comfort food beliefs, or to turning toward more formal but unfamiliar versions of faith such as Mormonism, or to a revival of a kind of non-denominational spiritualism portrayed today in popular television programs like *Ghost Whisperer*, *Medium*, and all the rest of the heartwarming, tear-jerking woowoo narratives warning us against the supposed coldness of reason and preparing us for the welcoming white light at the end of the après-death tunnel.

That's the puzzle I was approaching in my 1967 article with its deliberately mocking (and borrowed) title, which makes fun of rather simple attempts to persuade rather simple people that whatever we don't understand is probably best explained by the hand of God. Darwin put an end to that in biology a century and a half ago, but it's taking a while to filter through, not only in the Islamic theocracies but in Washington, DC. So one might fear that we haven't come far in nearly half a century, but the emergence of a vigorous defense of disbelief in unwarranted religious claims (by Richard Dawkins, Daniel Dennett, Sam Harris, Christopher Hitchens, Russell Blackford, and others) offers fresh hope, and commonsense instead of faith, and—

with a bit of reciprocity from the church, the synagogue, and the mosque—maybe charity.

Effing the Ineffable

Roughly halfway between Then and Now, the world entered a realm of signs and posts: postmodernism, poststructuralism, postfeminism. I spent several years immersed in social studies of science, semiotics, and deconstruction. The way to tell people who have studied deconstruction from those who haven't is that they never speak of deconstruction*ism*. Most people who sneer and rail at "deconstructionism" (a term as implausible as, say, "Christianism") don't know very much about the thing they are rejecting. I published my own critique of this deliberately obscure, frantically playful method of skepticism in the book *Theory and Its Discontents*, but there seems little point in rehearsing those arguments now that the fad is over.

One of its more inadvertent ironies is the way a number of prominent deconstructors embraced and contorted the religious or "religious" or quasipostreligious anti-Enlightenment opinions of Martin Heidegger and Emmanuel Lévinas. These revels stand at the opposite extreme from the ignorant stupidity of those convinced that humans never visited the moon, or that the United States government was behind 9/11, or that President Obama is a Muslim from Kenya, or, for all I know, a reptile alien from a flying saucer. (We'll come back to the flying saucers.) But they are all too often just as foolish in their ingenuity. Inevitably, one recalls the famous apologetic proposition of Church Father Tertullian: "Credo quia absurdum"—"I believe *because* it is absurd." Actually, because it is absurd the only thing you have any right to believe is that it is absurd.

A Chaos of Delight

With this chapter and the next two, I have abruptly launched us almost to the present day, because it is only recently that atheists have dared to raise their heads out of the foxholes. The topic of religion is a very old one, and the practice of science is still very recent—if 400 years is calibrated against a couple of hundred thousand.

A Comprehensible Cosmos

Spokesmen and women for the People of Faith (by contrast with, presumably, People of Reason) often insist that attempts to use science methodology to explore ethics, religion itself, or the origins of the universe are mere scientism. They can only be "reductionist," as the common slur has it. Why reductionism is thought to be such a crime is rarely explained. It is just a trick of cognitive hygiene or focus rationing, of the application of limited resources to any number of complex, even overwhelming problems.

If you are confronted by several bright red or green juicy, tasty fruit, and you notice that these are "seven apples," you have been reductionist. The number seven pares away almost everything distinctive and desirable and long-evolved in those apples, but counting them serves a purpose. Nobody in her right mind would suppose that this action is meant to summarize some supposed essence about apples. When the surgeon confronted with a life-threatening clot in the heart isolates it with an instrument, marking it off from adjacent healthy tissue, that is also reductionism at work.

Of course, if no attention is paid to the rest of the damaged body and mind, reductionism has gone too far *in that case*. And all too often, it is impersonal medical treatment, and expensive pharmaceuticals that can do as much harm as good, and ignorance or neglect of subtle psychological factors in healing, that convince us that reductionism is somehow intrinsically wicked and ineffective (compared with prayer and faith, for example—although Popes and ayatollahs are not famous for avoiding medical treatment when their health troubles them).

In any event, Victor Stenger's accounts of a God-free universe, drawing on his own appropriately reductionist physics and logic schema, seem to me to sketch the kind of answer the New Atheists provide, now that traditional gods have failed the test of existence. In 2010, Stephen Hawking and co-author Leonard Mlodinow, Professor of Physics at CalTech, belatedly announced the opinion that M-theory quite satisfactorily explains a self-creating eternal hyperverse bubbling out universes from the unstable nothingness, each with different laws and fundamental parameter settings, probably to the satisfaction of nobody except other M-theorists. So Stenger might not be correct; but his approach, like Hawking's and Mlodinow's, certainly suggests the fertile merits of appropriate reductionism.

Beyond Faith and Opinion

One of the more accessible recent books from New Atheists is *50 Voices of Disbelief*, commissioned and edited by my friend Dr. Russell Blackford and Udo Schüklenk, professor of philosophy at Queen's University, Canada. I expected at least 40 of those voices, and perhaps 49, to take a rather fierce and uncompromising tone (as I have done myself in places in this book). So I decided, in my contrarian way, to express a certain hesitation in my nonetheless explicit atheism. The older I get, the fewer topics I feel utterly confident about, something the elderly always tell the young—without, of course, convincing them for a moment of the virtues of this opinion. Yet, in a sense, I'm just continuing a hard-won attitude I adopted when I first confronted the possibility that the faith of my fathers, of all of our fathers and our mothers too, by and large, was just an enormously elaborate fairytale told again and again to comfort us in our ignorance and dread of death.

PART FOUR: POLITICS

THE SHAPE OF WARS TO COME (1967)

There was the glare in the sky, a red flare of heat and light and horror, A tall old tree on the hill turned brown, and sagged, and burst explosively into leaping yellow flame. Heat fell into the valley like a touch of hell and Beth screamed in terrible fear. And the sound crashed over them, like a world sundered, and 60 miles away a city melted into slag and a bright fireball grew into a white boiling mushroom.

...There were other cities, bombs and charred flesh and steel girders twisting like melted toffee before they vaporized, and the few who got away...

When I used those words in 1964 to describe in fiction the holocaust of a possible nuclear Armageddon, the threat of that Doomsday seemed terrifyingly real. *On The Beach* had been filmed in Melbourne, where I lived at the time, and its fantasy possessed a dreadful warning ring of truth. Cuba had, for long numbing hours in 1963, brought the world to the brink of atomic desolation—or so it seemed to millions as we waited out those hours. *Dr. Strangelove* took the fear to its ultimate conclusion, a vision of humanity exterminated at the hand of a maniac.

Yet today, in 1967, though the Arms Race has not slackened, the threat of final war seems no longer to loom over us. We have reached a watershed, an atomic impasse. The prospect is no longer merely terrible, it is too terrible. Words like megadeath and overkill in the military vocabulary of nuclear war have conjured so fearful a specter that we cannot believe in it. The apparatus for the suicide of the human race is readied and aimed, and nobody would dare to use it.

Mankind, though, is still the aggressive breed that clawed its way to the top. We love, build, believe and hope, hate and destroy. Our strange old human traits are still stamped into us by birth and by culture. We can fiercely protect what is ours and we can generously share it. We can greedily snatch what is not ours, and we can valiantly support idealistic causes. For reasons good and bad, brutal and decent, we still fight. We still wage war.

But, for the first time in history, an ultimate limit has been set. Thermonuclear warheads, sophisticated rocket delivery systems and ultrasensitive warning devices have drawn the line. Failure at the conference table still means war, but waging that war is getting to be the trickiest game in the book. In the last third of the twentieth century, a century which has discarded cavalry for near-intelligent missiles and shells for fusion bombs, we find ourselves gazing with astonishment at yet another new face of war.

The latest brand of war, of course, is the kind raging in Viet Nam, It has been called guerrilla warfare, yet its current implications sweep far beyond that ancient form of partisan conflict. Some see it as war of national liberation, a battle against both antiquated tradition and corrupt incumbent regimes. Yet its national character is often overshadowed by the ideological hostilities of West and Communist East. This new face of war is not easy to read. It's as enigmatic as the Mona Lisa, as compellingly complex as a Picasso.

"Forces of change," suggests John S. Pustay, a Major in the USAF, "will profoundly alter the international order within the next decade." His recent important study, *Counterinsurgency Warfare* (1965), lays bare the bones of the new warfare. (Pustay holds a doctorate from the Graduate School of International Studies of the University of Denver.) "The most drastic change will take place in the developing nations. It is safe to assume that the fundamental incompatibility between the ideologies of West and Communist East will tend mutually to invite conflict or, at the very minimum, active competition between member States...

"The situation in the underdeveloped countries is conducive to their becoming the battleground for such conflict. In the first place, the general political situation within these nations, whether or not they are committed by alliance to either camp, is somewhat blurred. This is inevitable, for the underdeveloped areas of Asia, Africa and Latin America are in the process of dragging themselves into the twentieth century by their bootstraps. Local leaders must violate age-old traditions in order to accomplish education and industrialization. Even when they are not corrupt, the ruling elites are in political hot-seats.

"Given the prescriptions of Communist ideology," states Major Pustay, "together with the nature of modern thermonuclear war and the unstable and exploitable nature of the developing States, it appears that the modes of conflict between the West and the Communist States will probably be indirect, muted and somewhat ambiguous. It is equally apparent that this conflict will be centered in the underdeveloped areas."

The guerrilla wars in our neighboring South-East Asian States, then, represent vastly more than the internal turmoil of newly emerging nations. They are the theater of an extension of the Cold War, an indirect play for the power and allegiance of these people by East and West. In this cautious (if bloody) war-within-war lies the emerging pattern of tomorrow's "non-nuclear, sub-limited" confrontations.

Perhaps the first indication of the shadowy profile of war's latest face was Khrushchev's now-famous speech of January 6, 1961. Reporting on a recently concluded conference of the Communist parties of 81 nations, he said: "Comrades, questions of war and peace were at the center of attention at the conference." Prevention of global thermonuclear war, and the limited wars which could escalate into it, was discussed as "the most burning and vital problem of mankind."

However, he was less hesitant on the topic of wars of national liberation. "Can such wars flare up in the future?" Krushchev asked the conference.

> They can. Can there be such uprisings? There can. But these are wars which are national uprisings. In other words, can conditions be created where a people will lose their patience and rise in arms? They can. What is the attitude of the Marxists towards such uprisings? A most positive one. These uprisings must not be identified with wars among States, with local wars, since in these uprisings the people are fighting for implementation of their right for self determination, for independent, social and national development. These are uprisings against rotten reactionary regimes, against the colonizers. The Communists fully support such just wars and march in the first rank with the peoples waging liberation struggles.

It was a gauntlet thrown down. On February 17, 1962, the US Secretary of Defense, Robert McNamara, suggested that it "might well be one of the most important declarations in the '60s by any world leader." Under the shadow of the Doomsday machine embodied in nuclear bombers, first and second strike atomic missiles, Polaris and USSR fusion-armed and powered submarines, the Cold War had to stay Cold or become very Hot indeed. Logistic support and "police-military" advisement to insurgents and counterinsurgents was the outlet. The two great power alignments of our time committed themselves to the new kind of war.

§

Is this the solution to the military problem of how to wage war in an age when war's very sophistication and horror had seemed, in some ways, to have banished or interdicted itself forever? What is this art and science of contemporary guerrilla warfare? Can, say, the Viet Cong hold the US at bay for much longer, pitting their meager physical strength against the might of the world's hugest industrial nation? Or will the Americans be forced into retreat, their highly-developed equipment and tactics grotesquely out of place in the new world of guerrilla insurgency?

The answers to some of these questions, of course, lie in the future. Nevertheless most of the factors that will provide their answers are part of today's world, and it is fascinating to try and forecast the emerging shape of these solutions. But before we investigate the future of guerrilla combat and its opposite, counterinsurgency, let us look somewhat more closely at the face, today, of the new strategy.

Insurgency warfare is, quite literally, the poor man's combat method. Like the ninety-seven-pound weakling who gets sand scuffed in his face by the hairy-chested bully, guerrilla techniques can exploit, karate-wise, the weaknesses of an opponent's strength. Lacking immediate political influence, weapons, supplies and numbers, guerrillas invoke what is called the *theory of substitution*. The principle has been explained strikingly by analogy: an intelligent, capable man, sitting behind the wheel of a complex and fast car, can be killed very messily by a tiny wasp stinging him at a crucial moment. The wasp's sting is insignificant in itself, a painful but minor irritation—yet if it distracts the driver as he guns his 400 horse power, ton-weight of metal and rubber, he can plough with fatal results into a vehicle speeding the other way.

The David-and-Goliath technique lies at the basis of insurgency warfare, although today's guerrillas are tremendously varied in the uses to which they direct the principle. The essential distinction between regular warfare and irregular or guerrilla approaches is that the first is an attempt to take terrain, by main force, from an enemy and hold it or deny it to him; the second is the attempt to prevent or avoid the exploitation of terrain by the enemy. As well as providing the wasp-type key irritation, therefore, the insurgents need the support of inhabitants of that terrain.

They must, as Mao Tse-Tung (the first modern genius of guerrilla methods) said, "live amongst the population as fishes live in the sea."

Generally speaking, guerrilla warfare can be of several kinds. It can be rebellion of an indigenous population, begun and supported from outside. It can be an organized and centrally directed popular revolt against enemy occupation. It can spring from local troops who have been passed by in the rapid offensive of an invader. In each case it must have, or obtain, at least the passive cooperation of the populace, and it must operate in terrain sufficiently difficult and broken to provide cover and security for bases and to discourage pursuit. Until Mao's formulation of rules for guerrilla war, it was believed that by itself insurgency was useless—that it could only serve to support a regular army. The success of the Viet Minh against the French professional soldiery demonstrated well enough the falsity of that analysis.

Today, particularly in South East Asia, guerrilla warfare is utilized by an amalgam of Nationalist and Communist insurgents anxious to replace a country's current government which is seen (rightly or wrongly) as colonialist or bourgeois-capitalist. "The path of recent history," remarks Major Pustay, "has been heavily marked by insurgency wars—not all of them successful—in which nations friendly to the US have become involved. In these internal wars the indigenous Communist parties, advocating either social reform or expulsion of the 'exploiting capitalists,' served as vanguard elements for insurgency.

"Some examples are the Greek Civil War; the Chinese Civil War; the Malaya Emergency; the Burmese Civil War; the Hukbong Magpalaya Nang Bayan (People's Liberation Army) rebellion in the Philippines; the Viet Minh, Pathet Lao and Vietcong insurgency in SE Asia; and the Castro Revolution in Cuba. However, not all insurgency wars with the Western and uncommitted areas during this period were Communist-dominated or even motivated. The Indonesian, Moroccan, Tunisian and Algerian revolutions are cases in point."

There is, however, a fundamental model for all of these revolts. Insurgency warfare is a resistance movement that develops in cells, directed against the incumbent political regime. It progresses in three phases. An initial stage of subversion and infiltration, which slowly undermines the enemy's basis of support, is followed by an intermediate stage of open resistance by small armed bands. These periods of subversion and insurrection have been termed by Mao the "strategic defensive" and the "stalemate." They may continue for years, wearing down the enemy and strengthening the insurgent forces in preparation for the third stage. This is the fruition, civil war or large-scale regular warfare.

Hanoi's present Defense Minister and Commander in Chief of the North Vietnamese army, General Vo Nguyen Giap, commanded the Vietnamese guerrillas, who in 1954 used these methods to drive out the French. For years the insurgents bided their time, building support, fighting and running away to fight again another day, finally trapping 12,000 French forces at Dien Bien Phu and liquidating them in third stage style.

Insurgents use preparatory measures in the first two phases, ranging from reforms in local economic and social welfare to torture and terrorism. The theory of substitution requires, in Mao Tse-Tung's words, "substitution of propaganda for guns, subversion for air power, men for machines, space for mechanization, political for industrial motivation." Terror, despite press reports of indiscriminate horror, seems generally to be aimed at political targets. The Australian University Study Group on Viet Nam suggests: "Once a state of civil war existed (in Viet Nam), those who occupied administrative or authoritative positions in the government must surely have known that they were marked men. Indeed, often the village headman had a semi-military position, and was protected by a squad of soldiers."

Eqbal Ahmad, an authority on revolutionary warfare, explains that the government representatives of the incumbent regime are "systematically eliminated from the countryside by the conversion or killing of village officials, who are then replaced by the political arm of the movement. The rebels must then build an administrative structure to collect taxes and provide some education and social welfare."

Systematic and calculated terrorism, nevertheless, clearly seems to be one of the weapons employed by insurgents. *Time*, reporting a March, 1967, statement by President Johnson contrasting inadvertent civilian casualties caused by US operations with the Viet Cong policy, remarked: "As if to punctuate the President's point, a Viet Cong plastic bomb erupted at a Saigon bus stop the same day, killing an old woman and wounding a young girl."

Dr. Thomas Dooley, in his book *The Night They Burned The Mountain,* has portrayed terrorist operations in North Viet Nam.

> I have seen what Communists do to Asians who work with Americans, for I had Asians working with me when the Communists took over. I knew that six or eight of my star pupils would be taken out and beheaded in front of the whole village and their heads, with the organs of the neck hanging down, would be impaled upon stakes. I knew that the Communists would take members of my Lao crew, stand them in a circle facing inwards, and with machetes would deftly cut the tendons in the back of their knees.
>
> When the crew would fall to the ground the Communists would walk around and hack them to pieces. I have seen the Communists do this and just leave the men in the middle of a room or in a field. When the tendons were cut, the Lao would not bleed to death. They would crawl like animals until they were caught and hacked to death. This is what they would do to

Chai, to Si, to Ngoan, and to Deng. To the girls of my staff they would do even more dreadful things.

Ironically, counterinsurgency measures may have led to an increase in terrorist activities. A *Time* report pointed out that the presence of Viet Cong in a village, the population of which provided protective coloration for guerrilla activities, now brought bombs from the US planes. "As a result, in many a village the Viet Cong are no longer welcome.... The Reds have been forced to step up taxation, rice levies and recruitment in areas they control, reaching down even to the fourteen-year-olds to keep up their 3500 men-a-month draftee rate in South Viet Nam. Once there was a kind of carefree banditry; increasingly, it is a grim way of life in which a village youth will very likely get killed.

"Increasingly," the report stated, "the Viet Cong are being forced to rely on terror and assassinations to keep their own village areas in line." On the other hand, counter-insurgents who seek to retain support (or create it) for the incumbent regime which is undergoing local subversion by insurgents have to do more than liquidate guerrillas. The University Study Group drew on Denis Warner's *The Last Confucian* to present the other side of the coin to terrorism: "The Viet Cong cadres stressed the immediate problems of the peasants—their desire for land, lower taxes, schools, and Self-Government. The party also began to attend to public health, sanitation, education and even the marketing of farmers' produce. It opened a first-aid station which was run by a public health cadre, who also visited the sick, and trained and appointed a mid-wife.

"It is small wonder that by the end of 1960 the Viet Cong had won such a measure of support that the village held a festival to celebrate its joining of the National Liberation Front."

Indeed, the French correspondent of *Le Monde* in Saigon, Max Clos, wrote in 1965: "The people have this picture to look at. On one side there is a real government, law and order, and responsible people. On the other side, chaos, anarchy and disorder. The people chose those who had won the contest."

The Vietnamese peasantry have little concept of the conflicting ideologies behind the war. Siding with the Viet Cong does not mean accepting the doctrine of Communism. All the same, counter-insurgents whose aim is non-Communist government for the people of Viet Nam (or any other similar state in insurrection) have a not-unfavorable guerrilla record to beat.

§

Counterinsurgency, and its development in recent years— largely by the Americans— is the other half of the new face of war. The guerrilla warfare of Mao Tse-Tung and Vo Nguyen Giap is on the whole a codification and adaptation of principles used by Spanish *partidos* in the Peninsular War of the early 1800s; one could trace the idea back to the Trojan Horse, probably. But counterinsurgency is a body of military theory and practice still under initial development.

Freedom of movement, superiority of military intelligence, familiarity with the locale, independence of arteries of supply, fanatical determination and endurance—these are the qualities which etch a portrait of the guerrilla's success. He is an enemy who can fade in and out of existence, who lives largely off the land, who is indistinguishable from the non-partisan peasants except when he has a gun in his hands. He fights with rifles fashioned out of old bicycle parts, Russian rockets, Chinese 120 mm mortars, steel-rimmed wooden wheeled pre-WW II machine guns, 12.7 mm anti-aircraft machine guns, Russian AK-47 30-round automatic assault rifles—and giant cross bows slamming six foot spears into helicopters.

Until recently, the celebrated ratio of counterinsurgent to guerrilla required to put down insurrection was ten or twelve to one. Even now the figure might not be much lower. But counterinsurgency is rapidly closing the gap between art and science. This is the new war; it is not just a macabre cross-history clash between the past and the present. This is the face of war for some time to come, and Americans and Australians are leaning how to fight it. This is the war in which choppers became the combat craft. Two years ago, just months after President Johnson sent US forces into Viet Nam in huge numbers to forestall the Viet Cong slamming into phase three and winning, low-slow helicopters showed their invaluable capability.

The 1st Air Cavalry, in a month of ferocious slaughter, claimed 2,262 Viet Cong at the battle of Ia Drang Valley. The division found a mobility which in some ways surpassed that of the guerrillas. During the campaign, it airlifted its 105 mm howitzers sixty-six times, fired 33,000 shells and flew 13,257 tons of supplies. Suddenly the air was a road, open to slow choppers.

Yet, despite the present monumental quantity of hardware in Viet Nam, despite the use of scientific detection devices, the insurgents are holding out. B-52s scream over the jungle, F4s and Skyhawks incinerate the petrol and oil supplies of Haiphong, but counterinsurgency is still very much a matter of search-and-destroy missions, "To find the enemy," writes Brig Gen S. L. A. Marshall, in a January *LOOK* article, "they will be tossed into jungle-covered highlands in groups ranging anywhere from five-man pickets to platoon size. They will be gone up to five days, sometimes twenty klicks (kilometers) from the nearest support element. For lightness, they will go with the Asiatic ration—boiled rice and a meat favoring. Otherwise, there is nothing light about the load; each man will carry 400-800 rounds of rifle ammunition, two to four hand grenades, a claymore mine, rifle and other gear.

"The ammo is slung Mexican-guerrilla style, crosswise over the shoulders. Carrying these loads, crouched over a choked jungle trail, they will walk five to seven klicks in a day. They get their water from the mountain streams, and consume three gallons daily to keep going."

Last year [1966], US Defense Secretary McNamara warned that the Communists were shifting "from a small arms guerrilla action against South Viet Nam to a quasi-conventional military action." Marshal agrees. "The fight," he continued, "in the main, is no longer guerrilla warfare. It is slugged out toe-to-toe, line against line. Mostly, they are company-size engagements, though there may be six or seven such fights going simultaneously within a belt of jungle no larger than Manhattan Island. More often than not, the sides close to within ten to 20 meters of each other, the shortest range at which Americans have ever engaged. The enemy seeks this embrace to escape our heavy weapons; the Americans close tight because in jungle there are no targets to be seen beyond the first snarl of bamboo.

"It is a death grapple at distances the width of a living room until one side or the other is destroyed or beaten into a blood-trailing retreat."

Insurgents, particularly infiltrators from North Vietnam, are no easier off. A march of 800 miles in danger from bombs, death from malaria, snakes, hunger, mud. They carry 70 lb packs in rugged slippery terrain, staggering and dragging themselves up 40 degree slopes. One man takes three months on foot to supply just one pair of eighty-one mm mortar rounds.

Beyond the current problems for both sides in fighting under such appalling and novel conditions lies the basic core of counter-insurgency. It is not enough to stop (if that is possible) the enemy from waging guerrilla and semi guerrilla war. Sub-limited wars only make sense in the context of a social and political revolution, a cultural revolution which in South East Asia and some African States is blasting underdeveloped areas from the feudal into the industrial age. Justification for the war is the concern of both parties for the way in which that fabulous transformation will occur, and the eventual political and ideological posture of the State involved. Broadly speaking, Vietnam and other crucial trouble spots will emerge either Communist-nationalist or Capitalist-nationalist; it is the business of counterinsurgency to ensure that the final strong and industrialized nation is well-disposed towards the West.

This being so, the main concern is the development, self-directed and non-totalitarian, of the State. Abuses and political outrages must be combated in the incumbent regime. "By correcting abuses, the government deprives the insurgents of sympathy, since insurgents base their appeal to the population on the desire for reform," explains one observer. (It is worth noting, by the way, the peculiarly coldblooded orientation of such a remark. It is to be hoped that the desire to assist reform, and a sound emergent nationalism, maintains a more humane motive than the mere defeat of insurgency.)

A preventative measure in counterinsurgency technique is the isolation of people from guerrilla infiltration. This serves the dual purpose of hindering insurgent propaganda and controlling terrorism. Unfortunately, while resettlement of villages for isolation purposes is ostensibly done in the best interests of the people and without their exploitation, it generates enormous resentment and resistance.

South Vietnamese, for example, are strongly attached to their ancestral lands for ancient religious reasons. The reluctance of outlying villagers to participate willingly in protective re-grouping makes psychological programs of great importance. One of the tremendous attractions to peasant farmers of the National Liberation Front is its promise of peasant proprietorship of one's own land. That the successful control of South Vietnam by the Viet Cong would eventually lead to State ownership of land is a concept counterinsurgency propagandists strive to convey.

Since one of the largest advantages of popularly based insurgency is its flash-fire rapid-intelligence network, counterinsurgents must endeavor to develop a unified national intelligence system of its own, giving peasants active participation. The Huk rebellion in the Philippines was crushed with the aid of such a system, which infiltrated or converted Huk ranks and eventually located the Communist Party's HQ and records, as well as top officials.

§

It is clear, then, that unlike ordinary war, counterinsurgency makes special demands and creates special problems. Sheer military prowess is not of first priority. It is important in the extreme, as a pacification measure, but it is simply ancillary to the job of establishing or re-establishing non-insurgent authority and order. The fundamental proposition of the new-faced war is (together with traditional pragmatic and cynical reasons) the need for the development of a people. That development will bear fruit of the most practical kind, of course: the Great Power which is allied to the victor earns vast potential markets and sources of materials. Nonetheless, the Communists are fighting for socialism and the freedom of men as they see it; the West is fighting so that the emerging nation will fully embrace our concept of the open and democratic society.

Consequently, counter-insurgents will find it especially important to assure civilians of their non-patronizing good-will. Troops, as well as the political and industrial-aid arms of the force, will of necessity take part in local civic projects. For what their bombs, their napalm, their war machines destroy of the land, they must give back in their active participation in the community. But while the element of crusade is a noble aspect of what everyone agrees is a "dirty" kind of war, it is yoked up to Western and Communist self-images of truth and prestige. The conference table, where insurgent and counterinsurgent will eventually sit to find the terms of settlement, is vacant; it may remain so until one party emerges victorious. What are the prospects of military victory for insurgent or counterinsurgent?

§

It has taken, according to one authority, perhaps 3,000 years and some of the most modern military equipment available today for the counterinsurgent finally to meet the insurgent on his own terms. The next advance for counterinsurgency seems to lie in the domain of instrumented detection of partisans, and methods of marking and identifying them.

One of the most intriguing possibilities has come out of space research. There are chemical by-products of the human system, known as effluents, which our bodies emit constantly. In the closed environment of a space capsule these effluents could literally poison an astronaut. In order to cope with disposing them, Dr. Thomas B. Weber, of Beckman Instruments Ltd, has identified all of them. Several of these trace contaminants are easily identified in the atmosphere with suitable instrumentation.

For example, ethanol and methanol are two by-products of the human body that are not normally found in nature. Specially designed instruments—using the principles of infrared light spectrum analysis or gas chromatography—mounted in aircraft, patrol vehicles or perimeter posts would signal the hidden presence of hostiles.

Low-slow air-mounted devices of this kind would locate and monitor the activities and movements of insurgents, point graphically the path to their homes or secret logistics stores. Other trace elements could detect motor vehicles creeping down visually camouflaged trails. Location of insurgents after curfew or in proscribed areas would be enormously simplified, and suspects could be picked up for questioning.

Furthermore, another counterinsurgency advance might be methods of marking suspects. Invisible dyes that fluoresce under excitation lights might be sprayed on the secretly located insurgent; other methods might involve spraying of non-harmfully radiating substances which would register on a Geiger counter, or visible dyes acting as a general deterrent as well as an identification device.

A bizarre notion is the micro-electronic "wiring" of trained animals, which would be released as roving and indistinguishable "agents." Their special circuits could send back sound and picture to a central computer which would tag anything suspicious for troop follow-through. But although some preliminary work as been done in this line, the whole approach seems too random—and pacification forces might find that their "instruments" are gobbled up by wild jungle creatures.

It is, of course, impossible to forecast developments that lie outside the range of present knowledge. As well, there is the chance that if counterinsurgency advances successfully block the use of guerrilla techniques, Russia or China might become more vigorously involved. Whether the threat of escalation into large-scale local war and, conceivably, hysterical thermonuclear global conflagration would be a sufficient buffer cannot be predicted, though it seems likely.

§

This, then, is the new face of war. It is the near stalemate confrontation of West and East, in an armed conflict involving some of the oldest human military procedures against the latest. If fresh pacification methods are evolved, they will serve to reduce the ratio of counter-insurgent versus guerrilla. Reconnaissance-locate-control may replace search-and-destroy. With the insurgent's traditional advantages removed or duplicated, the cost of counterinsurgency operations will drop dramatically.

The guerrilla will become a soldier of the past, for he is only credible as a military proposition while the enemy is both clumsy and expensive. The "new face of war" will give way to another as yet unforeseeable.

THE PRICE OF IGNORANCE (1969)

KILL THE SCIENTIST, proclaimed a recent front cover of this magazine. And amplified that graphic and remarkable injunction with the blunt justification: BEFORE HE KILLS YOU!

Geoff Wyatt, whose article on chemical and bacteriological warfare the slogan advertised, was rather more temperate. Although, he wrote, his views "are totally opposed to the views of the generals and the scientists in whose hands my life would appear to be contained... I cannot begin a campaign to murder the scientists and the generals because that would be indulging in their own madness," Wyatt's blood-curdling account of the new horror-weapons currently stockpiling in laboratory and arsenal was enough to make any sane man nauseated with dread, for both himself and his children.

All the more reason, then, for commending Wyatt in his refusal to take the easy way out, to demand (as that frightening slogan did) a policy of doing unto others what they would do unto you. It is my unhappy conviction not only that mankind is this day confronted by a number of threats to its continued survival, but that the public response which is emerging, as these threats gradually come to be recognized, is very often hysterical rather than rational. Hysteria is a peculiarly ineffective response to a demanding situation—unless that situation requires precisely a mindless, brutal exercise of sheer instinct.

A man in the extremities of physical and mental exhaustion

can, under deadly stress, call forth hidden reserves in a burst of hysterical strength and stamina. He can, anesthetized and driven by sheer terror, run on a broken leg. He can fight with the same hysterical intensity to preserve himself which will impel a trapped animal to gnaw off its imprisoned limb. The one thing he cannot do in that state is think, reason, evaluate, plan. The in-built switch that turns a cornered, defeated man into a flailing engine of last-ditch frenzy operates chiefly by bypassing the rational section of his personality.

This is fine, we must admit, in situations so stark, delineated so entirely in black and white, that hammer blows and fast feet are the final and correct solution. But human beings, by virtue of the complex and subtle self-constructed world we inhabit, are seldom faced with such primitive predicaments. Unfortunately, our ancestors were—for a million years or more. The hysterical reaction is stamped deep in our genetic heritage, waiting to be triggered by any threat too complex for our ancient, stupid reflexes to comprehend.

Luckily for civilization our magnificent intellectual capabilities are usually firmly in the saddle, holding those furious "fight-or-flight" instincts in check while we think the problem out—and realize, for example, that it's easier and more judicious to open a door by turning the knob than by smashing it down.

The danger in hysteria is that ninety-nine times in 100 it produces paralysis or futile and bloody rampages, communication breakdown, group imbecility, and a variety of other disorders. If we are successfully to meet the challenges which civilization has spawned in its own breast, hysteria is a luxury we simply cannot afford.

The bitter fact is that greater danger broods within the cry "Death to the scientists" than in all the hell-bombs and germ missiles our benighted guardians have ever built.

§

That said, it must be admitted that only a fool could face our botched world without putting his equanimity at risk. Like the Sorcerer's Apprentice (as we are just beginning to discover), our every attempt to bend nature to our will has been attended by unforeseen disaster. We have crippled the world and ourselves, in large ways and small, with each step of creative endeavor. Our lust to own the world, to forge it into shapes more suited to our comfort, has run far ahead of our capacity to predict and govern the side effects of change.

Let me offer some examples. One of the outstanding break-throughs in farming practice came in 1939 when a Swiss chemist, Dr. Paul Muller, created DDT. Recorded history, despite our urban prejudices, is largely the unfolding tale of man's relation-ship with the soil. Indeed, the invention and development of agriculture was the key to that food-surplus which made civi-lization possible. Until Muller's discovery, people had waged a ceaseless battle not merely with harsh climates and poor land but with periodic hosts of predatory and disease carrying insects.

The appearance of DDT and, later, such pesticides as diel-drin, aldrin and parathion, promised farmers a Golden Age of unravaged crops. With growing eagerness, the agriculturists of the world inundated their fields and orchards with tens of thou-sands of tons of dust and spray. Crop yields soared; the perils of insect infestation seemed on the verge of conquest. In 1948, Dr. Muller received the Nobel Prize, together with the gratitude of an ever-growing, ever-hungry world. Twenty years later, the nation that had awarded him that prize became the first to ban the wonder chemical.

The reason is by now fairly well known, though we have yet to grasp all the dire implications. In 1962, Dr. Rachel Carson brought to the world's notice the deadly fact that DDT and other insecticides are not particular about the victims they claim. Fish, plants, animals and birds have all suffered grotesque injury and death as a result. Human beings are not entirely immune. Cases are on record where farm workers have died or suffered serious poisoning from the supposedly safe chemical.

The critical factor, however, is not that individuals may be damaged by direct exposure to such substances. Accidents of this kind will occur under the most benign circumstances, and now that workers have been warned they can protect themselves. The central issue is the way in which DDT and its kindred molecules have acted on a whole chain of living creatures, growing more virulent with each new link.

Natural fauna—and some flora—concentrate certain poisons in their cells, rather than disposing of them as waste. It is easy to see how such an effect amplifies itself with each step in a complicated food chain.

An incredibly dilute spray of insecticide, dangerous only to its intended victims, will gradually build up in the soil. Earthworms living in that soil will soon concentrate 10 to 40 times that proportion in their own flesh. Birds feeding on the worms will distill about 200 times the amount to be found in the ground. Animals preying on avian life will continue the process...

An even more staggering example was reported from Clear Lake (ironic name!) in California, where DDT passed from plankton to fish to grebes and other diving birds; the final, and lethal, concentration in the birds was 100,000 times greater than it had been in the anti-insect spray.

Direct destruction via the food cycle is not the only way insecticides have wreaked havoc. One Bolivian town, plagued by malarial mosquitoes, was spray-treated with DDT. Most of the local cats were killed by it. As a direct result, the town was invaded by a wild rodent carrying Black Typhus. New cats were brought in as quickly as possible but before they could restore the previous ecological balance several hundred people were claimed by the hideous disease.

The list of depredations might be extended, and there is little doubt that all the ramifications of pesticide use are as yet unknown. An expert has summarized the position thus: "In the biosphere the whole is always greater than the sum of its parts; animals which absorb one insecticide may become more sensitive to the damaging effects of a second one. Because of such amplifications, a small intrusion in one place in the environment may trigger a huge response elsewhere in the system.

"Often an amplification feeds on itself until the entire living system is engulfed by catastrophe. If the vegetation that protects the soil from erosion is killed, the soil will wash away, plants will then find no foot holds for their seeds, and a permanent desert will result."

Another major cause of disruption to the biosphere is the massive pollution produced by the mere existence of vast industrial cities. A United Nations report released last year [1968] warned that modern cities and skills may soon make the earth literally uninhabitable. That appalling prospect, it claimed, is likely "within the lifetime of most people alive today" unless concerted action is taken to avert it.

That picture of an imminent global crisis is entirely realistic. Although we have lived for more than twenty years under the shadow of nuclear annihilation, the slender comfort has always been available that we do not have to push the button. Destruction of the human race by atomic suicide is at least only an option. To initiate that nightmare a long sequence of cool decisions is necessary, and so far our leaders have managed to restrain themselves.

The horror of pollution, however, is largely that it is already underway—and has been working its insidious damage for at least a century. We are steadily drowning in our own wastes, and what is worse we are poisoning the capacity of our planet to renew itself. The UN report pointed out that in the United States alone, industrialization pumps 142 million tons of toxic pollutants into the atmosphere every year.

Professor R. O. Slatyer, head of population biology studies at the Australian National University, stated that the world's atmosphere was being despoiled by the combination of fossil fuels equal in 1968 to a bushfire destroying the entire vegetation of the Australian continent. Within fifty years, he warned, we will all be breathing air containing twice the present amount of carbon dioxide. How did such a ghastly situation emerge without our noticing it until so late?

The answer is simple: we didn't know what we were doing. Most people still cannot comprehend the enormity of our risk. For we are caught in a cleft stick. We cannot maintain our present pollutive civilization without destroying our planet's biosphere—nor can we abandon the industrial base of that civilization without most of us perishing anyway.

§

Let us look more closely at how the problem arose. Far back in prehistory, our remote ancestors made two discoveries that set them on the path to ownership of the world. One was the use of tools, the other the use of fire. The significance of tools, even such simple instruments as levers and axes, was that they vastly extended the range of human muscle-power.

There is a fixed limit to how much effort any animal—including humans—can exert in a single burst (trying to lift a huge rock say). All other animals, too, are restricted by this very factor in the degree to which they can make large-scale alterations to their environments. The invention of tools, however, enabled human beings to apply tolerable efforts to one end of a long lever, and achieve a superhuman output at the other. Thus, a single man armed with a long stout pole can manipulate a one ton rock without assistance.

The taming of fire was an even greater advance. Even with the use of domesticated animals as powerful as horses and elephants, there is a limit to the energy available. The release and harnessing of chemical energy has taken us from the forest to the mechanized farm, the highway, the thermonuclear bomb, and the moon. The single drawback in the use of external energy sources (other than the risk of getting burnt to death or blown to pieces) is the fact that smoke, ash and heat must be vented as a side-effect. For hundreds of thousands of years this factor was practically negligible. The seemingly-unlimited store of fresh air and clean water available on our giant planet diluted and degraded all effluents with such ease that the cycle went unnoticed. Early on, it had become obvious that intensive crop cultivation drained the soil of nutriments, and the practice of rotational farming became established, leaving tired fields fallow until they had regained their vigor. Nobody noticed, however, the similar burden placed on the atmosphere and water supplies by pollutants.

Every single ton of wood, coal, petroleum or natural gas burned adds several tons of carbon dioxide to the air during production and use. Nevertheless, one might suppose, human beings are so minute a proportion of the earth's mass as to render any effect they might have insignificant. Not so; incredible as it may seem, the combustion of fuels between 1860 and 1960 is estimated to have raised the carbon dioxide content of the air by 14 percent. And so huge is the rate of advancing industrialization that the figure may exceed 100 percent [more than double] by the middle of next century.

The fantastic significance of carbon dioxide pollution is its effect on world temperature. CO_2 tends to pass visible light but absorbs heat radiation. Light from the sun, after it has passed through the atmosphere, is partly converted into heat energy by soil and plants and thus remains trapped within the atmosphere by a "greenhouse effect." As the percentage of carbon dioxide in the air rises, this greenhouse effect intensifies. Says Professor Slatyer: "It has not been possible to calculate the climatic effect, but some estimates suggest the temperature of the world will increase by several degrees. Even now it appears to have increased by at least one degree.

"Should this occur, dramatic changes will take place in cloudiness, rainfall and on the level of agricultural productivity."

Even more dramatic and daunting is the warning disclosed by the US President's Science Advisory Committee, whose report was published in November 1965. They found that the extra heat trapped by fuel-produced carbon dioxide might melt the Antarctic ice cap. Although there is no immediate threat of this catastrophe (estimates range from 400 to 4000 years for the effect to take place), it emphasizes the monumental problems we are bequeathing to our descendants. "The melting of the Antarctic ice cap," states the report, "would raise sea level by 400 feet. If 1000 years were required to melt the ice cap, the sea level would rise about four feet every ten years,"

It is almost impossible to picture such a cataclysm—yet we are inexorably laying its formations with every ton of fuel we burn.

§

Practically every element of our scientific way of life contributes to the contamination of air, soil, river and life. Our major transportation device, the internal combustion engine, has for 70 years befouled the air with waste fuel fractions. Exposed to sunlight, these fractions form the noxious components of smog—increasing the incidence of respiratory disease in most of the world's major cities. Tetraethyl additives in petrol have, since 1923, distributed lead particles into oceans, crops and human blood.

Sewage and farm runoff have loaded inland water supplies around the globe with excess phosphate and nitrates. Again we see the poignant paradox: substances introduced to raise crop yields for a hungry world have ended as a threat to health and life. "About 8 to 9 parts per million of nitrate in drinking water," states one authority, "causes serious respiratory difficulty in infants—cyanosis—by interfering with hemoglobin function. For domestic animals 5 parts per million is considered unsafe. Some wells in the US already have more than 3 parts per million, and the contamination levels will go up with the increased use of fertilizers and the growing density of population."

Perhaps the most striking recent case of technology biting the hand that creates it is the bizarre tale of The Wild Detergent Bubbles. The importance of this example is precisely to show how a seemingly minor "breakthrough" can result in a massive and sometimes disastrous intervention in nature.

Soap has been known during all recorded history. Fats and oils extracted from animals or seeds can, when cooked with alkali, react chemically to produce the double molecule mothers love and schoolboys loathe. This soap molecule works by filming its fatty part around droplets of greasy dirt and attaching its other end to water molecules. Sluiced away, the dirty soapy water is broken down by the action of bacteria in sewage outlets.

The trouble with natural soap is that in "hard" water, which contains unusually high concentrations of minerals, it forms a persistent and messy deposit. Economically also it leaves much to be desired, since animal and seed fats vary in availability, price and quality.

Chemical technologists in the 1930s, having successfully invented synthetic organic compounds such as plastics and artificial rubber, turned their minds to the development of a synthetic washing agent.

In short order, a family of cleaning substances was produced, by linking fat-like hydrocarbons with water-soluble sulfur groups. The new detergents were superior to soap in every way. They worked just as well in hard water, were cheap, pleasant to smell and touch, and could be stored for a long time. By the early '40s they had captured the major share of the American cleanser market, and by 1960 about 3.5 billion pounds of synthetic detergent was being used every year. Unhappily, the superior qualities of detergent did not end with its departure down the plug-hole. Mountains of foaming, gleaming bubbles began to appear in riverways. Faucet water drew a head, in some places, that made brewers gasp in envy. The tough synthetic bubbles simply would not go away; they lingered in their trillions, to the embarrassment and dismay of farmers, water-supply authorities and detergent manufacturers.

Stimulated by legislative action, the chemists ferreted out the secret of the delinquent bubbles. Natural soaps, as we have seen, break down readily under the attack of bacterial enzymes. The new substances, being based upon different molecules, resisted this action. Methods were eventually developed for synthesizing a degradable detergent, and on July 1, 1965, the multibillion dollar US detergent industry pacted to replace the offending ingredient.

Even these new detergents are far from perfect. They take longer to decompose in septic tanks. Some of them, after decay, add to the overload in surface waters of phosphate.

Amusing as the bubble saga may now seem, it highlights once again the critical failure of modern technology to predict the consequences of its actions. We may put aside from consideration for the moment the lunatic progression in destructiveness and inhumanity involved in the Arms Race; that particular horror follows a logic of its own. But there is a question we must face, the question on which—whether or not there comes a Third World War—our corporate survival appears to depend.

It has been aptly posed by Professor Barry Commoner in his book *Science and Survival*: "Are we really in control of the vast new powers that science has given, us, or is there a danger that science is getting out of hand?" Has it become, in short, not our savior but our greatest menace?

§

Already I can hear the voices rising in answer, like a great bell tolling, like a crowd of all the frightened men and women in the world chanting in rising hysteria:

"Science is the big steamroller, rushing over us, splintering our bones in the roar of its power."

"Science is the giant bomb, the searing flash, the heat that will eat our flesh."

"Science is the voice of the machine, the metal trumpet brazen with vulgarity, drowning the nuances of our human tongues."

"Science is the great beast we have made in our blindness, the moron monster groaning out our fate."

"Let us then, destroy Science, for it will not otherwise stop until it has destroyed ·us."

And the slogan they are bearing reads: KILL THE SCIENTIST BEFORE HE KILLS YOU.

To which I can only answer, with all the force and power of conviction at my command, "No. You are wrong. Your intuition is half-right, but you are wrong." For it is not Science with a capital "S" that has brought us to the lip of the abyss, nor indeed is it legitimate to blame scientists at large for the frightening mess we find ourselves in. Do not mistake me. I offer no absolution to those bloodless experts who poison us for profit, who foist on us with all the formidable power of the persuasive media those instruments, devices and narcotics which choke us and shorten our lives.

Nor do I hold a brief for those who, behind the masks of patriotism and honor, whore their minds to the merchants of death. Every society has borne the burden of men eager to profit from the gullibility and pain of their fellows; our own, at least, is perhaps the first in history to articulate publicly its skepticism of those men.

The non-military threats which now loom over us cannot, I believe, be ascribed to some amorphous force called "Science," nor to any particular body of scientific practitioners. We are caught, rather, in a trap shaped by the entire history of our culture. When we relinquished the harsh, archaic, and predictable ecology of the hunt, when we invented agriculture, cities and machine technology, we threw away the rule-book. We gambled on our own ingenuity to see us through as we moved farther and farther into an uncharted no-man's-land.

Today, we are not without charts, but they are incomplete and we often lurch ahead of our scouts into the unknown. The charts we do possess, built up painfully and sometimes incorrectly by generations of explorers, go jointly by the name "Science." There are, of course, other charts as well, called Literature and Art and History, but the maps most influential in our time are those labeled Science.

It is a bizarre notion that a man stumbling through strange

territory should burn the few maps he possesses. It is equally bizarre, and ultimately fatal, to suggest that our society turn its back on science, let alone kill its scientists.

§

Perhaps it might be felt that I am taking that last slogan too literally, that it is intended as no more than a graphic announcement of our over-reliance on charts that have shown themselves to be dangerously incomplete. My feeling, however, is that such slogans reveal more than they mean to—that their very hyperbole resonates with deep and near-hysterical fears latent in us all. The urge to find a scapegoat, to propitiate fate with an extravagant display, is deeply scored in our cells. There have been too many cases where the doctor is punished for revealing the patient's disease.

The situation is too complex to be encompassed by anyone's slogans, let alone mine, but if pressed I would argue that our present malaise is the result of too *little* science rather than too *much*. Our problem has been that the landscape charted by the scientists is neither simple nor static. It is intricate to the point where specialists cannot understand one another halfway through their training; it is fluid because of our very interventions in nature.

The communication difficulties are aggravated as well by the curious political madness known as "security," which has been known to deny a scientist access to the detailed results of work he has himself done! Another factor which increasingly isolates new information from a scientist's colleagues is the large amount of research done for profit-oriented corporations. Fearful of competition, huge companies deny the free flow of data which is absolutely essential if experts in divergent fields are to warn each other of the probable consequences of precipitate action.

The primary dangers confronting us, however—pollution, overpopulation, erosion, etc—stem chiefly from the urgent and continuing need to apply abstract knowledge to pressing problems. It would be absurd to blame scientists because their studies helped alleviate infant mortality, extended the average lifespan, destroyed disease-carrying pests, and raised the efficiency of agriculture. Each of these good and noble deeds has backfired on us to a horrible extent—but not through some malign plot or deliberate carelessness.

The universe is what it is; if our ignorance of its complexities brings disaster on our heads, the only remedy is more thorough knowledge, and the informed exercise of caution.

It is, needless to say, far too late in the day to call a halt to the entire enterprise. The global village cannot sustain its three billion human souls without the perilous use of scientific industrialization. The only choice left us lies in the kinds of restraints we are prepared to impose on our own immediate gratifications, in order that the biosphere might not become more irrevocably blighted than it already has.

At this point, the issue can be seen more clearly as one of planetary morality. Not, *shall* we use science, but *how* shall we use it? It is frequently asserted as a key to our predicament that advances in ethics have not kept pace with the explosive development of the physical sciences and technologies. This is nonsense. For at least 2,000 years, we have been in possession of an ethical theorem as powerful and elegant as Einstein's energy equation $E=mc^2$.

Briefly expressed, it is this: *Love One Another.*

Where we have, slowly but surely, been losing out in the race between our increasing disruptive abilities and our responsible command of them, is in our failure to act on that ethical insight.

The ethical technology we might have constructed upon the basis of that dictum does not exist—except in the tired cant of hypocritical leaders and the spokesmen of repressive theologies. Without such an ethical technology to guide and shape our endeavors, the other technologies have blossomed into a distorted and quite possibly lethal maturity under the impulse of such sordid motives as status-seeking, chauvinism, profiteering and militarism.

It is time for us to learn finally the toughest, most hard-headed lesson of all: that love may bring us joy, and that the lack of love may exterminate life forever.

HERBERT MARCUSE (1969)

"For a rational human being," raps Herbert Marcuse, philosophy Professor at the University of California's San Diego campus, "the right to be frightened is the most important one left today."

Fright, as a quick skim through the cinema advertisements will prove, is a most saleable commodity. Tales of terror and Gothic dread, films like *Psycho* and *Rosemary's Baby,* continue to captivate mass audiences who pay handsomely for the privilege of being shocked. It is easy to see why, of course. Fanciful horror has the wonderful advantage of delivering fright without risk. People who would faint away at the very thought of actual danger can purchase a few hours' apprehension safe in the soothing knowledge that the source of their terror is unreal, is a fantasy. Close the book, rise to shuffle into the cinema aisle, and you can be blithely certain that the stake remains firmly embedded in the vampire's breast. Breathe easily...it was all a delightful dream, irrelevant to your world of comfortable reality.

Doubly curious, then, that the fright Marcuse offers—the fright which has brought him fame and conceivably fortune in the past year—is centered solidly in this safe world of everyday reality. For Marcuse's claim is that *Nineteen Eighty-Four* is here already, that we are caught in a totalitarian trap we do not recognize, that the everyday world of Australia, Britain and the USA—no less than that of Russia and Czechoslovakia—is a concentration camp we may never escape.

Extraordinary? Ludicrous? We must face immediately

the fact that Marcuse's analysis and diagnosis of society has touched a nerve in millions of troubled young people throughout the world. Parisian students and workers invoked him as they fought fist-to-shield with riot police in the French Revolution of 1968. When the black and red flags of anarchy and socialism fly from the battlements of some campus under siege in Tokyo or San Francisco, Marcuse's name rings loud in tones of exultation and defiance. His ideas resonate with the profound sense of malaise that is thrusting youth in every Western country into fiery rebellion.

Marcuse, from the once-complacent ivory towers of the American intellectual establishment, has emerged at the age of seventy-one a crucial voice articulating the rebellion of the young. It would be a gauche mistake to see in him merely a demagogue, a pseudo prophet slavishly followed by rich kids seeking kicks. The thesis of Marcuse—elaborate, scholarly and hortatory as it is—becomes primarily a theoretical statement of what millions of middle-class youths are expressing directly in sit-ins, draft card burnings and the explosive extremity of street-fighting revolt. It is clear, therefore, that an understanding of Marcuse's ideas is critical in this hour. The possibility is not negligible that the thoughts of Herbert Marcuse might in the next fifty years focus revolution as shattering as that occasioned by the doctrines of Marx and Lenin in the fifty past.

II.

One-Dimensional Man, Marcuse's most recent major work, has been singled out by *Le Nouvel Observateur* as "the most subversive book published in the United States this century." It is all of that. Undeniably, the book is seditious, savagely subversive of every principal establishment in advanced industrial society. It is also on open sale in a cheap paperback edition in every principal Western country. Overt sedition, believe it or not, for $1.15.

Ironically, this very instance of the fantastic tolerance for dissent displayed by liberal democratic communities can just as readily be seen as a vindication of Marcuse's chief thesis.

The establishment, claims Marcuse, has an almost limitless capacity to contain and nullify effective dissent. "A comfortable, smooth, reasonable, democratic unfreedom prevails in advanced industrial civilization," his book begins. In this condition of "unfreedom," dissent is assimilated rather than suppressed, ridiculed rather than persecuted, given free voice in the secure knowledge that no-one will listen but the most impotent minorities. "The powers that be," said Marcuse wryly in August, 1967, "can take the fact that I can travel anywhere and say everything I want to, because they know quite well that they have nothing to fear from the Professor."

We are faced here by a paradox few observers have come close to elucidating. How is it that in America—which not long ago witnessed the sordid debauch of Mayor Daley's cops smashing everything that moved outside the barbed-wire enclosure of the Democratic Convention—radical black leaders like Stokely Carmichael freely preach bloody rebellion?

How is it that in a society which spends billions of dollars each year preparing for a nuclear holocaust while two-thirds of the world starves, men and women who call for a reappraisal of priorities are contemptuously dismissed as "nuts" and (in Australia) "ratbags"? What insane hypnosis has stupefied the sensibilities of those who democratically concur in the billion dollar orgy of waste known as "planned obsolescence," while one fifth of their neighbors subsist below the poverty line?

To Marcuse, these paradoxes are no mere accidents of history; they are part and parcel of the way industrial society is structured. More strikingly, they are the result of the way human consciousness has been systematically deformed, restricted and controlled. Such indictments are not in themselves new. We have heard before, from the most fashionable liberal commentators, that ours is the Age of the Organization Man, that increasingly we are mere cogs in a monstrous technological juggernaut, that we are alienated and dispossessed from our own full possibilities. Marcuse's distinction is that he does not simply catalogue these depredations—he seeks to explain them, and locate for us a more satisfactory path.

The roots of Marcuse's thought lie in the uncomfortable traditions of Marx and Freud. Do not be misled: he is far from Communism as it is understood today. His most scathing attacks are directed (in his book *Soviet Marxism*) to the Stalinist and neoStalinist dictators in the Kremlin and elsewhere. But the repressive logic of technological society, he suggests, is no less relevant in the Western countries than it is under communism. The foe is the identical repressive force at work in all these systems: the logic of technological domination.

We are talking, ultimately, about the quality of life. Marcuse is aware, as few of us could be, of the inhuman horrors men can inflict on men. A refugee from the Nazi barbarism in Europe, he certainly comprehends the distinction between the symbolic concentration camp of One Dimensional society, and literal reeking death pits. Spurious in one sense as democratic liberties might be, Marcuse does not take them lightly. It is only in view of his profound respect for the possibilities of total human freedom that we can begin genuinely to come to terms with him.

§

Marcuse's preoccupation is what he sees as the gradual, subtle and totalitarian erosion of dimensions of liberty in our civilization. And let it be clear: he is not talking primarily about the plight of minorities unjustly persecuted; nor about the need for abolition of nuclear weapons, nor any other specific issue of humanitarian or civic concern. These matters, grave as they are, appear to him symptoms of a larger illness. It is that general social disorder which he has taken as his subject.

If Marcuse has followed Marx in tracing the course of capitalism's alleged failure, it is to Freud that he owes his greatest intellectual debt. Like Marx, Marcuse employs the questionable method of historical dialectic in his attempt to comprehend the world. But he looks to psychology, as did Freud, for the basic key to societal disorder. And, since his special mode of thought is critical (or, as he sometimes calls it, negative thinking), Marcuse is quick to point up the weakness of his two masters and discern alternatives in their thought which history has found more cogent to our present situation.

Let us begin with Freud. The founder of psychoanalysis, in his study *Civilization and Its Discontents*, applied the insights of depth psychology to the analysis of a world which had recently suffered the bloody tragedy of World War I. His gloomy conclusion was that civilization is based on the permanent subjugation of human instincts. The travails attendant upon such suppression (such as war, neurosis, sexual restraint and so on) were unavoidable. Either one opted for civilization, paying for all its superb advantages at the cost of mental incapacitation for the few and intermittent spasms of insanity for the many, or one enjoyed a brief if sexy life in the trees. Indeed, Freud never really questioned whether the suffering inflicted on individuals by civilization has been worth the benefits. He considered the process both inevitable and irreversible.

Marcuse accepts with Freud that the free gratification of human needs is incompatible with civilized society, that renunciation and delay in satisfaction are the prerequisites of progress. More precisely, he accepts that this *has been* the case. Marcuse's central intuition was to question the invariance of this situation. He was the first to inquire in a thorough-going fashion into the possibility of a genuinely liberated nonrepressive civilization.

One of the difficulties in reading Marcuse is that many of his concepts are foreign to contemporary thinkers. For many years it has been unacceptable in polite academic circles to talk about instincts, particularly in reference to human beings. Modern psychology prefers to discuss specific drives, motivations and learning-patterns.

Recently, however, studies by ethologists of insects, birds and primates in their natural surroundings have led to a revival of instinct theory. Much of Freud's speculation must still be dismissed as confused, invalid and arbitrary. At the same time, certain of his postulations are regaining favor. It can fairly be said that his notions of culture and the supposed repression of instinctual drives remain enormously provocative. Freud's crucial idea can be expressed, over-simplified, as follows: humans, like all creatures, have certain innate impulses that must be satisfied if we are to remain alive and healthy. These primary impulses, or instincts, relate to sex, hunger, sleep and aggression.

Other animals satisfy these cravings directly and immediately. It is the peculiar distinction of humanity that the species has learnt to sublimate, or deflect to alternate goals, the energy which would "more naturally" be expended on the original instinctual goals. Sublimation thus permits and powers a diversity of sophisticated activities. In creating these "secondary impulses," however, we must strive painfully and continuously against the basic urge to satisfy primary goals.

"Happiness," summarizes Marcuse, in his book, *Eros and Civilization*, "must be subordinated to the discipline of work as a full-time occupation, to the discipline of monogamic reproduction, to the established system of law and order. The methodical sacrifice of libido (life energy), its rigidly enforced deflection to socially useful activities and expressions, is culture."

A basic example of this process can be observed in the social constraints on sexuality: "The conflict between civilization and sexuality," wrote Freud, "is caused by the circumstance that sexual love is a relationship between two people, in which a third can only be superfluous or disturbing, whereas civilization is founded on the relations between larger groups of persons... the pair of lovers are sufficient unto themselves, do not even need the child they have in common to make them happy."

Commonsense misgivings about this judgment are reinforced by modern ethology, which sees in primate pair-bonding one of the major elements of small-group solidarity. Nevertheless, the general point is well taken. Wholesale preoccupation with sex tends, at the very least, to eat into your time. Promiscuity, the most attractive form of sexual enjoyment, involves a slackness in the social bonds that precludes intense organization. A stringent mobilization of human resources, in turn, is necessary for the development of advanced culture.

The same applies to other primary instincts and their social sublimation. The development of work routines, task-specialization, forward planning and economy in the utilization of resources, all make the group that employs them more likely to survive a barren season, more capable of confronting attack effectively. At the most primitive level, it is reasonable to suppose that the family which preys together stays together. Abdication of immediate instinctual satisfaction, although it involves continual and unpleasant restraint, is the only feasible path for humans to follow.

"The sacrifice," states Marcuse, "has paid off well: in the technically advanced areas of civilization the conquest of nature is practically complete, and more needs of a greater number of people are fulfilled than ever before. Neither the mechanization and standardization of life, nor the mental impoverishment, nor the growing destructiveness of present-day progress provides sufficient ground for questioning the 'principle' which has governed the progress of Western civilization. The continual increase of productivity makes constantly more realistic the promise of an even better life for all."

§

This, roughly speaking, is the tortured paradox of today's liberal. He sees a world on the verge of possible total automation, disease almost entirely conquered, plenty within the grasp of all. And yet the price is terrible. We are in many respects becoming no more than cogs. Our education increasingly makes us and our children technically-proficient morons.

For the liberal, the price is not too great. He can put his faith in some distant future when the tax will be relieved, when technological achievements have made us so fully the Lords of the Earth that we will be spared a moment to learn to enjoy our heritage. Marcuse, however, is ruthless. He forces the argument to its unpalatable conclusion. If our present development is rooted in restraint, typically maintained by guilt which keeps us on the straight and narrow path of repression, how can we ever find authentic happiness? The rational control and coordination of ourselves and our resources certainly keeps us alive and physically healthy for our full natural span, but where is the sweet flavor of life?

Our lives are progressively more sanitized, deodorized, depersonalized and meaningless. In the extent to which we remove ourselves from our instinctual beginning, we destroy the savor in living which gives the whole enterprise point.

III.

If this were all, it would be chilling enough. But Marcuse sees more frightful implications than that anesthesia of our sensibilities.

"Intensified progress," he suggests, "seems to be bound up with intensified unfreedom. Throughout the world of industrial civilization, the domination of man by man is growing in scope and efficiency.

"Nor does this trend appear as an incidental, transitory regression on the road to progress. Concentration camps, mass exterminations, world wars and atom bombs are no 'relapse into barbarism,' but the unrepressed implementation of the achievements of modern science, technology and domination. And the most effective subjugation and destruction of man by man takes place at the height of civilization, when the material and intellectual attainments of mankind seem to allow the creation of a truly free world."

The chief horror for Marcuse is the way most members of industrial society have been seduced into closing their eyes to the danger. Sheer relief from want and overt oppression has obliterated our critical awareness. It is obvious that when your community is preparing day and night for years on end for nuclear war, personal anguish over that prospect cannot be sustained.

Indeed, the most evident and seductive fact is that in massive industrial societies the very existence of a huge military complex is one sure guarantee of a rising standard of living.

Observes Marcuse: "If we attempt to relate the causes of the danger to the way in which society is organized and organizes its members, we are immediately confronted by the fact that advanced industrial society becomes richer, bigger and better as it perpetuates the danger [of nuclear holocaust]. The defense structure makes life easier for a greater number of people and extends man's mastery of nature. Under these circumstances, our mass media have little difficulty in selling particular interests as those of all sensible men. The political needs of society become individual needs and aspirations, their satisfaction promotes business and the commonwealth, and the whole appears to be the very embodiment of Reason."

The advantages are so obvious, the disadvantages so seemingly remote. "And yet," urges Marcuse, "this society is *irrational* as a whole. Its productiveness is destructive of the free development of human needs and faculties, its peace maintained by the constant threat of war, its growth dependent on the repression of the real possibilities for pacifying the struggle for existence—individual, national and international."

This last implicit claim—that there are real alternatives to the Cold War technological society—derives more from Marcuse's Marxian philosophy than from his Freudian analysis. Marx taught that civilization developed as each individual, under the terroristic domination of an elite class, became more and more alienated from the totality of life and more and more efficient as a labor-cog. This use of most people as means rather than ends in themselves is always immoral, but has in a sense been historically necessary for the control or "pacification" of nature.

Periodically, one or another of the oppressed groups has rebelled and itself become master. This has, however, merely replaced one set of dictators and oppressors by another. Marx foresaw a final and ultimate revolution in which the body of the workers—the remaining exploited oppressed—would rise up and seize control of their own lives. This communist revolution would take place when the life of the workers became so terrible that they had literally nothing to lose but their chains.

Marcuse has, of course, developed his own ideas during the period in which Marx's prediction came conspicuously unstuck. Or did it? The liberal democrat may see the rise of unions and the breakdown of old-style capitalism as the genuine emergence of a democracy, the rise of the Welfare State as the non-revolutionary answer to communism. To Marcuse's critical eye, however, the workers—far from casting off their chains—have merely exchanged them for gold-plated bars. That analogy, indeed, is not strong enough: rather than risk death for freedom, they have gelded themselves and fallen fawning before their masters.

Nevertheless, Marcuse believes that the Marxian utopia is ready for building. Simply, no-one is prepared to take up the option. His explanation is fairly straightforward. The guilt which maintains the individual's repression has become a social phenomenon, preventing radical change.

Marcuse has pungently captured the essence of middle-class incredulity in the face of fundamental dissent and rebellion. But, he retorts, the "generous administration" are in no way the true source of society's benefits. Those are the fruit of science, effort and work by the whole human race. The specific organization of people and materials, the particular priorities we espouse today, are no more than one possible set of relationships among many—and far from the best, at that!

The still prevailing impoverishment of vast areas of the

world is no longer due chiefly to the poverty of human and natural resources but to the manner in which they are distributed and utilized, according to Marcuse.

This difference, he suggests, may be irrelevant to self-seeking politicians, but it is decisive in considering the feasibility of a non-repressive culture. For if scarcity and want can be minimized, if automation can replace repetitive and soul-destroying labor, then repression can also be minimized. Freud would be proved wrong; happiness in the form of free and unconstrained play of human faculties would not spell the end of civilization.

We would no longer be restricted to the spurious and inglorious choice between two brands of identical soap which so strikingly characterizes our "freedom" today. We would no longer be "free" to endure toil, insecurity and fear. We would not be forced to suffer the "freedom" that turns brilliant artists into advertising hacks, splendid craftsmen into waste-makers, honest citizens into blinkered dupes. We would gratefully forget the rigid "freedom" which represses the sensuality of sex into obsessive neurosis or baffled inhibition.

And yet, for all that Marcuse is a utopian, he is also a stern realist. "The closer the real possibility of liberating the individual from the constraints once justified by scarcity and immaturity, the greater the need (felt by the Establishment) for maintaining and streamlining these constraints lest the established order of domination dissolve. *Civilization has to defend itself against the specter of a world which could be free.*"

IV.

This vision of a world truly free was elaborated by Marcuse in a Czechoslovakian periodical, the Prague *Literární Listy*, on May 23, 1968. There is more than a little bitter irony in the ruthless crushing by Soviet tanks, three months later, of Czech moves towards a more liberal regime.

In a truly liberated world, Marcuse suggested, "scientific experimentation could become a play with the hidden potentialities of men and matter, society and nature; in short, with all the potentialities society has methodically hidden and blocked.

"This is one of the oldest dreams of radical theory and practice. It means that creative imagination and not merely the rationality of the efficiency principle would become a productive force aimed at the change of the social as well as the natural world. It would mean the rise of a new form of reality which would be the work and the medium of developing sensibility and sensitivity. And I am coming here to the earth-shaking concept: all this would mean the *esthetic reality of society as a work of art!*"

As we have seen, for all the attractiveness of this vision, Marcuse is skeptical of its chances. His own dialectical theory gives him little hope. "The human reality is its history and, in it, contradictions do not explode by themselves. The conflict between streamlined, rewarding domination on the one hand, and its achievements that make for self-determination and pacification on the other, may become blatant beyond any possible denial. But it may well continue to be a manageable and even productive conflict, for with the growth of the technological conquest of nature grows the conquest of man by man."

We return then, finally, to the colossal capacity of repressive society for containing and assimilating alternatives dangerous to the status quo. At the conclusion of his major book, Marcuse denies the efficacy of banner-waving protests and moves quietly into a position which is indeed subversive. "The totalitarian tendencies of the one-dimensional society render the traditional ways and means of protest ineffective— perhaps even dangerous because they preserve the illusion of popular sovereignty.

"However, underneath the conservative popular base is the substratum of the outcasts and outsiders, the exploited and persecuted of other races and other colors, the unemployed and the unemployable... Their opposition hits the system from without and is therefore not deflected by the system; it is an elementary force which violates the rules of the game and, in doing so, reveals it as a rigged game.

"When they get together and go out into the streets, without arms, without protection, in order to ask for the most primitive civil rights, they know that they face dogs, stones and bombs, jail, concentration camps, even death...The fact that they start refusing to play the game may be the fact which marks the beginning of the end of a period.

"Nothing," Marcuse somberly adds, "indicates that it will be a good end."

V.

One of his friends has characterized Marcuse's dominant mood as one of "buoyant pessimism." Certainly one is struck by the energy and vigor of his critiques, by his profound concern for humanity, by his final gloom.

Is he a false prophet, an ideologue blinded into dangerous negativity by the dazzle of his own spurious intellectual categories? Perhaps his adherence to dialectical logic, his espousal of some of Freud's more bizarre misapprehensions, is in error. But it is not easy to dismiss the profound intuitions at the center of his doctrines—the concealed totalitarian tendency of contemporary democracy; the need for, and technical feasibility of, a non-repressive civilization.

Could it be, if Marcuse is not entirely wrong, that perhaps we are on the lip of the greatest revolution of all human history?

FROM MANIAC TO MAN
(1969)

"IT HAS been said that the blood of martyrs fertilizes the earth. In fact," observes Arthur Koestler with brutal acidity, "it has been running down into the sewers, with a monotonously gurgling sound, as far as man can remember; and at whatever part of the world we look, there is scant evidence which would encourage us to hope that the gurgling will diminish or stop."

The voice is unmistakably Koestler's. It is the voice of a genuine twentieth-century magus, a space-age prophet. Its fine passion, its agony, is rendered in the compulsive tropes of popular journalism:

> So long as we believed that our species as such was virtually immortal, with an astronomical lifespan before it, we could afford to wait patiently for that change of heart which, gradually or suddenly, would make love, peace and sweet reason prevail. But we no longer have that assurance of immortality, nor the unlimited time to wait for the moment when the lion will lie down with the lamb, the Arab with the Israeli, and the Commissar with the Yogi.

If the style of the middle-brow journalist shows in his vocabulary, one detects as well the elegant complications of a cultivated European. Koestler delights in irony and metaphor. Despite his bitter renunciation of Marxist dialectics (he had been for seven years a Communist), he seeks out paradox and contradiction for the blazing unexpected star of truth that sometimes lies hidden within them. Chronicler of the Stalinist Terror, novelist, historian of ideas, journalist, scientist, Koestler stands at the opposite extreme to those dark hysteric egomaniacs who have in this century plunged the world over and again into bloody nightmare. Yet his diagnosis of our species, and the remedy he proposes, are as chilling as any Final Solution.

It is his belief that humankind is a doomed species. Forty years of brilliant, committed investigation into the human condition have led him inexorably to the conviction that the mind is fundamentally and tragically flawed. And he offers perhaps the most striking prescription for humanity's illness that any prophet has ever proposed.

For, he suggests, if humankind is doomed it is because finally we are insane. Literally, we are all mad, because the explosive forces of evolution have left us incomplete, forged us prone to a social insanity that is destroying us. And the conclusions, Koestler somberly points out, are, if we dare to draw them, quite simple:

> Our biological evolution to all intents and purposes came to a standstill in Cro-Magnon days. Since we cannot in the foreseeable future expect the necessary change in human nature to arise by way of a spontaneous mutation, that is, by natural means, we must induce it by artificial means.
>
> We can only hope to survive as a species by developing techniques which supplant biological evolution. We must search for a cure for the schizophysiology inherent in man's nature, and the resulting split in our minds, which led to the situation in which we find ourselves.

There are haunting overtones enough of myth in this brief passage, myth new as well as old, to make one's hair bristle and skin crawl. For what has Koestler said, if not that Man yet bears the sting of some Original Sin, that he is haunted by ancient ghosts, that only the elixir of life from the scientist-magician might now save us?

Your reaction may range from instant scorn to awe. But listen once again to Koestler. We must meet his challenge, for it concerns us all. "Our species," he urges, "became a biological freak.... It can only survive by inventing methods which imitate evolutionary mutation. We can no longer hope that Nature will provide the corrective remedy. We must provide it ourselves."

II.

There can be little doubt that we live in a world of ferocious and spectacular violence. The astonishing and finally sickening essence of this fact is that most of that violence is inflicted by men on other men.

For hundreds of thousands of years, the human race trembled on the brink of extinction. Man was, after all, a frail and vulnerable beast in an environment of specialized killers and natural disaster. He survived more often than not by running rather than fighting, by cunning avoidance of danger rather than heroic confrontation of it. Man has only become Lord of the Earth in the last six thousand years, and that more by accident than design.

When he gave up hunting for the greater efficiency and comfort of farming, a remarkable side-effect came into play. In clearing the land and planting his own crops, he triggered off a vast devastation of the ancient ecology: he inadvertently destroyed the ancient cyclic pattern of soil and grass and beast, prey and predator.

In relinquishing the hunt, Man slew a mightier host of his natural enemies than ever he could with spear or trap. The herbivores lost their traditional grazing grounds, and gradually perished. The carnivores were left in short supply of food.

More profoundly, the birds and insects that once had woven an intricate skein of interdependence with the trees and plants they had helped pollinate, disappeared species by species. We have created a world denuded of the rich diversity of plant and animal life which had both supported and threatened us.

Despite this mastery of the world, the human race has not achieved Paradise. Protected from the danger and misery of storm and drought in artificial dwellings, freed by artificial crops and herds and artificial medicine from early death, humankind discovered the most dreadful adversary of all in its own ranks. We conquered the world to make it a safe and comfortable dwelling place—and now men kill men by the hundreds, by the thousands, by the millions.

Could Koestler be right? Is humankind, as a species, insane? Consider these figures: "After the First World War, statisticians calculated that on the average 10,000 rifle bullets or 10 artillery shells had been needed to kill one enemy soldier. The bombs dropped from flying machines weighed a few pounds. By the Second World War, the block-busters had acquired a destructive power equal to twenty tons of TNT. The first atomic bomb on Hiroshima equaled 20,000 tons of TNT. Ten years later, the ·first hydrogen bomb equaled twenty million tons.... We are stock-piling bombs the equivalent of 100 million tons of TNT; and there are rumors of a 'gigaton' bomb, a nuclear weapon packing the power of a billion tons of TNT that could be detonated 100 miles off the US coastline and still set off a fifty-foot tidal wave that would sweep across much of the American continent...or a cobalt bomb that would send a deadly cloud sweeping forever about the earth."

Is it conceivable to a rational mind that such weapons should be used to establish a political point, no matter how lofty? Doesn't it seem plausible that some dire mass insanity has gripped us, when such monstrous calculations determine the direction of our civilization? We are most of us rational and humane enough in our daily lives. We deplore violence and brutality, we undergo hardship to gain security and comfort.

How can it be, then, that in our largest enterprises we encourage slaughter, lionize napalm-wielding heroes, proudly oil the wheels of war with our own children's blood?

Indeed, the issue is wider than even those grim statistics indicate. The explosive efflorescence in technologies for maiming and killing people, although it provides us with the opportunity to murder the entire human race, is ultimately no more than the grotesque enlargement of an ever-present tumor.

The basic condition, the tragic propensity which Koestler numbly refers to as "The Predicament of Man," is our joint preparedness throughout history to kill together. The variety of causes, occasions and justifications for war stands in the history texts as a blatant reminder of our corporate taste for injury and destruction.

Why? Why do we do it?

One short answer favored for its gristle, its hardheadedness, its tough-mindedness, is always popular in some circles: Man is an aggressive animal.

Man is the critter who can out-roar, out-lick and overkill any other beast on the surface of the planet. That's how he got where he is and that's how he stayed there. He fights because he must, because he's made that way. He fights for what he wants, he fights to keep it, he fights to get more of it. And finally he fights for the sheer joy of it, because it's the healthy thing to do, and the way to make a boy a man is to put him in the army.

That one short answer, to be blunt, is the fascist answer. The fact that many people find it a repellent doctrine is in a sense the only reply it needs. If it were true, we would always and everywhere rejoice in a world of jackbooted Gestapo stomping each other to ragged tatters. It is not true, despite the general addiction to vicarious violence via film, TV and book, despite the bashings and rapes that color our newspapers.

The doctrine has not, however, served merely as the backbone to fascist enthusiasm. It is held by many people who deplore violence but are driven to the fatalistic conclusion that it is wired in with the nerves and glands. They seek some way to discharge what they see as man's overwhelming aggressiveness; they look with William James for a "moral equivalent" to war.

"On this view," says Koestler, "the more sinister manifestations of violence and cruelty can be written off as pathological extremes of basically healthy impulses which, for one reason or another, have been denied their normal gratification. Provide the young with harmless outlets for aggression—games, adventure, sexual experimentation—and all will be well."

Unhappily, these remedies do not seem to have worked in the past. Is it because human self-assertiveness is simply too monumental a force to be side-tracked, or is something crucially wrong with the theory?

Koestler's startling explanation finds in the traditional doctrine "a series of fundamental misconceptions concerning the main causes which compelled man to make such a mess of his history, which prevented him from learning the lessons of the past, and which now put his survival in question.

"The first of these misconceptions is putting the blame for man's predicament on his selfishness, greed, etc; in a word, on the aggressive, self-assertive tendencies of the individual.

"...Selfishness is not the primary culprit... Appeals to man's better nature were bound to be ineffectual because the main danger lies precisely in what we are wont to call his 'better nature'."

III.

Man, in Arthur Koestler's scientific conjectures, shares with all living things a basic polarity, a double nature.

He is an individual, experiencing his private universe through his own distinctive personality, and at the same time he is a unit, a part, in one or more larger social organizations.

Like the very cells that make up his body, he is at once part and whole. Each of our cells is separate from the others, has its own, specialized structure and tasks, yet together with all the other cells in the living body it makes up the human being.

For entities that are both parts and wholes, depending on how you look at them, Koestler has coined the useful word "holon." In two recent and significant books—*The Act of Creation*, 1964, and *The Ghost in the Machine*, 1967—he has attempted to synthesize the findings of psychology, neurology, biology and cybernetics into a total scheme for understanding *Homo sapiens*. The notion of the holon is central to this attempt, and it is crucial to his account of the predicament of man.

The holon—whether muscle cell, individual human, or social group—faces, so to speak, in two directions. It acquires information from "below," filters and condenses it according to a variety of available strategies, and transmits it "up" to the next level of complexity. At the same time, messages pass "down" to it on which it acts within the range of its strategies. If it cannot handle the task, it either delegates the matter to more specialized and limited holons "beneath" it, or refers once more to the holon "above."

This dazzling image of a living creature as a web of constantly interacting feedbacks, from the most simple to the most complicated levels, is one of the truly beautiful products of modern scientific inquiry. Since the holon has two roles played once, it can readily be seen that two "forces" exist which must delicately maintain a mutual equilibrium. One is a tension that might be called "self assertive," which operates to ensure the holon's continued identity as a smoothly functioning entity in itself. The other could be termed "integrative" or "self transcending." It regulates the holon's activity within the larger context of which it is a part.

Without the self-assertive forces, there could be no specialized cells, and without them no complex entities. Equally, if there was no integrative force tying the individual holons harmoniously together, no complex entity could exist for very long.

Once stated, this presentation may seem trite enough. When

the theory is applied to human beings, however, *considered as social holons,* extraordinary implications follow rapidly.

We have considered the proposal that man's self-assertive, aggressive tendencies lead him to violence and carnage. Advanced civilization is largely based on the theory. The child, the criminal, the warrior must be disciplined and integrated into acceptable communal patterns of behavior. The self-assertive drives must be channeled into sport or business if there is ever to be an end to war. The only trouble is, it doesn't work. Says Koestler: "I would like to suggest that the *integrative* tendencies of the individual are incomparably more dangerous than his self-assertive tendencies. The sermons of the reformers were bound to fall on deaf ears because they put the blame where it did not belong."

The idea is disturbingly plausible. "Most historians would agree that the part played by impulses of selfish, individual aggression in the holocausts of history was small; first and foremost, the slaughter was meant as an offering to the gods, to king and country, or the future happiness of mankind. The crimes of a Caligula shrink into insignificance compared to the havoc wrought by Torquemada. The number of victims of robbers, highwaymen, rapists, gangsters and other criminals at any period of history is negligible compared to the massive numbers of those cheerfully slain in the name of the true religion, just policy, or correct ideology....

"The crimes of violence committed for selfish, personal motives are historically insignificant compared to those committed *ad majorem gloriam Dei,* out of a self-sacrificing devotion to a flag, a leader, a religious faith or a political conviction. Man has always been prepared not only to kill but also to die for good, bad or completely futile causes... No matter what period we have in view...the evidence always points in the same direction: the tragedy of man is not his truculence, but his proneness to delusions."

The revolutionary might object that Koestler lumps all military violence together; that, indeed, many wars have been fought for the simple and glorious reason that people enslaved by despotism will risk death to lose their chains. And, in a sense, this is true. The self-transcending bond works by no means only for the foolish and the wicked. And yet, few revolutions against oppression have not issued in equal or worse oppression, and none has given us Paradise. More crucially: no matter how just his cause, the rebel always confronts an army of fellow human beings dedicated to his extermination. Gulled they may have been by their exploitative war-lords, brainwashed, perhaps; but they march together in the aura of their self-transcending urge, and they kill and they kill and they kill.

The key, then, to man's dismal record must lie in the *kind* of social holons to which he gives his allegiance, or the *way* in which he gives it. The relationship between humans and the social holons of which they are parts must of necessity be a reciprocal one. A child is born. He carries in his genes a set of fundamental design specifications that describe and prescribe the shape of his body and to a lesser extent that of his mind and personality. Yet immediately he is part of a social holon in which his parents live and work.

The language he learns, with all its built-in biases, the education he receives, both formal and informal, the children he plays with, the companions he studies with, the associates he works with, the friends and family he lives with—all are devices for molding him as a specialized unit in the holon.

In return, his unique and unpredictable personality feeds back into the workings of the holon. And through it all, his own self-assertive and self-transcending tendencies maintain the particular balance appropriate to that social holon and himself as a part of it. He learns (at least in our society) to compete while refraining from major breaches of civilized conduct. He learns to value his own individuality, but not to the extent of being glaringly different. Gradually, he learns the exercise of judgment and discretion: not to follow blindly, not to stray extravagantly.

It is the nature of the integrative bond that we must investigate. Koestler describes a number of mechanisms, well known to psychologists, that operate to unite men, make them feel *"part* of some larger entity which transcends the boundaries of the individual self. This psychological urge to belong, to participate, to commune, is as primary and real as its opposite. The all-important question is the *nature* of that higher entity...

"One way of achieving this unity was through the transformation of magic into art and science. This made it possible for the happy few to achieve self-transcendence on a higher turn of the spiral, by that sublime expansion of awareness which Freud called the oceanic feeling...

"But only a minority qualifies for it. For the others, there are only a few traditional outlets open to transcend the rigid boundaries of the ego. Historically speaking for the vast majority of mankind, the only answer to its integrative cravings, its longing to belong and find meaning in existence, was *identification* with tribe, caste, nation, church or party—with a social holon."

Unfortunately, Koestler argues, the chief form this self-transcending identification took has been extreme, more akin to hypnosis than to the harmonious hierarchies of cells and organs. In practice, men and women have let slip their individuality at crucial moments and merged into an amorphous uncritical identity with the emblems and banners of their group. "The psychological process, by means of which this identification was achieved, was mostly by the primitive, infantile kind of projection which populates heaven and earth with angry father-figures, fetishes to be worshipped, demons to be execrated, dogmas to be blindly believed."

Again unhappily, this kind of "poor man's self-transcendence" does more than destroy our sense of responsible individuality. Self-transcendence, group empathy, can serve as a kind of carrier wave for a second-order aggressiveness. Just as identification with a fictional hero can elicit sympathetic panic, anger and shock, the more powerful identification with one's social holon can be the vehicle for rage, cruelty and unselfish heroism in support of one's group.

"The total identification of the individual with the group," writes Koestler, "makes him unselfish in more than one sense. It makes him indifferent to danger and less sensitive to physical pain—a mild form of hypnotic anesthesia. It makes him perform comradely, altruistic, heroic actions—to the point of self-sacrifice—and at the same time behave with ruthless cruelty toward the enemy or victim of the group."

Significantly, "the brutality displayed by the members of a fanatic crowd is impersonal and unselfish; it is exercised in the interests or supposed interests of the whole... In other words, the self-assertive behavior of the group is based on the self-transcending behavior of its members.... To put it simply, the egotism of the group feeds on the altruism of its members."

Since war is the kind of behavior that exemplifies this situation *par excellence,* it becomes possible to understand why personal guilt fails to overwhelm the individual soldiers. Koestler points out pungently that "sociologists who regard war as a manifestation of man's repressed aggressive urges make one feel at once that they have never served in the ranks, and have no idea of the mentality of private soldiers in war time... *Hating* does not enter into the picture."

What does, of course, is the bond of identification that the enterprise of war generates among comrades at arms. So strong at the time is that bond, so pallid the experience of life without it (for many men at least), that the fantastic notion is sustained which presents war as one's finest hour. Veterans' associations become, whether they admit it or not, lobbies urging the benefits of war and the preparation for war.

Beyond all this analysis broods the question, and Koestler's astonishing answer to it, why most social holons should operate in such an appalling fashion. How is it that man's rational capabilities have failed to solve the problems that lead to war? How did that most noble and poignant of sentiments, devotion to one's group, become perverted into the filthiness of mass slaughter?

Koestler looks to the history of human evolution for the explanation.

IV.

Somehow, the bulk of people in even the most literate countries do not really believe in evolution.

Despite the educational programs on television, despite *The Naked Ape,* the whole thing just seems a trifle too incredible. The idea of human beings evolving over millions of years from small grass-scurrying insectivores is no longer offensive—it's too banal to be offensive. Rather, the concept is so abstract and difficult to grasp that it owns about as much relevance as ghosts or life on other worlds.

To be more precise, I suspect most people think of evolution as God under another name. What they don't believe, or don't care to think about, is that evolution works by accident. That's the hard bit. Humankind and all our works, an accumulation of cosmic accidents.

As it happens, evolution *is* the way we came about, and if Koestler is right it may be vitally important that we thoroughly comprehend that fact. Because evolution, unlike God, unlike the Life Force, makes mistakes as well as triumphs. It may well be that humankind is a little bit of each, and the mistake part may be killing us.

Koestler describes two instances where evolution has consolidated itself into an impasse. The more chillingly charming is the sad tale of the arthropods, the phylum that contains the myriad variety of spiders and represents perhaps 700,000 species all told. It is a splendid example of what is meant by an evolutionary mistake, despite the fact that the combined species of arthropods make up by far the largest phylum in the animal kingdom. The kind of blunder we are considering does not by any means ensure total disaster; it is merely a foreclosure on further development. (In the case of humans, of course, thermonuclear weapons may be the clincher.)

The arthropods' whimsical error was to build their brains about their gullets. As their brains developed, the mass of nerves constricted their alimentary canal. In terms of further evolutionary development, it led to a droll dilemma: "either the capacity for taking in food without sufficient intelligence to capture it, or intelligence sufficient to capture food and no power to consume it." Australian authority Wood Jones has remarked: "The invertebrates made a fatal mistake when they started to build their brains around the esophagus. Their attempt to develop brains was a failure... Another start must be made."

To examine in any detail the evolutionary mistake Koestler believes occurred in man would require an account at the length he gives in *The Ghost in the Machine*. Briefly, there is evidence that the human brain contains a serious constructional error.

Anatomically, the brain can be divided into three major sections that differ radically in tissue, structure and purpose. The outermost of these, the cortex, contains 10 billion neurons, and is the apparatus for intelligent behavior. The cortex can in turn be divided into three areas, two of which make up the limbic system or "old brain," while the third is much more recent in evolutionary terms and is known as the neocortex or "new brain."

Following the studies of neurologist Paul MacLean, Koestler argues that the "old brain" —which is structurally similar to reptilian and primitive mammalian brains—actually does operate in a primitive and "pre-rational" way. Its main task concerns the control of taste, smell, and visceral sensations, as well as emotional reactions including sex, hunger, fear and aggression. The new cortex, on the other hand, has little direct neural link with the centers in the brain-stem concerned with those sensations and emotions.

Thus, although the neocortex is responsible for the clear rational thinking which distinguishes man from other creatures, it is not wholly master in its own house. The cruder, inarticulate limbic system occupies a "strategically central position for correlating internal sensations with perceptions from the outside world, and for initiating appropriate action according to its own lights."

It is likely, then, suggests Koestler, that the human brain suffers a built-in split, a "schizophysiology." "This," he admits, "is surely an odd state of affairs. If the evidence had not taught us the contrary, we would expect an evolutionary development which gradually transformed the primitive old brain into a more sophisticated instrument... Instead, evolution superimposed a new, superior structure on an old one, with partly overlapping functions, and without providing the new with a clear-cut, hierarchic control over the old—thus inviting confusion and conflict."

Professor MacLean believes that the lack of co-ordination between old and new cortexes might account for the differences between emotional and intellectual behavior. In terms of Koestler's theory, man is himself an incomplete holon, and the social holons he generates by group association and activity are prone to a similar disruption.

How could such a mistake have occurred? The major factor appears to have been the extraordinary speed with which the human brain evolved. Professor Le Gros Clark has written: "It now appears from the fossil record that the hominid brain did not begin to enlarge significantly before the beginning of the Pleistocene, but from the middle Pleistocene (about half a million years ago) onward, it expanded at a most remarkable speed—greatly exceeding the rate of evolutionary change which had so far been recorded in any anatomical character in lower animals.... The rapidity of the evolutionary expansion of the brain during the Pleistocene is an example of what has been termed 'explosive evolution'."

Somewhere in that explosion, a mutation occurred that took a short cut. The result was the human species—far from disabled, superior indeed to all other creatures, but flawed nonetheless. The mistake was not significant until perhaps 6,000 years ago, when humans began using the awesome power of the neocortex to invent culture—and weapons of increasing ferocity—and wars of conquest and exploitation on a vast scale. Until now we have within our grasp the power to ruin the Earth...

And still the sluggish superstitious limbic brain controls our passions while the neocortex cries its sane and impotent warnings.

V.

Assume MacLean and Koestler are correct. Is there, then, anything we can do to prevent the final fall of night, the doom of the human species, the suicide of the human race? Says Koestler: "All efforts of persuasion by reasoned argument rely on the implicit assumption that *Homo sapiens,* though occasionally blinded by emotion, is basically a rational animal, aware of the motives of his own actions and beliefs—an assumption which is untenable in the light of both historical and neurological evidence. All such appeals fall on barren ground; they could take root only if the ground were prepared by a spontaneous change in human mentality all over the world—the equivalent of a major biological mutation."

The population explosion represents an analogous problem. *Homo sapiens* is one of the few animals lacking instinctive controls to regulate breeding under conditions of overcrowding. In this particular case, the science that created the problem has also produced a solution—artificial birth control. Admittedly that solution has yet to achieve world-wide application. Even so, intrauterine devices and oral contraceptives amount to nothing less than an artificial mutation. Is it possible that we might find a scientific solution to our schizoid personality?

Such a cure is potentially available in the realm of the new psychopharmaceuticals. So passionate is Koestler's wish for a general mental stabilizer that he writes, "I believe that if we fail to find this cure, the old paranoid streak in man, combined with his new powers of destruction, must sooner or later lead to geno-suicide. But I also believe that the cure is almost within reach of contemporary biology; and that with the proper concentration of effort it might be produced within the lifetime of the generation which is now entering the scene."

Arthur Koestler is no Timothy Leary, longing for the acid apocalypse. "Neither mystic insights, nor philosophic wisdom, nor creative power can be provided by pill or injection." Koestler's goal is a basic human state of dynamic equilibrium in which thought and emotion are united, and hierarchic order made capable of achievement in individual and society.

"The psycho-pharmacist cannot *add to* the faculties of the brain—but he can, at best, *eliminate* obstructions and blockages which impede their proper use. He cannot aggrandize us, but he can, within limits, normalize us; he cannot put additional circuits into the brain, but he can, again within limits, improve the co-ordination between existing ones, attenuate conflicts, prevent the blowing of fuses, and ensure a steady power supply.

"That," says Koestler, "is all the help we can ask for—but if we were able to obtain it, the benefits to mankind would be incalculable; it would be...the breakthrough from maniac to man."

R. D. LAING (1969)

"The condition of alienation, of being asleep, of being unconscious, of being out of one's mind," claims Dr. Ronald David Laing, "is the condition of normal man.

"Society highly values its normal man. It educates children to lose themselves, and to become absurd, and thus to be normal.

"Normal men have killed perhaps 100,000,000 of their fellow normal men in the last fifty years..."

Ronald Laing is the forty-two-year-old Glasgow-born psychiatrist whose controversial theories have become the nucleus of a revolution in our understanding of sanity, madness and society. His exciting and extraordinary ideas are explorations into that dark forbidding land which is the interface between psychoanalysis and existentialism.

"We are," he dares to say, "bemused and crazed creatures, strangers to our true selves, to one another, and to the spiritual and material world—mad, even, from an ideal standpoint we can glimpse but not adopt." This is an extreme perspective. From a commonsense point of view, it seems most dubious. A man who states that we are all mad is, one might suppose, either playing with words or mad himself.

Yet it is a commonplace of popular psychology that we are all to some extent neurotic. Such generalizations are so readily available from even the most entrenched institutions of our society that we no longer recognize them as such. The churches, after all, teach that man is profoundly flawed, that we are each prone to sin and corruption. The doctrine of Original Sin remains a cornerstone in the ethics of the most powerful Christian confessions. At a more mundane level, our censors justify their efforts by pointing to a communal susceptibility to moral infection. Our policy-makers urge eternal vigilance against the threat of imminent communist subversion. (Communist policymakers, of course, proclaim the menace of imperialist capitalism.) Entire social institutions ceaselessly strive to deter us from theft, rape, murder and self-inflicted injury.

The underlying premise in every case is that human beings are marred by an intrinsic tendency to damage themselves, their neighbors and society.

The contention—despite the absurdity of some of its adherents—is a weighty one. Consider again those hundred million man-slaughtered men. Consider the two billion human lives condemned this very moment to slow, cruel death by starvation or malnutrition. Consider the normal people everywhere who acquiesce in the fearful absurdity of an accumulating arsenal of nuclear devices that could utterly destroy humanity.

We are surrounded every day by the joyous, satisfying aspects of life. We love them, cling to them, rejoice in them. But undeniably, some dark cancer looms and flames its corrosion in their midst. We know it by our reluctance to look at it, by our frenzied need for scapegoats to embody it, by our final impotence in dealing with it.

R. D. Laing has claimed that "normal" man is mad. Perhaps his claim is not so outrageous as first it seems.

II.

Laing is, first and foremost, a clinical psychiatrist. His major contributions have been in the study and treatment of schizophrenia, the most common form of mental disorder. His chief goal has been to plumb the nature and causes of madness, and to make intelligible the bizarre world of the psychotic.

As a result of his work with schizophrenics and their families, he has helped found the Philadelphia Association, London, which has established three experimental communities where sane and insane people live together in entirely non-institutional households.

It is via his work on schizophrenia that we can best come to grips with Laing's social theories.

Modern psychiatry is a bewildering explosion of hypotheses and techniques. Not surprisingly, in an age of experiment and technology, the emphasis tends to be on *curing* or *re-adjusting* mental disorders rather than on understanding the mad person. Psychology has become "Behavioral Science," its students learn largely by observing maze-running nets, by investigating the physical structure and operation of human nerve and muscle. Since the recent development of subtle psychochemical drugs, the behavior of patients can readily be manipulated through the entire spectrum from stimulation to sedation.

Control becomes the catchword, on the assumption that madness stems from a malfunction in the complex human mechanism that can be rectified by behavioral or pharmaceutical adjustments. The deep torment and anguish which has driven the person into madness is viewed as a byproduct of the machine's failure. The symptom, it is believed, *is* the disease; relieve the symptom and the problem vanishes.

There is startling evidence in support of this school of thought. Many personality disorders can indeed be traced to failures in early social learning, to traumata which inflict lasting phobias, to chemical errors in the hormonal system. London's Professor Hans Eysenck has argued, moreover, that the recovery rate of patients who undergo psychoanalysis (the chief psychiatric method seeking understanding rather than simply control) is no greater than that of patients who forego treatment. The implication is clear: correct psychiatric practice should intrinsically be identical with the medical treatment of, let us say, influenza or diabetes.

Laing is in sharp disagreement. "Psychiatry," he says, "could be...on the side of transcendence, of genuine freedom, and of true human growth. But psychiatry can so easily be a technique of brainwashing, of inducing behavior that is adjusted, by (preferably) non-injurious torture. In the best places, where straitjackets are abolished, doors are unlocked, leucotomies largely foregone, these can be replaced by more subtle lobotomies and tranquilizers that place the bars of Bedlam and the locked doors *inside* the patient."

The key to Laing's critical stance lies in the fact that man can legitimately be viewed either as a thing or as a person. Anatomists, statisticians, biochemists are not unjustified in studying humans as organisms, behavioral entities, *things* with specific properties. But human beings are also *persons*. We feel and experience, we have a subjective life which the vocabularies of anatomy or economics simply cannot encompass. Your behavior may reflect your experience—or it might not.

It follows that behavioral psychiatry is perpetrating an obscene and inhuman absurdity when it manipulates a person as though that person is no more than a thing.

§

A striking irony is evident in the fact that schizophrenics themselves typically view the world as a collection of detached, impersonal forces. In his book *The Divided Self*, Laing points out that the study of schizophrenics is "concerned specifically with people who experience themselves as automata, as robots, as bits of machinery, or even as animals. Such persons are rightly regarded as crazy. Yet why do we not regard a theory that seeks to transmute persons into automata or animals as equally crazy?"

Psychoanalysis falls into the same trap. Freudian theory splits the person up into abstractions which are then treated, to a large extent, as though they really exist. Journalistic language has to a surprising degree become permeated by this jargon: the whole person is split into "ego," "id," and "superego," psyche and soma.

Psychiatry, then, either rips a man out of his context as a human person in living relationship with other human persons, or it deals with him as though he were a combination of physical and mental apparatuses which an analyst can take to bits and reassemble more satisfactorily. The great primary reality of the I-Thou bond has been disrupted.

Is there any solution? Laing believes so. "Only existential thought has attempted to match the original experience of oneself in relationship to others in one's world" in a way that adequately reflects its rich totality.

III.

In Laing's development of existential psychiatry, the key to insanity lies in a study of *situations* and not simply of individuals.

Madness is not a disease, nor a series of broken cogs in some mental machinery. It is a way of being-in-the-world, of experiencing oneself and others, of acting and being acted upon. If the madman's words and actions appear bizarre and terrifying, it is because in a very real sense we do not inhabit the same world he does.

That is not to say, as many psychiatrists assume, that the madman is incomprehensible; merely, that an empathic understanding of his whole existential situation is called for. Such understanding is far from impossible. The published reports by Laing and his colleagues are a standing testimony to its feasibility. Once such an attempt is made, the results are remarkably illuminating.

To regard the odd gambits of schizophrenics, says Laing, "as due *primarily* to some psychological deficit is rather like supposing that a man doing a handstand on a bicycle on a tightrope 100 feet up with no safety net is suffering from an inability to stand on his own two feet. We may well ask why these people have to be, often brilliantly, so devious, so elusive, so adept at making themselves unremittingly incomprehensible."

Laing's answer to that question, borne out by intensive studies of the families of schizophrenics conducted at Palo Alto, in California, Yale University, Pennsylvania Psychiatric Institute and the National Institute of Mental Health, is a vindication of the existential approach. The studies "have all shown that the person who gets diagnosed is part of a wider network of extremely disturbed and disturbing patterns of communication." In practice, this means that the schizophrenic has been placed repeatedly in "damned if you do-damned if you don't" situations. Such situations are known as *double-binds*, and are specifically destructive of self-identity.

Together with Drs. Cooper and Esterton, Laing has investigated more than a hundred families of schizophrenics. With the consent of the families, they employed tape recorders in many sessions ranging over months, interviewing members singly and in various combinations. "Without exception," reports Laing, "the experience and behavior that gets labeled schizophrenic is a special strategy that a person invents in order to live in an unlivable situation... The person has come to feel that he is in an untenable position. He cannot make a move, or make no move, without being beset by contradictory and paradoxical pressures and demands...both internally from himself, and externally from those around him. He is, as it were, in a position of checkmate."

This is a critically important discovery about the nature of madness. If insanity is a series of strategies (conscious or unconscious, complex or otherwise) which reflects and reacts against a social group, then that whole social group is crucially implicated in the patient's madness.

"This state of affairs," Laing hastens to add, "may not be perceived as such by any of the people in it. The man at the bottom of the heap may be crushed and suffocated to death without anyone noticing it, much less intending it.... Nor is it a matter of laying the blame at anyone's door. The untenable position, the 'can't win' double bind, the situation of checkmate, is by definition *not obvious* to the protagonists."

This approach does not mean, as some critics have suggested, that Laing is biased in favor of the psychotic member of the group. "When I certify someone insane," he says bluntly, "I am not equivocating when I write that he is of unsound mind, may be dangerous to himself and others, and requires care and attention in a mental hospital." Laing's thesis does, however, raise serious questions about the *family's* "sanity," "normality," etc.

§

What is the response of the potential schizophrenic to such a network of untenable demands and possible reactions?

Full-blown psychosis is only the end-result of a long process of "schizoid" or pre-mad attempts to come to terms with the unbearable. Briefly, the schizoid individual is forced by the circumstances of her situation to speak and act at variance to her sense of authentic identity. All of us, of course, must behave at times in ways that seem false or hypocritical to us. Indeed, Laing points out, "we may remember how, in childhood, adults at first were able to look right through us, and into us, and what an accomplishment it was when we, in fear and trembling, could tell our first lie, and make for ourselves the discovery that we are irredeemably alone in certain respects, and know that within the territory of ourselves there can be only our footprints.

"There are some people, however, who never fully realize themselves in this position. This genuine privacy is the basis of genuine relationship; but the person whom we call 'schizoid' feels both more exposed, more vulnerable to others than we do, and more isolated."

The schizoid's extreme vulnerability is established in early infancy, maintained and exacerbated throughout childhood and adolescence by the kinds of relationships she has with family and friends.

Compared with the schizoid, the majority of people develop a strong sense of themselves as real, alive, whole; persons in their own right. Such basically "ontologically secure" individuals can encounter all the hazards of life—social, ethical, biological—from a centrally firm sense of their own and other people's reality and identity.

Not so with the potential schizophrenic. His achievements are often scorned by those closest to him, his fears ridiculed, his every move thwarted and rendered ambiguous by the unhappy network of his family's relationships. He develops a crippling sense of "primary ontological insecurity"; that is, he doubts his own valid impulses, and fears the confusing activity of other people. He comes to feel that the reality of the world is negating his reality, that it is imploding, crushing him into non-existence.

Under such fearsome stress, the schizoid may more and more present a "false self" to the world, a "self" who has less and less relevance to his own estimate of himself. Typically, schizoids are exemplary children. They do not scream, demand, throw tantrums like other children; they show careful "respect" and "affection" to their parents. The false self systems are at work, while the true self within grows increasingly isolated, despairing and detached.

When finally the mask breaks, and the schizoid begins a pattern of "bad," eccentric, distressing activities, the "true self" has become a trembling prisoner within the person— impoverished in its lack of real contact with the others it fears, dreading its very dissolution into non-being. The wild hallucinated madness of schizophrenia is the last ditch stand, the final impossible attempt to forge a viable universe of experience. Tragically, the volatilized self is trapped in its maze of "false selves." In the poignant words of one of Laing's patients, it has become the "ghost of the weed garden." If this account of the schizoid and psychotic modes of being-in-the-world is correct, behavioral psychiatry is making an appalling error in treating such disorders as diseases. Often, the due process of psychiatric committal, incarceration, tranquilization and therapy is simply *one more form* of the mystifying nightmare that has driven the embattled soul into madness. The very dialogue, the very empathy of person-to-person-in-society which the schizophrenic craves so hopelessly, is vitiated by the clinical context.

§

One of Laing's most controversial ideas, currently under-going experimental test in the Philadelphia Association's house-holds, is that some forms of schizophrenia are in truth healing processes. The desolate meeting with Nothingness which is the madman's fate may be the nadir of a journey back to wholeness. "Instead of the mental hospital, a sort of re-servicing factory for human breakdowns, we need a place where people who have travelled further and, consequently, may be more lost than psychiatrists and other sane people, can find their way *further* into inner space and time, and back again. Instead of the *degra-dation* ceremonial of the psychiatric examination, diagnosis and prognostication, we need, for those who are ready for it (in psychiatric terminology often those who are about to go into a schizophrenic breakdown), an *initiation* ceremonial, through which the person will be guided with full social encouragement and sanction into inner space and time, by people who have been there and back again. Psychiatrically, this would appear as ex-patients helping future patients to go mad."

Recognition of the way schizoid people adopt "false selves" in order to cope with unbearable social encounters—and the other side of the coin, successful voyages into inner space by some ex-schizophrenics—has prompted Laing to a series of piercing criticisms of our society. The traditional Freudian critique, he suggests, did not go far enough. "Our civilization represses not only 'the instincts,' not only sexuality, but any form of transcendence... In the context of our present pervasive madness that we call normality, sanity, freedom, all our frames of reference are ambiguous and equivocal."

We have, in short, relinquished the inner realms of experi-ence and creative freedom which are more than half our human heritage. If the schizoid comes to feel depersonalized, empty, unreal, it is at least partly because society teaches her that she is. "Thus," says Laing, "I would wish to emphasize that our 'normal,' 'adjusted' state is too often the abdication of ecstasy, the betrayal of our true potentialities, that many of us are only too successful in acquiring a false self to adapt to false realities."

IV.

The retreat from persons to objects that characterizes today's psychiatry is symptomatic of the prevailing mood of our entire culture. If some few campus rebels are driven to a cold hysteria of hate for the Napalm Society, their voices sound merely shrill and spiteful against the dull whir of our age. What perspectives has the new psychiatry to offer, in the era of one-dimensional man?

"The relevance of Freud to our time," raps Laing, "is largely his insight and, to a very considerable extent, his demonstration that the ordinary person is a shriveled, desiccated fragment of what a person can be." That, beyond question, is a striking assertion. We have so long been subjected to the frivolous and vapid sensationalism of the entertainment media that such a claim skips over our minds without raising a ripple.

But Laing means precisely what he says. The style of civilization we defend to our last drop of blood provides not only food, clothing, housing and work, but also a systematic womb-to-tomb program of repression and absurdity. "This state of affairs," says Laing, "represents an almost unbelievable devastation of our experience. Then there is empty chatter about maturity, love, joy, peace."

The alienation of contemporary humanity from our deeds and our very instincts is not an invention of the new psychiatrists. The intuition and analysis of that alienation is at the center of all current serious philosophy. It has been explored and expounded by thinkers as diverse as Marx, Kierkegaard, Freud, Heidegger, Tillich, Fromm and Sartre. Laing's importance lies in his power to make that intuition vivid, in his genius for unfolding its ramifications.

"We are born," he says, "into a world where alienation awaits us. We are potentially men, but are in an alienated state, and this state is not simply a natural system. Alienation as our present destiny is achieved only by outrageous violence perpetrated by human beings on human beings."

Even if we accept the contention of Arthur Koestler that an evolutionary flaw has predisposed us to a destructive pursuit of the irrational, it is clear that this tendency can be focused and amplified by social means. Herbert Marcuse's description of our culture as "one dimensional" is highly relevant. One-dimensional man is trapped in the compulsive repressive rhetoric of his flat universe. Like the schizophrenic, he is depersonalized and terrified to the point of desperation by the shadows dancing beyond the barriers of his own restricted mind.

And, like the schizophrenic, his world-view is the result of a desolating constellation of mystifying influences. "In order to rationalize our industrial-military complex," Laing observes, "we have to destroy our capacity both to see clearly what is in front of, and to imagine what is beyond, our noses. Long before a thermonuclear war can come about, we have had to lay waste our own sanity."

How does this come about? "We begin with the children. It is imperative to catch them in time. Without the most thorough and rapid brainwashing, their dirty minds would see through our dirty tricks. Children are not yet fools, but we shall turn them into imbeciles like ourselves, with high I.Q.s if possible."

Our entire education system, to tertiary level at least and often beyond it, is educated to the machine-production of individuals who embody many of the crippling characteristics of schizophrenia. Massive pressures are brought to bear to ensure a drab uniform regularity of appearance and lifestyle. Ostensibly, this protects equality of status and opportunity; in practice, it enforces the dull mediocrity of an atomized mob.

At the same time, premiums are placed on secrecy, slavish obedience, and extreme competitiveness. Techniques shorn of understanding are mechanically instilled. The gray, tedious atmosphere is, on the whole, bereft of passion, spontaneity, creativeness or any purpose save the efficient manufacture of reliable non-entities.

The enterprise, luckily, is not entirely successful. Yet the result of this violence masquerading as loving care is our world of H-bomb-shadowed "security."

The prevalence of violence in the guise of love, suggests Laing, is the root of our social schizophrenia. We are baffled to the point of craziness by the Orwellian paradoxes daily thrust at us. "Exploitation must not be seen as such. It must be seen as benevolence. Persecution...should be experienced as kindness... In order to sustain our amazing images of ourselves as God's gift to the vast majority of the starving human species, we have to interiorize our violence upon ourselves and our children and to employ the rhetoric of morality to describe this process."

Sociologists have told us long and loud, until their warnings have become boring and meaningless, that we increasingly inhabit a consumer society of hidden persuaders, status-clamberers, merchants of death. With effort, we can recognize the sour taste of defeat in our lives, the clash between remembered idealisms of youth and the dismal cynicism of maturity. The bureaucracies, technologies, institutions that provide us with health, comfort and security are simultaneously stealing our souls.

What wrong turning have we taken on the path from hope to reality? Laing cites the studies of Jules Henry, an American professor of anthropology and sociology, which show convincingly that education has seldom been an instrument to free the mind and spirit, but to bind them. "Children," observes Laing, "do not give up their innate imagination, curiosity, dreaminess easily. You have to love them to get them to do that. Love is the path through permissiveness to discipline; and through discipline, only too often, to betrayal of self."

The bloodless idiom of education and psychology bears him out. "The mother," writes a fashionable authority, Theodore Lidz, M.D, in his book *The Family and Human Adaption*, "can properly invest her energies in the care of the young child when economic support, status and protection of the family are provided by the father." Laing notes ironically that the economic metaphor is aptly employed. The mother "invests" in her child. The listed order of the father's "functions" is astonishingly revealing. "What one is supposed to want, to live for," Laing adds, quoting Lidz again, "is 'gaining pleasure from the esteem and affection of others.' If not, one is a psychopath.

"Such statements are in a sense true. They describe the frightened, cowed, abject creature that we are admonished to be, if we are to be normal—offering each other mutual protection from our own violence. The family as a 'protection racket'."

To what are we adapting in these "maternal investments," this "maximum utilization of the nation's human resources"? To isolation, colorless conformity, exploitation, hate, militarism? To a world gone mad? The family's function, and that of the education process, has become, says Laing, "to repress Eros; to induce a false consciousness of security: to deny death by avoiding life: to cut off transcendence...to create, in short, one-dimensional man: to promote respect, conformity, obedience: to con children out of play: to induce a fear of failure; to promote a respect for work: to promote a respect for 'respectability'."

The mystifications that double-bind and drive the vulnerable into actual schizophrenia can thus be seen as no more than an extreme form of the mystifications which make us all "good" and "useful" members of society. The man who says that They have taken control of his thoughts is certifiable. The man who runs a vast advertising agency is a respected member of society.

The child who says he is a broken machine is psychotic. The teacher who demands mechanical obedience and programmed study is an exemplary mother. The girl who believes that she is already dead is locked up, treated by electro-convulsion and tranquilizers. The technician who primes the instruments of massive retaliation is a lay-preacher in his church.

V.

In a world where terror and violence are so thoroughly confused with love—where patriotism, as Poul Anderson has written, is necessarily equated with necrophilia, in that the loyal citizen is expected to rejoice every time his government comes up with a newer gadget for mass-producing corpses—is there any hope?

"Only by the most outrageous violence to ourselves," admits Laing, "have we achieved our capacity to live in relative adjustment to a civilization apparently driven to its own destruction." But, he suggests, "perhaps to a limited extent we can undo what has been done to us, and what we have done to ourselves. Perhaps men and women were born to love one another, simply and genuinely, rather than to this travesty that we can call love.

"If we can stop destroying ourselves we may stop destroying others. We have to begin by admitting and even accepting our violence, rather than blindly destroying ourselves with it, and therewith we have to realize that we are as deeply afraid to live and love as we are to die."

In his most recent book, *The Politics of Experience* (1967), Laing offers at least a distant hope: "If nothing else, each time a new baby is born there is a possibility of reprieve...

"Who are we to decide that it is hopeless?"

POLITICS: LOOKING BACK FROM NOW

Guerrilla War

Politics is the human exercise of power.
Or: politics is the engagement of ideological prejudices.
Or: politics is the art of the doable.
Or...
Definitions roll endlessly off the tongue, and out of the tomes of political, diplomatic and historical theory, even from the journals of psychology, the scans of fMRI machines, and back again to the thundering presses and slick television mind-warp programming and the endless chatter and blather of the blogs.

Politics isn't just what happens when democracies and republics go to the voting booth. It's what used to go on in smoke-filled back rooms, and still does, although maybe the cigarettes and cigars are fewer in number, because while corruption and war is good for profit, cancer isn't so much fun, not when you're the one threatened by it. Politics is what determines the price and availability of oil and nuclear and solar and wind power. Politics is war and peace, and the ceaseless contestations bubbling chaotically below the surface of peace.

In the 1960s, two decades after the War against Fascism, the Great Patriotic War, the righteous global conflict that ended with Hitler dead and the evaporation of two Japanese cities, politics was again war and this time, shockingly, mass resistance to it by those whom the old men wanted to throw into harm's way half a planet away for no apparent sane reason, and by the mothers, many of them, in the Summer of Love, the Summer of Fear, the Summer of Furious Hatred, and a handful of summers and winters after that. Politics was the wind-up five or six years later when Vietnamese communists (or were they better seen as patriots on their own soil?) threw out the USA as they had earlier thrown out the French, using the methods I described above in this essay, and with just the outcome I predicted.

In the 2000s, right now, politics was the same thing all over again, in Iraq and Afghanistan, for reasons even more palpably bogus (Weapons of mass destruction! Weapons of mass deception!) or at best unspoken, unacknowledged ("The spice must flow," as Frank Herbert had reiterated in his Orientalized *Dune*, even as Vietnam was turning from a "police action" into a fated hopeless morass; yes, the oil must flow, the power must be held close, the world must be ruled, the blood must flow).

Forty and more years ago, the form that politics took in its military guise was new, giant helicopters contesting with men and women in pajamas: massed might versus guerrilla tactics. What was learned? Why, take a look at Afghanistan today. The same dismal confrontation, this time with vulnerable troops again in a strange land supported by smart weapons guided from a distance to batter cruel determined men in alien garb nothing like suits or jeans. The return of the unrepressed. Sooner or later, America will retreat once again from this god-awful landscape with its grotesque women-hating, poppy-growing fundamentalists ("The shit must flow!"), as Russia did, trailing the smoke of trillions of wasted dollars. Well, not necessarily wasted, not from some points of view. That's politics.

The Price of Ignorance

June 2010, according to a report in the *Christian Science Monitor*, showed the largest average global temperature in recorded history. The impact of global climate change had become undeniable (although the stooges of giant corporations continued to deny it). But as recently as 2009, only 49% of US respondents polled accepted that global warming, if it exists, is caused by human activity.

I find it interesting, in retrospect, that my essay from more than forty years ago took the greenhouse effect seriously, and used that term for it. I drew my evidence from sources such as Dr. Barry Commoner, a Harvard-educated environmentalist before the term had established its currency. (As I write, he is still alive, aged ninety-three.) In other words, back in the day, some of us were already alert to this danger, and saw scientific understanding as the necessary instrument to find a cure.

I do have serious reservations about one aspect of my 1969 article: the anxiety over DDT, which was widespread after Dr. Rachel Carson's *Silent Spring* (published seven years earlier) and led to banning in the US of this chemical insecticide in 1972. While it's true that DDT concentrates through the food chain, and in large quantities can damage eggs and even adult birds and other delicate animals, the amount of human misery caused by the ban has been enormous, and catastrophic.

By 1964, spraying in Sri Lanka had almost obliterated malaria, a debilitating and sometimes fatal malady. Halted for budgetary rather than ecological motives, consequences were almost immediate—hundreds of thousands of new cases. Granted, evolution rapidly increased resistance to DDT in the target insects, but green opposition to the stuff has been assailed as literally murderous. James Lovelock, the inventor of the Gaia hypothesis, has denounced the rejection of DDT as due to "selfish, ill-informed western liberals who have caused millions of people in poor tropical countries to pay a high price in death and illness from malaria."

Troubles with the shifting environment under the impact of human changes are political to the core; none of this began with Al Gore and his 2006 *Inconvenient Truth* movie and Nobel Peace Prize in 2007, but that moment was perhaps the point at which the politics of power tried hard to crush its opposition, and ever so slowly is failing. An August 25-26, 2010 Rasmussen Reports poll of a thousand US voters showed 45% persuaded that warming is the result of planetary trends, with 40% considering humans largely responsible. Still, in the same week, a poll by the Natural Resources Defense Council showed 60% in favor of regulating emissions thought to contribute to heating and climate shifts. I don't know of any poll asking whether prayer or science is the more likely to ameliorate global warming, and I'm afraid to look.

Marcuse

One of the notable German Marxist theoreticians of the Frankfurt School, "Father of the New Left," who had found in the USA sanctuary from Hitler's totalitarianism, Herbert Marcuse died at eighty-one, ten years after this equivocal tribute appeared in, of all places, the lowbrow men's magazine where I pontificated among the coarse cartoons, fake tales of adventure, and pastel, inoffensive porn. Marcuse's star had already faded by then, in 1979, and the political upheaval begun in 1968 with such desperate hope and utopian rage in the Paris streets, students flinging cobblestones at the *flics,* had quieted down into the dullard beat of disco, bling, and the Village People. And yet—in another ten years, the Berlin Wall would fall apart under its own weight, collapse in a sort of resigned sigh. No revolution needed, and none of the fruits of a revolution (for good and ill) available to onlookers some distance around the rind of the world.

And yet, and yet—to repeat a perspective from more than 40 years ago: "Perhaps Marcuse's adherence to dialectical logic, his espousal of some of Freud's more bizarre misapprehensions, is in error. But it is not easy to dismiss the profound intuitions at the center of his doctrines—the concealed totalitarian tendency of contemporary democracy; the need for, and technical feasibility of, a non-repressive civilization." In the intervening decades, the western world of oligopolistic corporate "capitalism" (hardly that any longer, in a world where "free market" is more a myth than a reality, if it ever was) has outsourced not only its proletariat but much of its white collar workforce to the Third World. How that will all work out has yet to be seen. But in the meantime, the emergence of the World Wide Web has created the space for some of Marcuse's dreams to come true. What else is the Open Source movement, than "the rise of a new form of reality which would be the work and the medium of developing sensibility and sensitivity…the *esthetic reality of society as a work of art!"*

From Maniac to Man

Probably Arthur Koestler is still best-known (among those who recall his name) as the anti-Stalinist ex-communist author of *Darkness at Noon,* and as one of those who first carried word to the West of the gulag atrocities. The Hungarian Koestler was also much more than that: a true polymath, novelist, journalist, theorist of consciousness and laughter (not that you'd get a grin out of the kinds of jokes he liked to cite because they fitted his model of humor), historian of Kepler and Newton and the birth of the scientific revolution, notable for his extraordinarily ambitious bid in *The Act of Creation* (1964) to unpick the secret architecture of the sciences and the arts, and perhaps of DNA and the entire universe while he was at it.

His analysis of the evolutionary and neurological roots of barbarity, discussed in the article above, was provocative in its day, a sort of forerunner of sociobiology and evolutionary psychology. In retrospect it bears about as much resemblance to what we now understand as the crude pencil sketches of Schiaparelli's "canali" on Mars bear to the reality of the crater-pocked, colossally fissured surface of that planet. But it was a start, a companion to other marvelous attempts from the same epoch: Jacob Bronowski's *Science and Human Values,* Alex

Comfort's *Darwin and the Naked Lady* (which looked for the evolutionary and Freudian roots of art and other baffling human behaviors). Years after Koestler's death (he and his wife killed themselves) he was denounced as a multiple rapist, and certainly as wildly and roughly promiscuous. Whether this perhaps criminal flaw had any bearing on his intellectual endeavors is unclear, but I wonder if his own soul-searching might have led him to a rather despairing estimate of the condition of humankind.

In all this, Koestler remained entranced, I think, with the interactive systems theory of his early Marxism; his model of holons is just such an attempted structure, an explanation that anticipated chaos theory and the endlessly flowering Mandlebrot set generated from a simple equation. He denounced reductionism and behaviorism while championing a blend of instinct and creativity, with something almost mystical folded into the process. In later years he wondered if standard genetics was wrong in denying the direct inheritance of characters acquired from practice by a child's parents. It turns out that some properties are indeed marked in the DNA by father and mother, and some immunological responses can be handed down directly. He became convinced that the phenomena studied by parapsychology are real (as indeed they are), but got muddled with his mathematics. When he died at seventy-eight, in 1983, he left his considerable estate to the University of Edinburgh to establish a professorial Chair of Parapsychology.

Laing

One of the founders in the 1960s of the scandalous "anti-psychiatry" movement (a term he disliked), Dr. Ronald Laing was born in Scotland in 1927 and died in August 1989, several months before the Berlin Wall was opened like a parable of a divided mind recovering itself. His lucid book on schizophrenia—which he saw not so much as a mental disease or disorder as a healing journey, properly regarded—was *The Divided Self.* I read it in paperback in 1965, alongside other existential treatments such as Alan Watts' *Psychotherapy East and West,* and fell for Laing's paradoxical and crazy ideas. When I ended up living with a woman who went through a psychotic break in 1968, I berated her parents on the basis of Laing's argument that madness results from a sort of cruel familial scapegoating, driven mostly by a double-binding schizophrenogenic mother.

This unkind and mostly untrue Laingian account of madness became immensely popular in the late '60s and '70s, especially after his oracular, poetic political opinions and manipulations appeared in paperback: *The Politics of Experience and the Bird of Paradise* (1967), *Knots* (1970), and the works of his disciples. Like most of those entranced by Laing's brilliance, I later felt ashamed of my infatuation. This was helped along by the emerging experimental disciplines that showed what was really going on inside people's heads, how our genetic inheritance, development, social and other environmental stressors, and day-to-day neurochemistry mediates and influences our feeling and thoughts and actions (as we shall see in the next chapter), and how easily bamboozled we can be, especially when a poet of genius and fluency like Laing shows up.

Yet finally all of us, however we are made, by whatever encouraging or disturbing pathways, build our minds and our selves in a context of other humans: loving or hating, speaking or being silenced, welcomed or ignored or crushed. So a lot of what Laing wrote still makes quite a bit of good sense—taken in moderation.

PART FIVE: WEIRD SHIT

THE MIND REVOLUTION
(1973)

The new mind sciences are not the latest findings in management psychology, decision theory and the subtle area of communication known as "body language." Those are doubtless important—but the mind sciences I will discuss are so new the experts are still busy tidying up the basic principles. The discoveries are going to turn us all on our ear, shake up the world like it hasn't been shaken since the invention of writing, though they may not emerge full-blown from the laboratories for five, ten, perhaps twenty years. But they are coming—and now we know they're on the way we can get an edge by preparing for the shock when it hits.

More importantly, it's precisely because we can't pinpoint exactly when to expect these developments that we have to start preparing *now.* The fringe areas of research move in startling jolts. Remember the shock of the first heart transplants? Laymen weren't alone in their surprise. In the very year Christian Barnard performed his epoch-making operation, a conference of specialists was told by Dr. Richard J. Cleveland to expect the feat "within five years."

Similarly, present dating on predictions for direct human/computer linkups, brain grafts to enhance intelligence, pills to increase memory and concentration, and a hundred other wonders, may well prove to be underestimates.

Chemicals designed to improve memory dramatically are already on sale in the US. The pills have been field-tested on students at Stanford University, California—and they work. And that's just the emerging tip of the iceberg.

According to the claims of scientists such as Professor Georges Ungar, of Houston, Texas, experiments on animals have actually resulted in specific memories being transferred in chemical form from one animal to another. The memory involved was very general—in one case a "fear of the dark" acquired during conditioning by the donor animal—but it is easy to foresee the beginnings of a whole new pharmaceutical technology of education.

Indeed, despite the remarkable leaps forward we must yet anticipate in conventional technology, others more important, more directly affecting humankind, will occur in every branch of the mind sciences. This is a comparatively recent shift of emphasis. Most people have barely adjusted to the need to keep abreast of radical innovations in the orthodox sciences. We are starting to realize how greatly the constant changes in our physical and technical environment are altering us. But the effects of the mental revolution are going to be even more staggering.

One man who has attempted to map the coming shock front is Dr. John G. Taylor, Professor of Physics at the University of Southampton. "It has been in the past few decades," he stated in his book *The Shape of Minds to Come* (1971), "that a truly revolutionary development in man's understanding of his mind has occurred. We seem to be in the middle of the mental revolution, with still more startling developments about to take place.

"Already this new understanding of the mind has given birth to fantastic methods of controlling a man's behavior, or his feelings, or his intelligence. Every aspect of his behavior and thought processes can now be controlled, either by himself or by others, in a gross fashion and in some cases, in detailed fashion."

Control of the mind has both terrifying and exhilarating potential. With what is now known—leaving aside the discoveries we can expect within five years or so—science fiction horrors like the brainwashing in *A Clockwork Orange* are already old fashioned and inefficient.

Kubrick's film is only a couple of years old, but the supposedly supermodern methods of aversion therapy it portrays are not essentially novel. One method which is—and which we have far more reason to dread—is direct electrical stimulation of the brain.

Neurologists today have a fairly precise knowledge of which sections of the brain control which kinds of behavior. For example, parts of the hypothalamus—at the top of the brainstem—regulate the body's reactions to heat and cold, as well as appetite and other functions. A minute electric current, directed into the correct area of the hypothalamus via a tiny wire embedded in the brain, can cause animals to sweat or shiver, drink up to half their own weight of water, or avoid food even when they are starving. And these findings have already been applied to humans.

Certain curious cases of spasmodic berserk violence in otherwise reasonable people are now known to be caused by breakdowns in the "aggression circuits" of the brain. Dr. Robert G. Heath, of the Tulane Medical School in New Orleans, in an attempt to save such people from their episodes of unwished-for psychosis, has successfully implanted electrodes in his patients' brains. At the onset of a berserk fit, the raging patient is plugged in. A current is passed into the docility center of his brain. Instantly, he subsides. He does not become unconscious. He does not even need to know that the current has gone on. He simply relaxes, all hostility vanishes, and he is capable of chatting and joking with the medical staff.

If a transistorized power pack were permanently attached to the electrode, he could become a completely free agent. Knowing the symptoms of an oncoming attack, and wishing to avoid it, he could stimulate himself out of the fit. This is being done right now with other electrode implants, such as the DCS or dorsal column stimulator. Intense disabling agony in the back can be shunted out of existence by applying do-it-yourself stimulation to an implanted electrode through a portable device pioneered by American surgeons C. Norman Shealy and William H. Sweet.

It's only a matter of time before electrical stimulation is devised for other, perhaps more crucial parts of the brain. It is known that attention, alertness and sex drives are all localized in various areas of the brain, and there seems little doubt that "black boxes" will be built to allow override command of these functions. Without recourse to drugs, the flagging executive will be able to keep his mind keen and active for extended periods. Alternately, the over-tired but insomniac businessman will achieve instant relaxation and sleep with the push of a button.

Nasty visions of the ultimate dictatorship naturally arise. If everyone was compelled by law to have remote-controlled electrodes placed in his pain centers, the foulest clique could reign unopposed by serious rebellion forever.

The logistics of such a program, fortunately, are so immense that we are probably spared that grim prospect. But computer technology is advancing so fast we cannot completely dismiss such fears. It is only by taking these marginal possibilities very seriously indeed that we can be sure we will not find them leering at us out of the headlines.

According to Professor Taylor, the significance of the mental revolution is chiefly to be seen in terms of evolution. Because humans developed intelligence, memory and speech, which combine to allow each generation to gain from the accumulated mistakes of all who went before, we are masters of the earth. Admittedly, human tinkering with the world's resources and ecology, and even its wholesale devastation, might yet result in universal disaster. Nonetheless, if intelligence and drive have produced these problems, it can only be through these same characteristics that we will solve them.

In a sense, then, humanity's special aptitudes have enabled the species to evolve at breathtaking speed. It takes at least a million years for one species to evolve into another, under the spur of changing environmental demands. But human beings have evolved from the primitive to the technological in a mere one hundredth of that time. We did so by amplifying our individual intelligence through group information and skill retrieval. The human brain won its superiority by exchanging instinct for flexibility, inherited skills for learning.

Today we stand on the threshold of a new revolution. If that ancient innovation passed up biological specialization for the benefits for group success, we are now beginning to use the fruits of that breakthrough to create unprecedented changes in individuals.

It could be said we are performing mutations on our own minds (rather than our brains), no longer randomly, but with purpose and increasing expectation of success. And those mutations are then being selected or discarded through the agency of intense social competition.

"The competition for survival," stresses Taylor, "is still continuing, if not increasing. But in the present day it does not mean that only the fittest will survive, but that only the fittest will succeed. In their mastery the fittest will determine the cultural patterns that will shape society; it is the successful who will mould the future."

Consider the following extraordinary facts. It is known that intelligence is related to the size or complexity of the cerebral cortex—in humans, the densely packed rind of gray cells on the outside of the brain. Autopsies show that rats raised in a complex, demanding environment have developed a thicker cortex than those raised under dull, uninteresting conditions. The various obstacles these more intelligent rats had been forced to handle have had a direct effect on the complexity of their brains, even if the enriching experiences occurred only two hours a day.

As well, the chemicals that help transmit information from nerve to nerve are also found in greater abundance in rats from a demanding environment. The implications accord well with findings from the Department of Studies in Behavioral Disabilities at Wisconsin University. Forty newly born children, whose mothers had IQs of less than 70 (feeble-minded), were exposed to an intensely stimulating environment. An automated teaching device produced the word for any object the babies looked at. So successful was this program that these children, who would be expected on genetic grounds to have impaired intelligence, were being prepared at two and three for reading and arithmetic.

In other words, the brains of infants are much more flexible and capable of dramatic response to training than we commonly suppose. But does this mean the only difference between genius and feeble-mindedness is one of early environment? By no means. We might imagine that an enriched environment *plus* extra cortical tissue would produce a super-genius. And this, at least in experiments with animals, has been shown to be true.

It is impossible to graft spare cortex cells into a fully grown animal, both because of the immune-response rejection that plagues organ transplant surgeons and also because an adult brain has already developed specialized functions for each group of cells. But in early life such grafts are feasible. Two Americans, David Bressler and M. Bitterman, recently removed the equivalent of the cortex from ten young tropical mouth-breeder fish and implanted the tissue in ten others.

The experimenters tried to train the fish when they grew to maturity in much the same way rats are trained in the laboratory. The essential difference was that such fish are not sufficiently intelligent to respond to training. This time, though, four fish actually demonstrated the desired learning—and two of them exceeded the researchers' wildest hopes. Post-mortems proved that only in those four had the transplants taken, and in the better two the cortex had doubled in size.

How long will it be, then, before human infants are the subjects of similar brain grafts? Many will find the very concept nauseating. Certainly, there are far-reaching ethical problems involved which will make the uproar over heart-transplants seem a mere quibble. Where is the spare tissue to come from? Even if societies that largely believe abortion is no crime (86% in a recent Australian poll), how many will stomach the idea of deliberately killing fetuses in order to transplant their cortical tissue to some more fortunate child?

Even so, it is well to heed the words of Dr. Rollin Hotchkiss of the Rockefeller Institute: "Many of us feel instinctive revulsion at the hazards of meddling with the finely balanced systems that make an individual what he is. Yet I believe it will surely be done or attempted. The pathway will be built from a combination of altruism, private profit and ignorance."

Still more bizarre problems are tangled up in that particular can of worms. Suppose that, to circumvent the moral issue of tampering with human beings, the brain grafters concentrate instead on producing animals with enough intelligence and dexterity to handle the lousy jobs automation can't cope with. Arthur C. Clarke, the science fiction writer, envisages a breed of "super-chimps," the slaves of the future. But at what point does a super-chimp gain the same moral rights as a person? How long would it be before an augmented chimp cried: "Let my people free?"

Fortunately, the mind revolution has other tricks on the way that, hopefully, will help many and injure none. Have you heard of alpha feedback?

We've known for years that the brain emits a range of electrical rhythms that vary with different states of mind. One which has attracted plenty of attention recently is the alpha rhythm, a comparatively slow cycle of 10 pulses per second with high voltage. EEG (electroencephalograph) studies demonstrate that the alpha rhythm corresponds to a mental state of relaxed attentiveness—the same state much lauded by yogis and practitioners of meditation in both East and West.

Now we find we can learn to turn this tranquil state on and off if an EEG is wired during the training program to signal the presence of alpha. It's a form of self-conditioning, like all learning, with the added remarkable feature that brain rhythms have always been thought virtually inaccessible to conscious control

The arduous techniques of the yogis can do it, but that path requires years of effort. Now, for the cost of a cheap portable EEG feedback unit, you can bypass that rigorous regimen and quickly learn to master the alpha state. Still, is it worth doing? Many psychiatrists believe so, arguing that in this age of frazzled nerves and high anxiety, voluntary entry to the alpha state is superior to any chemical tranquilizer. More—that the alpha state helps clear the mind's cluttered furniture, aiding the processes of creativity.

Alpha feedback control is merely one of the forms of self-mastery recently shown to be possible. Another is control over high blood pressure. Pioneered by Prof. N. E. Miller, at the Rockefeller Institute in New York, this new front line offensive by the mental revolution has driven deep into the hitherto inviolate *autonomic systems* of the brain.

Animals have been taught voluntary control by feedback and reward of heart beat rate, blood pressure, brain cycles and even such incredible nuances as the amount of blood flowing into either ear! When you recall that the supreme sexual delights are always ultimately dependent on the orgasm reflex—until now an almost totally autonomic function—you can appreciate that Miller's unlikely discoveries are the harbinger of a true sexual revolution.

Brain rhythm research can also teach us the best use of the natural periodicities of the body. That mysterious third of our lives, the hours of sleep, is regulated by large cyclical shifts from alpha to low-voltage fast rhythms characteristic of wide-awake attention. These latter periods of cortical arousal during sleep correspond to flickering of the closed eyes, and tell us that the sleeper is dreaming. Both fast- and slow-wave sleep are essential to our well-being; deprived of either, experimental subjects become irritable, erratic and finally plagued by hallucinations.

This sequence, which averages ninety minutes to complete, also has its equivalent during waking hours. Drs. Oswald and Merrington at Edinburgh University spent many days observing student volunteers relaxing in a room fitted with one-way mirrors. They found that eating and drinking showed strong evidence of a ninety-minute cycle. Obviously, as this new data continues to mount up, we are going to have to rethink our adherence to timetables based on units of an hour.

Other experiments show that close attention can be paid to a lecturer, or a task, only for about twenty minutes. It's necessary at that point, for best efficiency and to prevent restlessness, to take a few minutes' break. Adroit public speakers and teachers have always known this unconsciously, interleaving their important remarks with jokes and other inconsequential chatter which give their audience time to switch off briefly.

§

Perhaps the most fascinating facet of the mind revolution is the novelties it promises to introduce into our sex life. As we've seen, conscious control of the autonomic system will have immediate benefits on a man's erectile prowess. Even more startling, though, is the possibility of chemical or electrical stimulation of the brain centers that co-ordinate our erotic responses.

There are two sex centers in the hypothalamus that play an important role in activating sexual behavior, and removing them castrates a man more totally than a gelding knife. Other centers in the nearby limbic system inhibit sexuality. A British surgeon, Dr. Falconer, found that fifteen patients whose inhibitory centers were destroyed by cancer operations became sexually overactive "either by intercourse or masturbation."

Another expert reports, "One female patient was so tortured with vivid sexual imagery and sensations in the clitoris several times a day for periods lasting one to two hours that even achieving an orgasm through masturbation twenty times in succession did not relieve her of the unendurable sexual tension."

Now the sex centers have been located, it is possible to employ such effects deliberately and with more control. Electrode stimulation of the hypothalamus in male monkeys and rats has produced constant erections. "One monkey studied was reported to have experienced twenty ejaculations in one hour of stimulation." The mind revolution will certainly offer us such abilities very soon, either through hormone aphrodisiac pills acting on these centers, or via implanted electrodes.

But will so "unnatural" a method as brain implants appeal to any but the most jaded or depraved? In a review of the data, Taylor remarked: "It is very likely that these various methods will be used by normal men and women to increase their sexual powers. This would particularly apply to cases of sexual incompatibility between married couples.... And in a permissive society, where there is a great deal of changing of sexual companions, the most favored would be those with enhanced powers. They would be the flames around which the moths would dance. But more people would want to be the favored flames with their sexual powers burning brightly; such treatment would most likely spread very rapidly."

So the mental revolution will be well and truly launched into public awareness. Like all revolutions it has its dangers—as the sorry episode of LSD frenzy in the late '60s has shown—and we may be burdened with a new cult of "wire-trippers" and "brain junkies." But the possible benefits are incalculable. In learning the new dimensions of self-control and self-enhancement, we shall be building a future of human beings with powers truly like the gods of legend.

WEIRD SHIT (1978)

I.

It probably hasn't escaped your razor-sharp attention that the 1970s has been bonanza time for the purveyors of paranormal phenomena (known technically in the trade, by me at any rate, as "weird shit"). Most people who see themselves as committed deeply to the integrity of ideas have failed to express delight at this fact. Devotees of the occult, after all, generally evince a marvelous gullibility, usually tempered by a single proviso: they steadfastly *won't* believe it if it's in the regular textbooks.

I have an equivocal standing in this scandalous failure of sober Western rationality, because I spend a lot of my time eagerly poring over ESP test results and tabulations of UFO reports. By and large, though, I'm just as aghast as the rest of us folks raised on a solid diet of hypothetico-deduction and standard deviations. We can only shake our heads ruefully and tell one another, "Crikey, Bert, I don't know, if you ask me *the world's gone bloody mad.*"

If you make a practice of believing six impossible things before breakfast (even if it's organic muesli), you'll end up with an extraordinary quantity of nonsense in your head. But of course in an important sense none of us *really* knows what's impossible and what merely seems unlikely at the time. Recall the gruesome tale of the venomous persecution ladled out less than 20 years ago to the heretics who thought there just might be something in the idea of drifting continents. Today, plate tectonics is established truth; less than a generation ago, offensive delusion. (Yet any fool, looking at a map, could see that at one time the continents had fitted snugly together. There's other weird shit staring us in the face today, waiting for the belated nod and the establishment of University chairs.)

Scientific understanding, Thomas Kuhn tells us, advances by revolutionary lurches. Each dislocation of the standard maps is followed by lengthy, boring consolidation. Then, just as the heretics are settling their academic gowns about their shoulders, some bastard does it again. Mopping and mowing and gnashing of teeth.

I think we're on the edge of one or more such revolutions. The rogue data from some investigations of some alleged paranormal phenomena are screaming for inclusion in a fresh paradigm. I suspect the UFO evidence is one of these barely contained volcanoes. I'm quite certain that parapsychology is another. And there's even a wisp of a hint (although it pains me to admit it) that the two are linked, and not just as the outpourings of mad minds and the stoned work-shy.

For a start, during the last decade or so, while Vietnam burned and the ecosphere choked and hundreds of millions starved and people with cash for paperbacks teased out baroque hopes of salvation from extraterrestrial Pygmalions, something stupefying seems to have happened in ESP research. A handful of investigators appear to have done for psi phenomena (pronounced "sigh," not "pissy") what Marconi did for radio waves and Von Braun did for rockets. They got it working with acceptable reliability, and in doing so I believe they've paved the way to a new post-industrial revolution.

By a curious irony, the recent upsurge of credulous enthusiasm for the occult makes this assertion at once banal and unbelievable. When the skies swarm with divine chariots, when plastic pyramids confer nameless energies known only to the ancients, when the woman up the street changes her name by deed-poll so the letters give the most propitious numerological configuration, we all yawn and turn to the sports pages.

What's the point, after all, even if psychic supermen do daily cause the detumescence of cutlery? Even if weird shit is not entirely shit it's undeniably weird, and where's the percentage in weird already?

Oh you dull swine. Have you no imagination?

Arthur C. Clarke's *2001* dealt with a science so far advanced as to be indistinguishable from magic. It's my belief that any sufficiently advanced magic will be indistinguishable from technology.

In general, though, there's no call to get all grim about it. Weird shit, like science fiction, is primarily intellectual play for the zest of it. Still, when Clarke published his haunting, flawed novel of a psychic apocalypse, *Childhood's End*, he prefaced it with the extraordinary note: "The opinions expressed in this book are not those of the author." Since science fiction is a species of fantasy where wild irresponsible speculation is grist to the writer's mill, this disclaimer seemed peculiarly redundant. Evidently the man felt threatened by the occult drama he portrayed so movingly. I can sympathize with his forebodings. The vistas of weird shit are dizzying, and for anyone schooled to the tenets of orthodoxy the predominant emotion must surely be dismay. A journey into the borderlands of science and parascience begins with furtive thrills and often concludes in sour sardonicism.

I was much taken when I read in *The Social Contract* a comparable disclaimer by Robert Ardrey, whose stock in trade after all is a conceptual recklessness to infuriate any scholar. Sometimes even his nerve fails.

"There is a surmise so wild," he wrote, "that none with a reputation to lose dares publish it. Yet it is a story so good that to deny it to readers becomes a criminal act. And so, since I lose my reputation anyway as regularly as oak trees their leaves, I present it here.... I do so, however, with the strict understanding that I do not believe a word of it."

Let his words be the keynote to this column.

II.

Allow the possibility for a moment that human beings are sometimes the agents of paranormal psi phenomena: flashes of telepathy, premonitions of the future, metal-deformation, you name it. This daring act (unless you're a Believer) will no doubt produce a hot screeching in the cogs of your prejudice, but probably won't rupture anything permanently.

Okay—weird shit specialists concur that such phenomena are sporadic, unscheduled and unreliable, but that they can be demonstrated. So what value do they have?

According to Stuart Holroyd, in *Psi and the Consciousness Explosion*, psi research has two main benefits. "It is an established principle of science that a small event produced in the laboratory may give us important information about much larger events that take place in the universe." Psi in the lab, even when it's just a one percent deviation from chance expectation in a card-guessing test, could lead to the understanding of universal forces thus-far unaccounted for. Maybe we'll revolutionize the theory of evolution, and build a psi-machine for long-range disaster forecasting.

Holroyd, in common with many Believers, has bigger fish than that to fry. Psi will change our consensus view of reality, bring us together around a Kumbaya camp-fire holding hands and vibing out auras of peace and love. "It turns up well-proven facts," Holroyd asserts, "that are incompatible with the mechanistic and materialistic image of man that has predominated in our culture. It provides factual and theoretical material to create a new image to supersede the old in which man's psychic and spiritual dimension will be restored."

Wow. Can you *dig* it. Well, frankly, I'm far from persuaded. Sociologists might discern here the seeds of a fresh unifying faith, and philosophers thrill to the possibility of an authentic phenomenology with apodictic psi insights. But when it comes to the bottom line I can't see much difference between the metaphysics of a loving telephone call and a brain-to-brain flash. In the long run, when all the bugs are worked out of telepathy (assuming that's possible), maybe we'll all swim together in the pellucid collective unconscious, unhampered by the snares of language and deceit. I doubt it'd work that way (*get out of my head!*). Today's psychics aren't always noted for their acuity and loving-kindness.

If psi is a reality, it will certainly shake up our current paradigms. The resistance from orthodoxy to the data of parapsychology is proof enough of that. But the immediate practical consequence, as I've said before, is going to be a new technology.

§

For a truly provocative look at what's going on in this field, I recommend *Mind Reach*, by Russell Targ and Dr. Harold Puthoff. They're the laser physicists who—by current standards—blew their reputations out by studying Uri Geller in the Stanford Research Institute labs. But their work with Geller (whom they couldn't get to bend metal under strict controlled conditions) is the least of their efforts.

Targ began with an automated ESP-guessing machine, designed to generate random targets and automatically record the guesses of subjects. When a NASA-funded study using this device was published (showing, overall, no significant psi effects), Targ was pulverized by *Scientific American*'s Martin Gardner. The attack by Gardner turned out to be fun for the psi scientists, because they were able to show that his critique was based on malicious hearsay with no foundation in fact.

By 1973, Puthoff and Targ had launched an extraordinary series of experiments which cut right away from boring card guessing. Several alleged psychics and some non-psychics were invited to try "remote viewing": to describe a distant scene, selected at random, while locked under double-blind conditions in an SRI office. After a series of such verbal outpourings, independent judges were taken to the remote locations and asked to blind-match the several descriptions with the target areas. They did so to a striking and statistically significant extent.

Later still, certain subjects were asked to describe locations in advance of their random selection. You have to see the photographs and descriptions cited in the book to appreciate the impact of these experiments. For example, one subject "saw" a scene she didn't understand: a "black iron triangle that Hal had somehow walked into." She "heard" a "squeak, squeak, about once a second." The location, chosen *later* and without reference to her hallucinatory free-association, was "a children's swing at a small park about six miles from the laboratory."

Could this technique be used to identify the location *prior* to blind-matching of disclosed locations? Targ and Puthoff tried the method I believe is the path to reliable psi application: they overlapped the guesses of several subjects at the same target area, and looked for the points in common. The results were very promising.

Is it reasonable to apply cold, dispassionate statistics to a mysterioso phenomenon like psi? Why not? It's the only way yet devised to co-ordinate fuzzy, unreliable hunches and turn remote viewing reports into a solid piece of useful communication.

The metaphysics comes *after* we've got it working.

III.

When scientists of distinction deride reports of occult phenomena (and most of them do), they frequently ask: "Where is the evidence?"

This is a baffling question, for when a tally of the best reports for ESP or UFOs is presented, the data are generally dismissed unread. This could suggest that to the astute eye these data are plainly phony, that time spent proving their inadequacy is time squandered.

Consider a recent question-and-answer routine penned by Dr. Isaac Asimov, a science-writer not famous tor the paucity of his imagination. "There is certain direct evidence for flying saucers are spaceships... Some claim even to have been aboard the ships. Have you investigated these reports?"

To which Asimov responded with magisterial authority: "No, I have not investigated any of these reports. Not one.

"My justification in dismissing them out of hand is that eye-witness evidence by a small number of people uncorroborated by any other sort of evidence is worthless...."

The same goes, by and large, for ESP. It's hard not to feel sympathy. I have never investigated the evidence for a hollow Earth, or for goblins, or the revelations of Mary Baker Eddy. Neither am I likely to, and that admission of bias hardly makes me cringe in shame. But I *have* done experiments in ESP, and got powerful results. And I've read enough substantial reportage on UFOs to be convinced that *something* the hell weird is afoot, and it's not all witless loonies and weather balloons.

The prime objection of scientists, I judge, is the apparent absence of evidence in all the rest of their own data.

If Geller-style kids can derange Geiger counters, how is it that anyone can ever use the things reliably? If ESP some-times fetches your heart's desire against all the odds, why do bad theories get trashed when it comes to the test? Surely their adherents are in there rooting. Why doesn't psi step in and foul the instrument readings, making the scientists' dreams come true? Instead, all around the world, scientists are falsifying their own favorite hypotheses every day, and gritting their teeth, and going back to the drawing-board.

One answer is that these intrusions *do* occur from time to time. The little-reported truth is that scientists are constantly throwing away data which don't fit their models or which fit too well to be persuasive. Such results are written-off as glitches, instrument failures.

Then there are the people who get just the right jolt on the needle to give them priority in the discovery of the quark or the tachyon (hypothetical subatomic particles which can only be detected by complex machines). Other scientists can't replicate the claims. Sorry, fellas, it must have been an incredibly unlikely breakdown in the bowels of your detecting equipment, just the right kind at the right time to give you a pulse that looked like your Nobel Prize.

The answer: Psi is *rare*—that's why it doesn't happen all the time. Still, one flash from the future might be all it takes to receive an idea that nobody has yet thought of. If psi is a fact, why did the idea of moveable type fail to spread by telepathy from China to the west? Once the concept of zero had been achieved, and the simple Hindu numbers we use today instead of LXVIII, why didn't mathematicians in more laggardly nations instantly perceive the breakthrough?

One reason lies in the antagonism between logical thought and intuition. The very people best equipped to use psi-mediated blockbusters seem to be those least likely to register them. What's more, while ancient scholars were not averse to "supernatural" inspiration, techniques interlock. You can't introduce moveable type, and thereafter newspapers or cheap books. without first providing paper, ink, presses.

Mystics who live in a daily haze of psi flashes are having themselves on. Lab studies show how spasmodic and unreliable psi is—which is why statistical methods had to be devised to concentrate ESP to the point of visibility. So telepathy or precognition might add a partial insight to a prepared mind but, lacking an infrastructure, the brief glimpse would evaporate. There'd be nothing to anchor it in.

You'd be better advised to look for such paranormal flashes in art and literature than in science. Myth, satirical romance and modern science fiction are all worth studying for psi intrusions. It might take a stringently designed computer search to separate any pattern from innumerable "noise" factors: contemporary scientific expectation, archetypes, readers' tastes, editorial prejudice.

Structural analysis is called for. By isolating the dynamics that make up the framework of both myth and fantasy, any psi intrusions could be thrown into relief. An index of consistent overlays (if there are any) needs to be drawn up. In scrutinizing our past through such a grid, we might discern the shape of things to come.

This kind of thinking can, of course, get out of hand.

One outlandish speculation I can't keep to myself (though I don't really believe it) concerns the caduceus— ancient symbol of entwined snakes. It's long been the emblem of medicine. In Roman mythology it was the herald's staff of Mercury, messenger of the gods. The caduceus is in fact a double helix.

How piquant that it should have possessed in antiquity the dual significance of information exchange and healing. Did someone get a glimpse, across the depths of time future, of that primal double helix: the DNA molecule...?

IV.

On May 1, 1952, the weather at Davis-Monthan Air Force Base, in Tucson, Arizona, was balmy, clear, with visibility to eighty km. At 9.10 am, Air Intelligence officer Major Pestalozzi and another airman watched from the ground as two round, symmetrically convex metal craft overtook an incoming B-36. One, according to Pestalozzi, stationed itself "just behind and to the port side of the B-36. The second stationed itself between the pusher-type prop spinners and the leading edge of the starboard elevators."

All the crew, except the pilot, crowded the starboard observation port. The disk was about eight meters in diameter, four meters high at the center. The pilot remained on-course, and after twenty seconds the shiny craft turned sharply and accelerated to three or four times the speed of the military plane. Before reaching the horizon, one disk stopped dead and hovered. Shaken, the B-36 crew obtained permission to land immediately.

The aerial objects observed by Major Pestalozzi and the other airmen could not be identified in 1952, and still elude explanation. The report of the multiple sighting is just one of some 640 high-quality descriptions of flying objects listed as *unidentified* in the revised files of the U.S. Air Force Project Blue Book.

Recently, under the U.S. Freedom of Information Act, all restricted Blue Book files have been opened for the first time to public scrutiny. Other important information has come to light from House Select Committee hearings. Much of this documentation, and careful scientific analysis of its data, is now being published. And the evidence is disturbing. The UFO question has been blown wide open again.

That evidence details hundreds of brilliant aerial luminosities, and apparently solid "craft," which fly at speeds beyond the technology of the day, execute incredible instant turns, and occasionally disgorge unearthly crew. Ridiculous? Perhaps not.

The era of UFOs seemed to end in 1969. After two decades of fantastic claims and pained official denials, the whole sorry charade was apparently resolved by a 1,485-page University of Colorado report. According to the study's eminent Director, Dr. E. U. Condon, his government-sponsored committee had found "no direct evidence whatever of a convincing nature...for the claims that any UFOs represent spacecraft visiting Earth from another civilization." The U.S. Air Force, with great relief, immediately closed down Project Blue Book. Flying saucers were a dead issue.

But the UFO sightings didn't stop. In 1973, for example, there was a major influx of new reports to civilian investigative organizations, rivaling previous sighting peaks. Despite ridicule, people kept seeing impossible aerial phenomena.

Startlingly, the man spearheading current demands for renewed intensive study of UFOs is Dr. J. Allen Hynek, chairman of the Department of Astronomy at Northwestern University. From 1949 on, Hynek was the chosen scientific consultant to Blue Book. As an expert astronomer, it was his role to isolate from the cascades of reports those which were due to misidentifications of stars, planets, meteors and other recognized celestial phenomena. During the bulk of his consultancy, he was seen as an official axe-man, the man most likely to debunk.

It was utterly astonishing, therefore, when Hynek published an outspoken article in the *Saturday Evening Post*, in December 1966, denouncing Blue Book's negative assessments. Bear in mind that Hynek was the one scientist at that time conversant with sufficient detailed case-reports to evaluate the scale of the problem. Then, as now, the broad scientific community was hostile to the idea that UFOs might represent a major anomaly. Hynek had little to gain (other than the suspicious interest of "believers"), and his professional reputation to lose. But the accumulating evidence had obliged him to change his mind.

Still, even if Dr. Hynek's singular credentials give us pause, do UFOs really *matter* that much? Surely we have practical problems enough, with resource depletion, pollution, hunger and strife battering at the door, without wasting our time on lights in the sky. Of course the same seemingly hard-headed attitude could be taken to all pure research, yet it is on such research—and its unexpected and lucrative products—that technological society depends.

Hynek considers the UFO phenomena "something that really *is* new, something not yet encompassed by our present science." In calling for more study, better funded, he is scrupulous *not* to advance any flashy hypotheses. If the small residue of truly unexplained cases really is alien craft, of course, the significance of establishing that fact is self-evident. But the phenomena are so extraordinary, if genuine, that they appear to place our scientific foundations in jeopardy. And the resolution of such anomalies yields powerful breakthroughs, as the history of science shows.

"Today," Hynek states in his latest book, *The Hynek UFO Report*, "I would not spend one additional moment on the subject of UFOs if I didn't seriously feel that the UFO phenomenon is real and that efforts to investigate and understand it, and eventually to solve it, could have a profound effect—perhaps even be the springboard to a revolution in man's view of himself and his place in the universe."

Hynek's important new book is a general examination of the recently declassified Blue Book files. He gives brief summaries of some of the most striking of the 13,134 reports, some key statistics, and a critical analysis of official U.S. policy up to the Condon study. Without unseemly passion, he highlights the scandalous and unscientific antics that characterized military and CIA response through the two decades.

To get full value from *The Hynek UFO Report*, it helps to read it in conjunction with two other recent crucial studies. One is *UFOs Explained*, by American avionics writer Philip J. Klass, a stinging stylist whose brilliant skeptical forensic research has exploded some of the more celebrated "classic" UFO cases. In some instances, Klass offers plausible accounts for reports which even Condon's investigators found mysterious.

(It is a bizarre fact that the Condon report, widely thought to have given the *coup de grace* to UFOS by explaining the unexplained, lists as still unexplained thirty of the ninety-one cases it looked that. Of one alleged photo of an alien craft, the Condon committee specialist concluded: "This is one of the few UFO reports in which all the factors investigated...appear to be consistent with...an extraordinary flying object, silvery, metallic, disk-shaped, tens of meters in diameter, and evidently artificial...." Klass's reappraisal, on the contrary, indicates that the photo is a hoax. Yet the Condon report thought it was genuine!)

The other essential book is *The UFO Controversy in America*, a sociological study by Professor David M. Jacobs, of Temple University, published in 1975 as a monograph by Indiana University Press. With impressive scholarship, Jacobs traces the UFO debate from the perspective of a historian of science.

Jacobs' chief contribution has been to elucidate why, if the UFO data are as impressive as Hynek and other specialists claim, it has taken so long for the fact to surface. Why the official opposition to unobstructed research, why the often-ludicrous and bungled attempts at debunking? Is there, as UFO enthusiasts often claim, a sinister "conspiracy of silence"? (An assertion, it must be remarked, not nearly so odious in these post-Pentagon Papers, post-Watergate days).

No, answers Jacobs. The answer is three-fold. First, the military were in charge of the data, and they asked the wrong question ("Are UFOs a threat to security?").

Second, UFO characteristics are inconsistent with the accepted paradigm—or consensus view of reality—of physics, and such anomalies tend to be shelved by scientists.

Third, the CIA stepped in early in the piece, convening a panel of distinguished scientists in January 1953, and after ten working hours recommended a policy of public education and stringent debunking. Convinced that UFOs were of natural origin, the CIA panel was alarmed at the possibility of a panicky public clogging crucial intelligence channels with useless reports, to possible Soviet advantage.

A climate shaped by such forces was hardly conducive to cool scrutiny of the phenomenon. Customary scientific standards slipped grotesquely, most tellingly in the *Blue Book Special Report No. 14.* In 1952, the U.S. Air Force commissioned the highly reputable Battelle Memorial Institute to analyze available data, specifically to learn whether "Unidentified" cases differed significantly from the great abundance of reports that could be assigned a natural explanation.

This is a most important question. Skeptics, typified by Dr. Isaac Asimov, maintain "that if each puzzling UFO report were subject to thoroughgoing investigation, then the more that would be found out about it, the less puzzling it would seem." This is the working maxim of such investigators as Philip Klass, and in certain cases it has served them well. But is it generally true? Are the "unidentified" residual UFO reports those most deficient indetail? In that case, a better assessment would be "insufficient data." Or are they those cases which remain extraordinary on close study, markedly different from simple cases of this observation?

The Battelle study, cited in Hynek's new book, looked long and hard at 2,199 reports. Independently, it assigned the reports to various categories. Of those rated "Poor" in quality, 16.6 percent remained unidentified. Yet, at the top end of the scale, 213 "Excellent" reports yielded 33.3 percent unknowns. Contrary to Asimov's speculation, the more that is known about truly anomalous UFO sightings, the harder it is to account for them.

What's more, Battelle were able to compare the Identified and the Unidentified, using six separate parameters or measures. In all but one parameter, the likelihood of the two groups of reports stemming from similar stimuli was "less than one percent," in two parameters "very much less than one percent." Combined, the probability that Unidentified aerial objects were the same class or phenomenon as those with a reasonable (though not obvious) explanation is *much less than one chance in a billion.*

Yet, stunningly, the Battelle report (delivered after the CIA panel's recommendations) admitted in its conclusions only that "The results of these tests are not conclusive since they neither confirm nor deny that the UNKNOWNS are primarily unidentified KNOWNS, though they do indicate that relatively few of the UNKNOWNS are astronomical phenomena." The press printed the conclusions, but failed to note how utterly they flew in the face of the analysis.

One can only conclude that to date there is no solution, either simple or complex, to the UFO conundrum. Talk of alien spacecraft is both premature and broadly consistent with the data. We are left with Hynek's summary that UFOs—the inexplicable residue—display "apparently intelligent characteristics (of a rather puerile kind)."

One possible hint, appalling to the conservative scientist hovering at the edge of conviction, is their resemblance to alleged psychic phenomena. My own research, which concurs with the estimate by Dr. Jacques Vallee, a NASA computing specialist, locates the most widely witnessed and thoroughly documented UFO sighting in Portugal on October 13. 1917.

A silvery disc reportedly cavorted in the sky above 70,000 people, of all ages and creeds, for ten minutes.

The crowd had been advised two months in advance to expect a remarkable event at that precise hour. The phenomenon is enshrined in the doctrines of the Catholic Church as the "miracle of Fatima," and as a result of an authorized devotional cult the sighting zone has become a place of pilgrimage and, allegedly, paranormal healing. Yet the "miracle of the dancing sun," stripped of piety, is absolutely consistent with statistically-derived UFO profiles.

Are Hynek and his colleagues correct? Do UFO reports, after the sifting which banishes ninety-five percent of them, contain a clue to an epoch-making conceptual breakthrough? There is evidence enough for the possibility. Can we afford not to investigate the problem?

V.

When I was only *that* high, chanting out the intellectual principles that cement the life of the Catholic faith, the nuns at St. Gabriel's rather liked this catechism mantra:

"Q. If there is a God, why do we not see Him?

"A. We do not see God because He is a Spirit, having no body, and cannot be seen by us in this life."

Trenchant, and pretty well unsinkable. It's a convenient line of argument and one with countless applications. Modified slightly, it helps to explain Unidentified Flying Objects, unless you're one of those people who need injections and the nurse has skipped the rounds this week.

Such, at least, is the conventional wisdom. It falters a tiny bit when you pick up your *Sunday Telegraph* on 12 September, 1978, and see the disclosures of a former USAF sergeant, Duane B. Piciani. A crewman on an Apollo Range Instrumentation Aircraft, "which is crammed with super sensitive electronics equipment," Piciani *has* seen a UFO in this life.

"The saucer shaped craft snuggled right up next to our wing. It was round and flat, about 40 feet in diameter, with a raised surface in its center that might have been a crew's quarters."

The information officer for the air force's systems command, according to the *Telegraph,* confirmed that the space program jet had encountered "unknown aerial phenomena" more than once.

Well, Piciani was—at the age of twenty-seven—"recently retired" from the air force. Still, if there's the slightest chance that we are being nosed by alien spacecraft, it's worth tucking our grins away and checking out the available facts.

I took my newspaper clipping to a well placed science journalist and sought his opinion. He's a busy man. He put a few feelers out, but a month later he had no feedback pro or con the story's reliability.

Logic alone insists that the issue is an improbable folk rumor. If the little buggers are buzzing NASA we'd have been told, wouldn't we?

(Right. And if the Americans had been bombing Laos we'd have been told, wouldn't we? But we *were* told, despite the official screams. If Nixon couldn't save his own ass, he couldn't keep the lid on real live extraterrestrial spaceships. Could he?)

§

Photographs then. Where are the watertight photographs to back up the myriad civilian sightings?

Dr. Don Herbison-Evans, a computing specialist at Sydney University and a cautious UFO believer, offers some interesting arithmetic. There are substantial grounds for thinking that only one in ten UFO sightings is reported to official authorities. The USAF Project Bluebook (defunct since 1969) lists an average of 500 reports a year, with a mean sighting duration of ten minutes. If as many as ten percent of these sightings are not "trivial misidentifications and hoaxes"—twice as many as Bluebook's ultraconservative residue—we're left with a single non trivial sighting *per year* per 20,000 square kilometers in the USA.

Can we catch that UFO on film, and thus test the spaceship hypothesis? With 2,000 automatic cameras optimally deployed, Herbison-Evans points out, each taking a picture once every ten minutes, just *one* UFO would appear for every hundred million pictures.

But surely we'd want more than one virtually context-free picture. Suppose we increase the shutter rate to a shot every six seconds. That way, we could build up a time-lapse profile of the UFO's trajectory and appearance. Now we need to take and examine ten billion pictures. For an adequate modest coverage of the year's 500 aerial unknowns—many of which are doubt-less explicable in orthodox terms, once the data is in—we're up to five trillion pictures from an array of a million expensive instruments.

Compared to such an undertaking, the hunt for rare sub-nuclear particles in streamer chambers is kid's stuff. In 1948, P. M. S. Blackett got the Nobel after scrutinizing 20,000 cloud chamber photos for eight confirmatory events; "surely," as Isaac Asimov has declared, "an example of superhuman patience, faith and persistence." If Herbison-Evans' estimates are anywhere near the mark, confirmation of UFOs at the same level would take 40,000 times Blackett's endurance.

We're stuck, it seems, with a statistical *reductio ad absurdum*. To carry out such an essentially mindless exercise would be preposterous, even if it were practicable (and it could be made so with the aid of video-tapes and on-line computer control). Rigorous investigation of the data to hand, by information specialists, has revealed no useful systematic pattern. We need to look in another direction.

§

"If there are UFO pilots, why do we not see them?" But many people *do* claim to have seen them. Recently Dr. Claude Poher, of the French National Center for Space Studies, went through 35,000 sighting reports. Ten percent involved landings or near-landings of unidentifiable craft; five percent claimed sighting of UFO personnel.

Poher selected the most promising thousand cases, ran them through a factor-analysis employing eighty variables and announced that the printout conclusively demonstrated the alien reality of UFOs. Unless we begin by ruling all "close-contact" reporters insane, which somewhat begs the issue, maybe some clue might be sought here.

A 1975 made-for-TV movie, *The UFO Incident,* dramatized the alleged flying saucer kidnapping in 1961 of two Americans. As psychodrama, the film is gripping. Under hypnosis, Betty and Barney Hill were repeatedly regressed to a two hour amnesic period which followed their observation of a strange aerial light. In trance they evinced authentic terror as they "relived" their capture and on-board examination by aliens.

No effort was spared in the film in presenting the antecedents to what their psychiatrist clearly diagnosed as *folie à deux* delusion. Even so, a single feature was mentioned in the closing seconds that strained against this interpretation.

In 1964, under the posthypnotic instruction of her psychiatrist, Betty Hill attempted to reconstruct a three-dimensional star map allegedly shown her by the UFOnauts. The drawing (map 1) was published in John Fuller's *The Interrupted Journey* in 1966. Despite one abortive attempt neither Betty nor Fuller could make any convincing sense out of the diagram.

UFO map 1: Betty Hill's post-hypnotic diagram

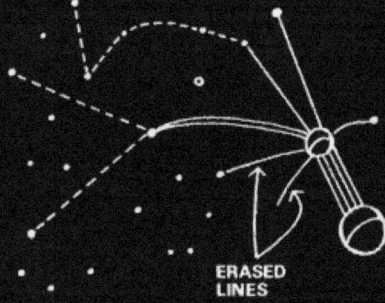

ERASED
LINES

UFO map 2: The Fish map

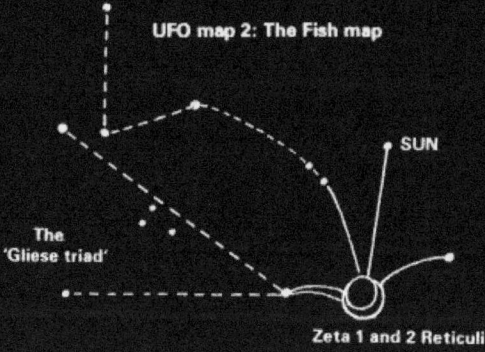

SUN

The
'Gliese triad'

Zeta 1 and 2 Reticuli

The Hill map shows twenty-six stars, several more prominent than the rest, of which twelve are linked by lines indicating
trade and exploration. Several erasures are still visible, and it
seems clear that the "background stars" were dotted in more
carelessly than the linked stars.

From the therapy transcripts, it appears that one of the stars is
our sun—but there is no indication of which. If it were feasible
to map Betty's diagram on to a similar array of stars in the solar
neighborhood and to evaluate the "goodness-of-fit," we might
have some measure of the reliability of her otherwise utterly
outrageous tale.

That's not as easy as it sounds unless you have a computer
program specifying the coordinates of the thousand stars within
a radius of fifty-five light years of the sun (something not generally available in the 1960s). Why that figure? There are forty-six
stars similar to the sun in that volume, a reasonable set of candi-
dates for an alien road-guide.

A then-thirty-four-year-old Mensa member and school
teacher, Marjorie Fish, became captivated by the problem.
She began the hard way: building beads-and-string star maps
in three dimensions, using only Sun-type stars (technically,
"single, nonfluctuating, main sequence stars between F8 and
K1"), based on reputable astronomical catalogues. Her search
took six years. It culminated so fruitfully that her findings
merited a lead story in the December 1974 issue of a respected
popular science magazine, *Astronomy.*

The crucial twelve linked stars (map 2) were provisionally
identified by Fish. One of them is our Sun. According to Walter
N. Webb in 1974, "A continuing inspection since then has not
uncovered any (other) pattern remotely resembling the original
discovery."

The "trade routes" on Betty's map seemed to radiate from
a pair of stars which, as the editor of *Astronomy,* Terence
Dickinson, pointed out, "is practically in the midst of the
cluster of solar type stars." These stars are Zeta 1 and Zeta 2
Reticuli, suns which are about thirty-seven light years from the

solar system and about one-twentieth of a light year from each another.

What's more, the stars on the Fish/Hill map have an internal coherence that only becomes apparent when they are viewed in cubic relationship. Dickinson showed that of the forty-six sun-like stars within reasonable range, fifteen are clumped together. The most economical and rational route for an imaginary inter-stellar expedition leaving Earth to explore such stars would follow a sequence containing ten of the stars identified by Fish as fitting the Hill configuration.

Fraud? If Fish could do it, might not the Hills have set about in the same fashion, perhaps with the advice of some UFO-fanatic astronomer? It's doubtful. The most captivating feature is not the straightforward identification of the trade-route stars. When the 1969 Gliese *Catalog of Nearby Stars* was published, containing fresh and more accurate estimates of stellar coordinates, Fish revised her cube. Another three stars instantly fell into place: Gliese 86.1, 95 and 97.

The triangular fit was not precise, of course, but the structural relationship seemed amazingly persuasive. Here is the most compelling aspect of the entire bizarre episode: Betty Hill could not have drawn these stars fraudulently, since in 1964 the star 86.1 had not yet been listed in any catalogue, while 95 and 97 were listed in erroneous parallax positions. They would not have produced a visual triangle like that in the Hill diagram.

A fluke? Dr. David R. Saunders, a one-time member of the University of Colorado UFO study group—and a statistics expert who built up a computer program containing over 60,000 UFO reports—evaluates the match as "rather persuasive." He disputes Fish's identification of the star Tau 1 Eridani, for example, preferring YBS 448. "The odds are about 10,000 to one against a random configuration matching perfectly with Betty Hill's map. But the star group identified by Marjorie Fish isn't quite a perfect match, and the odds consequently reduce to about 1,000 to one...."

Others, including Cornell's Carl Sagan (an open-minded

skeptic), disagree. Responding to the *Astronomy* article, Sagan argued that the resemblance is tenuous, *produced* rather than merely *displayed* by adding the Hill "trade routes" over the Fish stellar perspective. Robert Sheaffer has stressed recently that the benefits of including the Gliese stars are offset by Fish's failure to identify the remaining eleven Hill dots.

Frankly, I was pretty impressed by the Fish effort. She appeared to have the guts of the Hill map covered rather thoroughly, and given that it was produced from memory in a state close to automatic drawing, I figured that a greater degree of detailed accuracy would indeed have looked suspicious.

Of course, I was not utterly opposed to the possibility that the Hills might have been telling the truth during hypnotic regression, though I was sure that many of the incidents described were more of Freudian than exobiological interest. It boiled down, then, to two questions: how reliable is post hypnotic suggestion in eliciting accurate visual recall after several years, and how likely was it that the Fish/Hill congruence could be due to chance coincidence?

For the first, I sought the opinion of Len Kane, MA, a clinical psychologist whose Australian National University thesis dealt with time distortion under hypnosis. He felt there were severe limits to the accuracy of trance-enhanced memory, though it was true that the condition helps retrieve repressed material. The high emotional charge associated by Betty Hill with the salvaged memory would certainly contribute to accuracy, but her recall would be by no means eidetic.

In short, the major structural elements of such a map (assuming it ever existed) might be remembered, though in a distorted form, while the background elements would almost certainly be lost. The clump of stars at the bottom of Betty's map would therefore be arbitrary, though perhaps the "Gliese stars" might be better recalled, due to their enclosing lines, than other backdrop lights.

Reading the therapy transcripts in Fuller's book, it's obvious that Betty's psychiatrist never considered the possibility that the map might be authentic. Had he done so, according to Kane, he might have used a whole battery of techniques for eliciting a more accurate representation. This might include an "Identikit" approach, moving various counters around a board until their mutual relationship seemed right; concentrating on different segments of the map independently; scoring numerous random arrays of dots for familiarity, and so on. By now it's probably too late to try such methods.

Given that there is a fighting chance Betty got the main features right (assuming the incident did occur), how likely is it that Marjorie Fish has found the right stars? Saunders says it's a thousand to one against chance coincidence—but is it?

Suppose we stay with Fish's fifteen stars...and simply flip them upside down (map 3). An array emerges which, while not as nice a fit as Fish's own, has several superior features. *All* the major points in the Hill diagram are accounted for, with the exception of the clump Fish also leaves out and the "Gliese triangle." Moreover one of the erased lines fits quite neatly into the inverted map, replacing the line Betty produced with conscious intervention. In brief: win two, lose three. (My version, incidentally, shows the Sun at the end of an "exploratory" not a "trade" route—surely a plus.)

A more savage objection has been raised by Robert Sheaffer, who has brought to public attention another contender, produced after much labor by Charles W. Atterberg (map 4). The Atterberg attempt looks still more like Betty's original than does the Fish version, and identifies not fifteen but twenty-five of the twenty-six stars. Bearing Kane's strictures in mind, this is not necessarily an advantage—it seems too good to be true, given the doubtful nature of hypnotic recall—but it is rather startling.

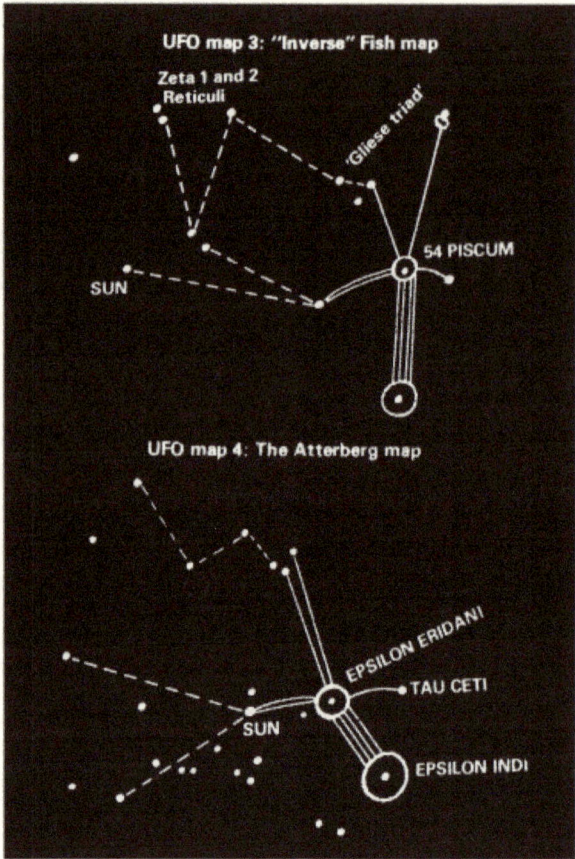

UFO map 3: "Inverse" Fish map

Zeta 1 and 2 Reticuli

'Gliese triad'

54 PISCUM

SUN

UFO map 4: The Atterberg map

EPSILON ERIDANI

TAU CETI

SUN

EPSILON INDI

Atterberg began by considering *all* the stars in the Sun's vicinity, rather than restricting himself, as Fish had, to those with a high likelihood of carbon based planetary life. Incredibly, even so, on his map "of the eleven stars supposedly visited by the aliens (not counting the Sun), seven of them are listed in Stephen H. Dole's Rand Corporation study...as stars 'that could have habitable planets'." Not a bad percentage for stars selected at random from the solar neighborhood.

"Even more surprising," Sheaffer adds, "...the three stars that form the heart of the Atterberg map—Epsilon Eridani, Epsilon Indi and Tau Ceti—and which are connected by lines supposedly representing the major 'trade routes' of the ufonauts, have been described by Dr. Carl Sagan as 'the three nearest stars of potential biological interest'."

It is important to note that Sheaffer is not championing Atterberg over Fish, but arguing that zealous aficionados can always find apparent sense in random noise.

There are, so far as I can see, no neat conclusions to be drawn from the Hill star map saga. Ben Bova, editor of the magazine *Analog,* observed, "If the Hill/Fish map can be shown to be nothing more than a random coincidence, then the case for UFOs as alien visitors suffers another setback. If the map holds up, the UFO believers will gain at least one slightly skeptical adherent: me. And we'd better tune our radio telescopes to the vicinity of Zeta Reticuli." To which we might now add: "and 54 Piscum...and Epsilon Eridani...and...."

Several years ago a young Scottish amateur astronomer, Duncan Lunan, tried plotting into graphic form some anomalous radio echoes recorded in 1927-8, and thought he'd hit the jackpot with a time-shifted star map of the constellation Bootis, presumably from a probe dormant in Earth orbit for the past 13,000 years. It was a nice try, made in good faith, and *New Scientist* was sufficiently impressed by the legitimacy of his basic endeavor to print his retraction when the whole thing fell through. Maybe *Astronomy* will do the same for Marjorie Fish and Charles Atterberg.

Or maybe not. In which case all our think-tank scenarios, good times and doomsayers will go out the window. Admit it... don't you secretly *hope* so?

VI.

Not long ago, an Australian public intellectual named Phillip Adams had a nasty shock. He was viewing Spielberg's *Close Encounters of the Third Kind.* In the midst of explosions of color, Adams found that he was surrounded by a nest of metaphysical deviants.

It was just awful. A well-dressed woman in the audience cried out in recognition at a commonly reported Unidentified Flying Object. Worse, the film's technical adviser was Dr. J. Allen Hynek, who believes in UFOs. "I am uncertain," Adams commented, "as to his attitude to Father Christmas and the Tooth Fairy."

It was a telling analogy. Children believe in those myths for two reasons. First, inexplicable presents and gifts of money are observed, and confirmed by other witnesses. Then reliable authorities (parents and TV advertisers) explain these unusual events in the well-known fictitious manner. Just so, thousands of ordinary people have reported inexplicable aerial phenomena. Authorities have then accounted for these sightings by reference to weather balloons, the planet Venus and hysteria. For the hard-core of anomalous sightings, those explanations have all the force and value of a parent's appeal to Santa and the Tooth Fairy.

Is there anything to UFOs? Many intelligent people, I suppose, would go along with Phillip Adams. Poor old Prof. Hynek concludes after twenty years as the principal scientific advisor to Project Blue Book that the phenomenon is an authentic challenge to consensus verities, so Adams dismisses Hynek, *on that basis alone*, as "St. Peter to the [UFO] movement." This mock-theological rhetoric forecloses on rational discussion. Hynek cites evidence, not faith.

Of course, obsessive UFO believers are an irritating distraction. They cavort through the data with the glad hope of salvation gleaming in their eyes. To the open-minded, what's lacking is a cogent hypothesis or two. Puzzling data lacking a harness of hypotheses are an embarrassment to any scientific discipline. Indeed, the need for an acceptable intellectual home for these reports can be so painful to the trained mind that grand schemes, testable or otherwise, flap like bats in the dark hours of the night.

The sad and curious case of Captain Bruce L. Cathie is a fascinating cautionary tale against these dangers. Cathie is no fly-by-night mountebank. A Boeing 737 captain working for the National Airways Corporation of New Zealand, he is exactly the trained, straight observer beloved by responsible UFO researchers. Cathie's notoriety in the UFO field is not, however, occasioned by his several sightings of inexplicable aerial objects.

You see, ten years Capt. Cathie revealed that he had breached the mystery of the saucers. The UFOs were here to repair an ancient global "magnetic grid" functioning on "harmonic" principles. In his third book, the stakes have escalated. Unblushingly, he tells us that he now has "a harmonic unified field equation expressed in terms of light—or pure electromagnetic waveform—the key to the universe, the whole of existence."

Underlying this captivating discovery were quite sensible attempts by Cathie and others to reduce the messy UFO data to some geographical and temporal order.

To date, the most impressive published work of this kind has been done by NASA computer specialist Dr. Jacques Vallee, and certain French colleagues. Prof. Hynek claims to have gone further, but declines to announce his findings for fear of generating spurious reports in line with his predictions. Statistical computer studies have yielded some important broad generalizations supporting the reality of artificial, craft-like UFOs.

Is the UFO hysteria the result of mass-media provocation alone? Is the phenomenon a kind of collective psychosis generated by the pressures of big-city living? Vallee intensively studied "close contact" reports from France, and his figures clearly implied that the phenomenon behind the sightings was *craft*: not ball-lightning, not high-flying birds, not malfunctioning radar equipment. Within a broader compass, he found many regularities of "flight characteristics," peak diurnal activity, and so on.

More recently, Dr. Claude Poher director of the French National Center for Space Studies, scrutinized 1000 world-wide cases selected from a batch of 35,000 reports, and he argues that the results conclusively demonstrate the alien reality of UFOs. The French have a talent for this sort of work. Two decades ago, Aimé Michel proposed a most haunting regularity in certain batches of UFO reports.. When independent sightings for a given day were plotted on a map, they seemed to fall on a series of straight lines, several lines intersecting. The alignments were not stable; they altered drastically from day to day. Nor could they be interpreted as flight-paths (whether of meteors or spacecraft) since the sightings along a given line were not arrayed chronologically.

Subsequently, Michel suggested extension of such "local" alignments to incorporate sightings across the world. His hypothesis, plausibly, was that they would fall on great circles, that is, curves bisecting the Earth's sphere.

Michel's attempts came under immediate attack. How many people viewing all aircraft, let alone an unidentified aerial object, can offer reliable estimates of its distance and height?

Dr. Vallee set out to test the null hypothesis. If truly random dots were positioned on a map of France, how many lines would be needed to join them up? Would asterisk-shaped constellations appear by chance, like those which had excited Michel? They did. The computer simulation wrecked Michel's scheme. Moreover, attempts to tease out world-wide alignments were highly discouraging. It was all a fluke, a false lead.

§

The tortuous path by which Captain Cathie also progressed from gridding UFO reports on a map, to his revelation that the Earth is enmeshed in an ancient network of magnetic devices, is retraced in his book *The Pulse of the Universe: Harmonic 288.* As an exercise in obsessive-compulsive psychology, rational expectations deforming under the relentless desire to find meaningful, portentous patterns in the UFO data, the book is fascinating. It is also very funny, if you can stop yourself from screaming with rage and frustration.

Not surprisingly, the Pyramids, Stonehenge, Krakatau, the Siberian meteorite of 1908, and Australian aboriginal stone patterns in the Outback all possess mathematical affinities (measured in Cathie's own "new feet" and "new seconds,") with Cathie's "harmonic grid." Like compulsive brick-counters, occult syncretists *can't stop.*

A minor by-product of Cathie's discovery (taken up, alas, by some of the more baroque enthusiasts for leaving uranium in the ground) is that textbook accounts of nuclear energy are in error. Nuclear fission and fusion, it seems, are dependent on the "harmonics" of the magnetic grid, and can only take place at certain times. The politics of nuclear retaliation to a first strike is therefore a massive hoax.

Cathie's work epitomizes the split between the new Two Cultures, between the staid technologists of squalor and the bright, deracinated magicians of apocalypse. Cathie has sold an extraordinary 30,000 copies of his books, in hard cover, mostly in Australia and New Zealand. His inane ideas are influencing a lot of people.

His books exemplify splendidly the results of approaching the (authentically puzzling) occult with an unstable tool kit of dogged imagination and rudimentary scientific methods. If we can judge by his continued employment as a pilot, Cathie's technical skills have not been impaired by his remarkable adventures. Yet the most astonishing facet of his magnetic grid hypothesis is precisely the nature of his mathematics. The graphs of UFO sightings that started him on the trail might or might not be legitimate. But the manipulation of numbers that created the "magnetic grid" is preposterous. Consider just these cases:

"In harmonic calculations of this kind decimal points as well as zeroes to the right of the figure can be ignored; so it could be said that the square root of 695 was 2636." But of course the square root of a whole number must be smaller than itself.

"1703—this is the four-figure harmonic of 170,300,000,000, which is the expression in cubic minutes of arc of the *mass* or *volume* of the planet Earth and its surrounding atmosphere." (My italics.) In short, a cubic foot of lead has the same mass, according to Cathie, as a cubic foot of feathers.

"The speed of light reciprocal harmonic of 695 is incorporated in a harmonic of 2695.... It appears that the factor 2 preceding the 695 serves to harmonically double [695]...." That is, for Cathie, two times 695 equals 2695.

The highpoint comes with Cathie's disclosure of a unified field equation—a formulation for which Einstein famously spent his last years looking. Cathie's algebra is gibberish. For example: confronted by the expression $\sqrt{(4E+1)/4}$, he tidies it up into $\sqrt{E} + \frac{1}{4}$. And this is the least of his blunders.

He tells us, though, that "an excellent mathematician... checked the equation" and found it good, which suggests that someone was rather unkindly pulling the luckless Captain's leg.

It is important to stress that Cathie's notions did not spring fully armed from an empty forehead; nor is his voice that of one crying in the wilderness. His laughable model of "harmonic nuclear physics" has striking overtones of ideas promulgated in the inner sanctums of Rosicrucianism. And he is speaking to a comparatively large audience not merely willing to pay for his books but prepared to slog through his pages of murky pseudo-mathematics.

If it is difficult to be sympathetic to Cathie, the sad image of a man wasting endless years in the laborious adumbration of the preposterous must cause a pang in even the hardest heart.

WEIRD SHIT: LOOKING BACK FROM NOW

The Mind Revolution

At the start of the 1970s, Freudian accounts of the mind were already being forked onto the trash heap, but nobody was quite sure what sort of thing might replace them. Gruesome memories of the literally mindless behaviorism of John Watson and B. F. Skinner loomed as frightful warnings but often enough went unheeded by the experts in "rats and stats." Mental processes were still ignored or abstracted away by the new computer-modeled disciplines of cognitive science. But other unprecedented instruments and probes were coming to the rescue.

The MRI or magnetic resonance image scanner (originally called "nuclear magnetic imaging" until that term frightened everyone who supposed their heads would be fried, although no X-rays or other ionizing radiation were used) came into labs and research hospitals in the late 1970s. More subtle variants such as fMRI (functional magnetic resonance imaging), which tracks blood flow changes in the brain every few seconds, didn't arrive until the '90s. Studies of neurotransmitters and interactive hormones grew ever more sophisticated, although they still remain fairly crude. The case presented in my 1973 article reminds us how this emerging science of the mind could even then be seen dimly on the horizon.

"Dimly" is probably the operative word. For example, those experiments on transferring and inducing scotophobia (fear of the dark) remain somewhat dubious. Ungar died in the mid-1980s, but not until he had isolated the peptide, scotophobin, he had transferred in his experiments. Methods for direct human/computer linkage are only now becoming reliable, in a primitive way. Drugs for memory enhancement are known, but their status remains borderline. Sexual enhancement does not use wires embedded in the brain but drugs such as sildenafil (on the market as Viagra since 1998), and emerging pharmaceuticals designed for women. So these disruptive innovations were not "five, 10, perhaps 20 years" away in 1973, but more like 25-40 years. Still, by the standards of history, these leaps are almost instantaneous—and seem to be accelerating.

My article mentioned potential risks with these brain technologies, but I was unaware of some creepy realities. Dr. Robert G. Heath did more than surgically implant therapeutic devices; he reportedly took part in secret CIA experiments using LSD and bulbocapnine, often on black prisoners, information revealed in August 1977 in the *New York Times*. One has to wonder, in the age of Abu Ghraib, what equivalent new brain science atrocities are being cooked up as part of the twenty-first century "War on Terror."

Meanwhile, though, keeping pace with the continuing breakthroughs in knowledge and paradigm (long a favorite word among philosophers of science and others who wish they were) was a rising surge of notions from the fringe. In recent years, they have reached their apogee in the American radio program Coast to Coast, with a nightly audience of tens of millions, where *soi disant* authorities passionately divulge the latest news about Bigfoot and crimson-eyed Mothman, past life regression, crystal skulls with uncanny energy fields, sunken Atlantis, the healing power of intention, reptilian aliens and grays who abduct people from their cars and beds and perform ghastly indecencies on them, and do worse still to their mutilated cattle, Mayan calendars and the end of the world in 2012, prophets of financial woe and ecological collapse, zero point fields, climate change skeptics, purported psychic remote viewers who keep getting it wrong, students of the Pyramids and of ancient wisdom able to levitate great blocks of stone with a chant and a musical note, chemtrails, crop circles, Truther 9/11 conspiracy advocates, and (on one occasion) me. Weird fellow travelers, indeed: the true offspring, in a demented and sometimes genuinely challenging way, of the acid-stoned and politically oppositional '60s. Bring it on, but keep your powder dry!

Weird Shit

As I mentioned in the Introduction, in the late 1970s I briefly wrote a column for the weekly Australian alternative newspaper, *Nation Review*—a.k.a. *The Ferret,* "lean and nosy," as the masthead had it—under the deliberately aggressive heading "Weird Shit." If you were around in the 1970s, you'll recall that these were the days of Hunter S. Thompson's *Fear and Loathing*, of *The Fabulous Furry Freak Brothers* comic, of R. Crumb's voluptuous Jailbait of the Month, Honeybunch Kaminsky, and his small beaten-down sexually obsessed men with huge "keep on truckin'" clodhoppers, of the Mothers of Invention chanting William Blake lyrics about mystic sunflowers, of aliens with gigantic pincers landing in Pascagoula, Mississippi, and terrifying a couple of fishermen, of Richard Nixon's humiliated resignation. Weirdness was everywhere, and not only among the speed freaks and acid droppers. Most of this weird shit seemed certain to be absolute nonsense, delirium, stupidity, prankishness. I decided to make fun of that, more in ridicule than in anger.

I leave my musings to stand on their own merits, as a reflection of a puzzled habitué of the weird looking about him with a certain admiration at the craziness. What of the remainder, though? Don't we now know that the US government spent tens of millions of dollars over two decades looking into extrasensory perception and prophecy (otherwise known in the trade as remote viewing and precognition), with repeated operational taskings conducted for many years by trained military experts? Why, yes, we do know that, despite the guffaws and sniggering. You can find a lot more about it in my book *Outside the Gates of Science.*

Depressingly, if inevitably, Captain Cathie's innumerate numerology has now given birth to an online-marketed "Gridpoint Atlas" that maps his ancient power grid onto Google Earth. But some UFO sightings seemed absurdly believable, after all due allowance was made for rational factors and throat-clearing, and yet.... My article cited a newspaper report of a remarkable 1978 close-up UFO sighting by "former USAF sergeant, Duane B. Piciani." Alas, Google doesn't recognize him, thirty-two years later. Nor Picciani, which it suggests as an alternative. Total yellow journalism bogosity? It seems likely, in that case. Then there are simple errors, or even complex errors of perception by expert witnesses. Surely UFOs have been debunked long ago? Not so fast. Whatever the phenomenon is, it keeps on keeping on, and it looks as if the long 70 year cover-up by various governments finally might be cracking open. In May, 2010, the French GEIPAN group (Study and Information Group on Aerospace Unidentified Phenomena) released a quasi-official preliminary report endorsing the reality of UFOs and their possible extraterrestrial origin.

It was equally surprising in August 2010 to find a notable string theorist and broadcaster, Professor Michio Kaku, endorsing Leslie Kean's *UFOs: Generals, Pilots and Government Officials Go On the Record.* Dr. Kaku agreed that the 5% of reports which resisted conventional explanation might well be some kind of craft from a culture thousands or millions of years in advance of our own. This is an opinion you might have heard often enough in the 1950s and 1960s, but hardly from notable university professors with a public platform. Still, why take the reports in Ms. Kean's book any more seriously? Kaku noted: "We're talking about generals, we're talking about air force pilots, we're talking about governors of states, that claim, 'Hey, this is beyond our understanding of the laws of physics.'"

Maybe so (although state governors are perhaps not the ideal assessors of advanced physics). Interesting times, then, even more interesting than we might have anticipated, back there in the quondam-present that became the past, looking blurrily into an indistinct future that is now today, crisp and clear except where pests try hard to obfuscate the windscreen, and any minute now will be yesterday, again.

PART SIX: LIFE BEFORE WIKI

READING THE
BRITANNICA (1985)

In his memoir *Wisdom, Madness, and Folly*, the controversial psychiatrist R. D. Laing told how he learned to read rather early, and of the hauntingly Socratic consequence of this skill:

> A lot of my time was spent absorbing two sets, several volumes each, of an illustrated history of the world, and of an illustrated history of world literature. By the time I went to school I was beginning to read the texts of these encyclopedias. Parts of literature and history are two subjects I've always felt I've always known but largely forgotten. Finding out about these things always felt as though I was simply refreshing my memory.

Few of us are as smart as Ronald Laing, but many (that modest constituency who actually *enjoy* reading books) do seem to treasure the image of some fat, battered volume, usually at least a generation out of date, choked with the stuff of wonder and expectation: gigantic gleaming locomotives, strange animals nothing at all like pussy cats or puppy dogs; atoms and bacteria too small for the naked eye; or mysteries so distant only the telescope's lens might reveal their shape—the rings of Saturn, say, or a spiral galaxy like flour strewn on Mother's bench top.

I relish such memories, though I can't put a name to the multi-volume set, owned by an elderly neighbor of my grandparents, which I was permitted to borrow, just one book at a time, during visits.

When I was eleven or so, a friend of my toolmaker father made the lucrative move to selling, approaching all his mates with the Newnes encyclopedia. Ten volumes for thirty-nine pounds, and an eight-guinea dictionary, the thickest book I'd ever seen not excluding the *American Woman's Cook Book*, thrown in at a bargain six pounds. There was no high pressure; my parents were happy to buy the lot, and today one of my brothers has it still on his own shelves.

When the row of red leatherette-bound books duly arrived, though, it was immediately (and justifiably) stockaded behind a fence of prohibitions and warnings. The glamour quickly wore off anyway, and though I delved into the things for homework, I never developed any real love for the Newnes.

I must have seen the *Encyclopaedia Britannica* in the municipal library. Great heavy volumes in embossed leather, imposing and terrible. But as a kid I wasn't much interested in anything I couldn't borrow. What would it have been like, living in a household that owned a set? Surely one's parents would have felt impelled to place it out of reach, which is exactly what you must not do with knowledge, messy fingers and torn pages or not. Knowledge has to open its arms to you. Ideally it should slouch against the wall with a roguish gleam in its eye, whistling slightly out of tune.

By the time I got to university in the early sixties I had picked up a vague distrust of encyclopedias. They were vulgar (thought this kid from the rough, working-class suburb of Reservoir, then near Melbourne's outer boundaries). Certainly their reputation wasn't advanced by the night I arrived home at two a.m. to find my exhausted parents trying to evict a Britannica salesman who'd started his spiel five hours before. A fellow St. Gabriel's parishioner, this worthy labored through an entire memorized routine, replete with punishing and unanswerable thrusts: Your kids would be hard pressed to get through Matriculation without a set of the Britannica in the home, and they'd certainly never make it through University. I listened to this claim with some astonishment.

When at last he could no longer deny the galling fact that he'd wasted his time and theirs, that he wasn't going to unload his 200 pounds' worth of truths, he caved in and got them to sign a chit to prove to head office that he'd strutted his stuff. No commission, but a pittance for trying. So you can see, perhaps, why I took the Britannica to be pretty *déclassé*—homogenized knowledge for the plebs. I read Isaac Asimov instead.

Of course, twenty years earlier, Isaac Asimov hadn't had that option.

> For years I had wanted an *Encyclopaedia Britannica* and finally my father managed to scrape together the money to buy a copy, and on March 11 [1942] it arrived. I began a project of reading it from cover to cover—not every word, to be sure, but lots of them, and at least I looked at every entry.

Asimov was twenty-two at this time, America had entered the war, and the recent graduate was about to take up war-related work as a civilian chemist in the Navy Yard. He left home on May 13, 1942.

> I was in the third volume when I left, and my last words as I left were, pointing to the encyclopedia, "Gee, now I'll never know how it came out."

A smartass as well as a damned know-it-all. But notice: when the call of duty snatched him away, he was already into Volume Three...a little more than two months after the set had arrived! A volume a month! Perhaps this is the clue any budding know-it-all needs for a life of success.

At the end of the seventies I did some writing for a children's encyclopedia. Quite a lot of this was recycled from the material so richly set out in the Britannica—not plagiarized, I hasten to affirm, but it would be absurd not to acknowledge a major debt. Day after day I found myself up to my elbows, at the local library, in everything you could possibly wish to know about kaolin, or dynamos, or Leonardo da Vinci, or light, or machines guns.

I began to wonder what it would be like to have a set in the house.

Where would you keep it? In the study? (But in my case that was at the bottom of a narrow spiral staircase. You couldn't really rush up and down the stairs every time you felt like checking a minor fact, like the location of Indonesia.) In the living room? Too showy, surely, too...uncool...if not uncouth. The ideal place, to be honest, was the bathroom—shelved between the toilet and the bath, so you could pluck a volume at random as you sat and strained, instead of propping a magazine or paperback on your knee, or flip idly through topics you'd always meant to learn more about while soaking in the tub. No, that was unthinkable. Lèse-majesté, for one thing; too heavy and unwieldy, for another. You'd never forgive yourself if you dropped volume nineteen of the new edition Macropaedia (EXCRETION to GEOMETRY) into the porcelain.

I'm a book reviewer. In 1979, I decided to review a set—put it through the equivalent of an honest, grueling road test. Six years later a better analogy would be a home computer evaluation, but in 1979 the idea that the ordinary householder might afford such a thing would have been laughable. This should remind you of the appalling change of pace in technology and daily life. Indeed, the 1979 set of Britannica I obtained for my road test did not contain an entry on "microprocessor," though the 1985 version does.

Well, you can't rush these things. I decided I needed to use it (or neglect it, if that's how things fell out) for at least five years. During that time, of course, some of the information would date—but this was precisely the kind of thing I was looking for.

How much of what we wish to know is current, the stuff of up-to-the-minute journalism? In 1985 or 1986, I mused, how much value would there be in owning a huge collection of articles written at the start of the seventies and updated somewhat patchily to 1979 standards?

True, Britannica supplied yearbooks (for a fee), including one specially concerned with "Science and the Future"—but those had the drawback, which an integrated encyclopedia is supposed to remedy, of standing alone. (Not quite. Each index referred back to the last two volumes as well. Still.) The 1979 Micropaedia index would not tell you useful things about the Ayatollah Khomeini, whose hour was not quite come, though his biography in the 1980 Book of the Year certainly did. (Of course, you might not wish to keep buying an extra volume each year at $30 a throw....) The 1985 edition gives him almost an entire Micropaedia column.

Last year, the thirty-volume "Britannica-3" set in brown vinyl binding would have cost you $1,328. For Heirloom binding, you paid an extra $70. This year, a major upgrading of the Britannica has been released, in which some of the radical innovations of the fifteenth edition are rescinded and some extra features appear.

One of the big differences introduced in the changeover from the "traditional" 14th edition was the relocation of many small entries into the index, which was thus expanded by a factor of five into ten substantial, illustrated volumes—the Micropaedia. Teachers, it seems, disapproved of the loss of the separate index. There were other problems, too, so Britannica spent an extra $24 million in reorganizing, revising and generally revamping the once-ballyhooed 1973 framework. A two-volume index is again part of the set.

Today's [Australian] price is $1,478 ($1,548 with the leather coat). A further price rise—attributable to the slump in the Australian dollar—is due before Christmas.

What do you get for your fifteen hundred dollars?

My 1979 review set comprised three unequal parts. (We'll come back to the upgraded version.) The whole caboodle added up to forty-two million words provided by more than 4,000 specialist contributors, checked by an advisory staff of some 200, and put together and probably rewritten by hundreds of staff editors.

The first part was the ten-volume alphabetically-arranged Micropaedia, or composite Ready Reference and Index, full of nifty little articles, maps, diagrams and photographs, often in color. The lack of a separate index meant you had to hope your thought processes were in tune with the indexer's or you'd risk juggling heavy volumes for minutes on end.

The second part was the nineteen-volume Macropaedia, 4,207 major articles, from AALTO (the post-geometric twentieth century Finnish architect) to ZWINGLI (the only major Protestant reformer of the sixteenth century without a sect to his name), and interspersed with glossy pages of colored illustrations.

Finally, there was a curious volume called the Propaedia, or Outline of Knowledge, meant as a structured guide to all the information in the rest of the set.

The principal revision in the current Britannica, apart from the triumphant return of the General Index, with its 172,400 "entry-points" and 411,500 references, is a further migration of a fair amount of information from the Macropaedia to the Micro Ready Reference books. Now there are seventeen slimline Macro volumes, containing 681 full-scale topical pieces which usefully consolidate articles previously scattered to hell and gone by the alphabet. That still leaves twenty-three million words and 8,000 illustrations.

Thousands of the briefer Macro entries, complete with bibliographies, have moved to the Micro (now with twelve volumes, for a total of eighteen million words), with the previous limit of some 750 words per reference abandoned. Many quick references have gone up to 1,500 words, a decent length in my view; some run as high as 3,000 words. Both Aalto and Zwingli rest these days in the Micro; ACCOUNTING now begins the Macropaedia, which closes with ZOROASTRIANISM, arguably a related discipline.

Britannica wish us to perceive their 1985 World Data Annual as an integral component of the new style. The statistical addenda from the Micro has gone here, all 352 data-jammed pages of it. Good thinking. Why structure-in a heap of facts which go out the window every twelve months? To flesh this stuff out, the Book of the Year is included, an America-focused "year in review" and some Reader's Digest style features on important background issues. Of course we are meant to buy one each year, a neat regular marketing trick.

The Propaedia is essentially unchanged, though all page references have been banished to the General Index and a splendid series of anatomical transparencies has been slipped in. With commendable good sense, these do not shrink from showing the naughty bits of each sex.

In its original format, one was led to believe that the Propaedia allowed an autodidact to trace a path from the simplest starting points through to a comprehensive grasp of any field. Sadly, this was balderdash—not necessarily in principle, but certain in practice—and still is.

Here's an example of what used to be suggested for the home student who wanted to bone up on, say, KINSHIP. (I'm drawing on my 1979 set in most of what follows, to retain the authentic flavor of my six-year live-in relationship with the Britannica.)

The major Macropaedia article on KINSHIP was a comprehensive bit of work by Jackie Barnes, Professor of Sociology at Cambridge and a former Professor of Anthropology at the Australian National University. His article was about 9,000 words long, but if you wished to pursue the Propaedia's guide to total education it was just the first step in your trek.

Barnes's article was broken into seven sub-headings, from "Kinship systems: their functions and types," to "Kinship and theories of social evolution: kinship as an evolving social institution." To keep what follows bearable, here's your suggested 1979 road-map to the last-mentioned sub-topic only:

You are instructed to start with three-quarters of the last page of Professor Barnes's reference in volume ten. Jump from there to page 426 of Volume Two, thence to page 1120 of volume three, thence to page 731 of volume five, thence to page 711 of volume fourteen, finishing with three-quarters of page 128 in volume seventeen. Actually, if you're an absolute completist, there's an ancillary list of lesser references to volumes six, eight, another part of eight, thirteen, and seventeen.

This is madness, of course. I think even the editors now admit as much, for the new format directs readers largely to two or three major "alphatopical" entries. Of course, these new consolidated articles have brought together much of the material previously scattered through all nineteen Macro volumes. Still, the Propaedia remains a kind of verbalized computer flow-chart. If the Britannica is ever released on computer disk (as is quite feasible, since it's edited that way) the Propaedia will disappear into the invisible software and do its job nicely without ever implicating us poor devils in its grotesque exertions.

So why do Britannica make such a fuss about this strange component? Well, because the Board of Editors for the fifteenth edition was headed by the University of Chicago's Mortimer J. Adler. You must understand that the Britannica has nothing to do with Britain any longer; much to the horror of devout Anglophiles, it became an American citizen years before Rupert Murdoch realized the advantages.

Mortimer Adler was the Aristotelian philosopher of law responsible for another publishing bonanza, the fifty-four-tome *Great Books of the Western World*—reviewed famously by the scathing polymath Dwight Macdonald in 1952 as "The Book-of-the-Millennium Club." These multifarious works are strung together by a Propaedia-like volume Adler devised entitled the *Syntopicon*, which is meant to access and organize the 102 Great Ideas in the Great Books.

Dr. Adler, you see, like his spiritual mentor Aristotle, is a demon for putting things in categories and bringing stray thoughts to heel. Robert Pirsig's *Zen and the Art of Motorcycle Maintenance* is notable for some less than complimentary remarks aimed at Dr. Adler and his team of Rational Christian educationists at Chicago, who stopped with Aristotle.

Adler's study of evidence, cross-fertilized by a reading of classics of the Western world, resulted in a conviction that human wisdom had advanced relatively little in recent times. He consistently harked back to St. Thomas Aquinas, who had taken Plato and Aristotle and made them part of his medieval synthesis of Greek philosophy and Christian faith. The work of Aquinas and the Greeks, as interpreted by Aquinas, was to Adler the capstone of the Western intellectual heritage. Therefore they provided a measuring rod for anyone seeking the good books.

It would be going a little too far to suggest that Adler's fifteenth edition of the Britannica is a modernized, face-lifted version of a medieval monk's *Summa Contra Gentiles*—but it wouldn't be going all that far. Despite the association in the back of our minds with slick salesmen, Britannica is clearly put together with a conservative moralist's fervor.

"When the Eleventh Edition was published in 1910 and 1911," observes the latest Editorial Report, "the Victorians' world seemed secure and subject to capture" by encyclopedists. By contrast, the 1985 edition "must not be edited with a national view. In a world under nuclear arms and ecological stress, the easy judgments and parochial self-confidence of another day no longer serve."

Nice work if you can get it. Yet it's strikingly revealing—in a document where the section on NUCLEAR FUSION is by Lev Artsimovitch, late Head of the Plasma Physics Division in the Kurchatov Institute of Atomic Energy in Moscow—that the major article on MARXISM should have been provided by the Reverend Henri Chambre, of the Society of Jesus.

This spirit of ecumenism doesn't operate in reverse, alas: the bumper article on CHRISTIANITY is by a convocation of ecclesiastics and church historians, including Archbishop Iakovos, Linwood Fredericksen of Rotary International, and the Rev. Massey H. Shepherd, Jr, of (naturally) Berkeley, California.

§

Even if you knew nothing of this background, it'd be clear from the outset that Adler's ambitions go beyond any mere compendium of data. His Editor from 1964 to 1975, a man with the wonderfully Tolstoyan name Warren Preece, detailed three ways an encyclopedia might be used:

> First, there are occasions on which a reader desires to look something up...the size of the whale, the feeding habits of the robin, the achievements of Rudolf Virchow...
>
> Second, ...he may...be more interested in the causes of the war in Vietnam than in the casualty statistics of the Tet offensives...; he may want to know how interest rates can be used to control the volume of currency in circulation rather than how to define compound interest...
>
> Third, users may on occasion seek that genuine understanding that in itself somehow defines what the world means by the word "education." On such occasions, his interest is in neither the size of the whale nor the taxonomic characteristics of the family to which the lion belongs, but in an insight into what has been known and conjectured about the whole sweep of life on Earth...an understanding of the objects of studies of all the sciences as they relate to something grander than the disciplines themselves.

Heroic stuff. The *Encyclopaedia Britannica* is engaged in nothing less than a crusade to civilize us all by turning the tools of mass production to the service of the human spirit, as understood in the light of St. Thomas Aquinas and his rational but pious Greek chums.

By the way, if you've never heard of Rudolph Virchow, here's some of what the Macropaedia says:

> A German pathologist, statesman and anthropologist, Rudolph Virchow pioneered the modern concept of pathological processes by his application of the cell theory to explain the effects of disease in the organs and tissues of the body. He emphasized that diseases arose primarily, not in the organs or tissues in general, but in their individual cells. Moreover, in line with his liberal political views, he held that the body is a free state of equal individuals (its cells). He was active in the reform of medical education and contributed to the development of anthropology as a modern science.

The sub-text is not entirely without interest. (The entry was not written by Ayn Rand, in case you were wondering.)

And the cause of the Vietnam war? The 1979 account given in VIETNAM, HISTORY OF (by journalist Joseph Buttinger) is by no means predictable to those who might expect establishment forelock-tugging from the Britannica:

> The French long ignored the real political cause of the war—the desire of the entire people, including the anti-Communist leaders, to achieve unity and independence for their country.

After the defeat of the French,

> Except for some local revolts in 1956 against a brutally conducted campaign to collectivize agriculture, and for some periods of food shortages, no serious social or political obstacles interfered with the north's steady economic progress between 1955 and 1965.

By contrast, the south remained chaotic. Ultimately, we read,

> Diem used totalitarian propaganda methods together with police and army terror... Buddhists were alienated

by a policy of preference toward Roman Catholics; the intellectual elite was embittered by the denial of civil liberties and an ever harsher persecution of all critics, even those who were prominent anti-Communists... Elections were conducted in a manner reminiscent of totalitarian states... These conditions favored a Communist-led insurrection, which started in 1957, a year after Diem had refused to hold the all-Vietnamese elections called for by the Geneva Agreement.

In the end,

> ...years of intensive bombing in the north and of fighting in the south with the massive modern equipment America was able to supply had devastated vast regions of Vietnam, both north and south, but seemed unable to weaken the enemy's will and strength.

Buttinger's frank assessment, now part of SOUTHEAST ASIA, MAINLAND, has been somewhat muffled in the 1985 version. And in the Micropaedia entry on VIETNAM WAR, Diem's methods have become "authoritarian" rather than "totalitarian," as befits a volume dedicated to Ronald Reagan. Still, the Britannica's treatment remains overall refreshingly candid, clear-eyed and not without its moral undertone, though hardly the note one might have feared.

A high moral tone (though one suspects a whiff of irony) frequently steals into Anthony Burgess's splendid essay on the NOVEL, now swallowed up as part of THE ART OF LITERATURE:

> ...the term novel still, in some quarters, carries overtones of lightness and frivolity. And it is possible to descry a tendency to triviality in the form itself. The ode or symphony seems to possess an inner mechanism that protects it from aesthetic or moral corruption, but

the novel can descend to shameful commercial depths of sentimentality or pornography.

How awful. This is serious business, folks. Still, we come to understand that the crusty Tory rhetorician knows whereof he speaks, more than can be said for non-creative critics:

For even the most experienced novelist, each new work represents a struggle with the unconquerable task of reconciling all-inclusion with self-exclusion.

All-inclusion is, of course, something every encyclopedia must aim at, despite the bitter understanding that it's utterly impossible. One way to handle this problem is for each expert to emphasize the issues and authorities with absolute centrality in his or her topic. Consider the long entry on PSYCHOSES (now included, along with essays on "Neuroses" and "Concepts of Psychiatric Treatment" under MENTAL DISORDERS). Writing about madness is, as Laing and others have made plain, always a political act. We usually declare people mad not just because they are dreadfully unhappy, but because they upset the rest of us. So any attempt to reduce this labeling to a scientific taxonomy, to a theory of madness and its cures, raises issues of interest. Who's saying this? Why are they saying it?

But the Britannica article caused me to ask that question for a different reason, as I read about the "predominantly psychological theories" of Emil Kraepelin (nine lines of summary text), Freud (fourteen lines), Jung (eight lines), Harry Stack Sullivan (nine lines), and Silvano Arieti (twenty-one lines).

Silvano who?

Well, the Britannica told me that Arieti, an Italian-American psychiatrist born on June 28, 1914, believes that while in the first three stages of madness the developing psychotic responds to an unhealthy environment in ways which further distort and magnify the underlying stress, by the fourth stage he or she actually starts thinking in a strange way: "The patient follows a particular way of thinking, called palaeologic, which is not reconcilable with Aristotelian logic." Good old Aristotle once more. As I turned the pages, this fellow Arieti kept cropping up in longer and longer passages. A modern genius, evidently. I should not be unkind. What he says sounds reasonable enough; alternative views are given a bit of a run for their money; and I'm assured by those in the game that Arieti is indeed a psychiatrist of considerable stature. For all that, I'm bound to say I wasn't entirely taken by surprise when the identifying initials at the end of the article revealed it to be penned by none other than S. Ar.

Speaking of the mysteries of the mind and its explorers: one is accustomed to being told (usually by psychoanalysts) of the unexampled brilliance of Sigmund Freud's retinue. The 1979 Britannica agreed so enthusiastically with this estimate that I learned of Ernest Jones (psychoanalyst and history of Freudian thought) that he was born in 1897 and obtained his medical degree in 1903. Six years old! Prodigious indeed. That date of birth should be, of course, 1879. The mistake's still there in the 1985 Micro.

On the other hand, the Britannica is a hoard of small joys and pleasures, of unexpected discoveries and bright items to please the jackdaw mind.

I'd never even heard of the independent republic of San Marino (1984 population estimate 22,000 citizens), smallest in the world until the 1968 independence of Nauru, San Marino which perches within Italy at about the same place a garter decoration would ride if Italy were a stocky dancer's leg....

Of course everyone wants to boast about the errors and misprints they've found in the Britannica. The chief hobby of Ford Maddox Ford's celebrated character Christopher Tietjens, I am reminded, was correcting the Britannica. So yes, I've dug some up—but by golly they're few and far between, and most of the 1979 bloopers I found have been corrected.

There are simple literals—the Micropaedia entry on the SEVEN SLEEPERS OF EPHESUS misspelled "legend" as "lengend," which means absolutely nothing except that even so gigantic an enterprise is made by fallible humans with tired eyes. That gremlin's now been ejected, but popped up in another form in the 1985 reference to the literary critic Eric S. Roblein (his name is Rabkin).

A worst pest is this sort of thing: while Britannica tells me a little about Riemann-ChristOFFel tensors, it fails to spare me the horrid shame of pronouncing them "Christo-FELL." Other less expensive encyclopedias do provide pronunciation keys. This omission is one of my major criticisms of the thing as a learning tool.

And there are important blunders—the 1979 Micro entry on "synthetic division" was badly wrong about polynomials of degree n, giving "a0xn + a1xn-1 + ... + an," where the correct format should begin "$a_0x^n + a_1x^{n-1}$." I worked this out from the context and confirmed it in the Macropaedia article on ALGEBRA, ELEMENTARY AND MULTIVARIATE, and I don't suppose too many mathematicians will be thrown into confusion by finding the wrong formula. But of course the ambition of Britannica is to get it right (as they've now done in this case)—to be a repository of human knowledge and a guide to the self-taught.

Then again, material palpably dated by fresh research tends to be chucked out entirely. Separate entries on the Sun and planets have been merged into a powerful and comprehensive Macro article, SOLAR SYSTEM, with post-Voyager space craft details correct to about 1980 and reading guides up to 1982. It would be hard to do better than that. A comparison between the 1979 treatment of the planet Mercury, shadowy penciled guesses at topography and all, and the 1985 full frontal flyby photos, feels like a breathtaking exercise in time travel to the future. Micro entries on individual topics and scientists are still more current. High-energy physics, say, is accurate to mid-1984, with experimental evidence of the "top" or sixth quark.

§

Dr. Adler, you'll recall, hoped readers might occasionally be tempted in so deep they'd seek to understand Life Itself. The article in question is by none other than that plosively-enunciating Jeremiah of global nuclear Death, Dr. Carl Sagan. Incidentally, while nuclear winter is too recent a concept to make it into the Britannica proper, it is portrayed colorfully in the 1985 WORLD DATA ANNUAL, along with the "Star Wars" initiative which might well precipitate it.

Sagan's long Macropaedia article on LIFE ranges from the very general question of life's definition—that traditional poser for metaphysical philosophers, now nicely solved by molecular physics and information theory—to its genetics; evolutionary history; the flabbergasting variety of life in Earth's many environments; its extraordinary range of behavior and adaptation.

Besides the senses of sight, hearing, smell, taste and touch, various animals have a wide variety of other senses. We have an inertial orientation system and accelerometer in the cochlear canal of the ear. The water scorpion Nepa has a fathometer sensitive to hydrostatic pressure gradients. Most higher plants have chemically amplified gravity sensors. Fireflies and squids communicate with their own kind by producing time sequences or patterns of light on their bodies.

And so on. One problem here is that not every reader will instantly grasp the meaning of such terms as "inertial," "hydrostatic," or "cochlear." However, the great thing about an encyclopedia, if you have the patience, is that all these concepts are likely to be defined and explained in their own little sections. HYDROSTATICS, for example, used to be described this way:

> A branch of fluid mechanics that considers the properties of liquids at rest and their effects on immersed bodies.

If that was not enough to give you the general idea, you were directed to Macropaedia, where you read about "fluid statics principles." It wouldn't be a very rewarding exercise for the puzzled neophyte, alas:

> By consideration of the fluid forces acting on a small element of fluid, as in Figure 1, with gravity acting in the vertical, or -y direction, equations for rate of change of pressure in the coordinate directions are obtained. The pressure is p at the centre of the element and is assumed to vary continuously in any direction.

I'll spare you the partial differential equations that followed.

Now you can't do any of that, because the entry and its references are gone from the Micropaedia. Instead, the baffled neophyte looks up the General Index and tries to guess where to go among some ten alternatives, none very promising. I don't know which is worse.

A second problem is that Sagan sometimes makes outrageously broad jumps, partly the result, no doubt, of his excessively generous brief:

> Rats that pass through mazes easily can be interbred, as can rats that pass through with difficulty; eventually two populations with inherited characteristics called "maze-smart" and "maze-dumb" are produced.... Similar genetic determinants of behavior exist in man. Possession of a supernumerary Y-chromosome in males is strikingly correlated with aggressive tendencies—which may, however, have been a selective advantage in more primitive societies.

This item of scientific folklore is almost certainly false, being derived from a few badly designed experimental surveys of prisoners in jail. More worrying than the reporting of an error is a general objection: that Sagan is here using a rather simpleminded model in his analysis of human behavior, if he really thinks aggressiveness is a "thing" capable of being passed down like a Mendelian trait.

But these are, in the context of his substantial and wide-ranging article, only cavils. Ask, rather: is Sagan a characteristic contributor to the Encyclopaedia Britannica? For aren't encyclopedias known to be generally boring, dry-as-dust compilations of raw, dull facts—the principal imports and exports of Bulgaria, that kind of thing—unrelieved by the human touch? Surely (despite Burgess) the *Encyclopaedia Britannica* is the last place anyone'd look for humor and wit?

Well, let's turn to that very topic in the Macropaedia. Hmm. Granted, the introductory paragraph would tighten the lips of any hardened cynic.

> ...Humor can be simply defined as a type of stimulation that tends to elicit the laughter reflex.

If that wiped the smile off your face, wait for the next bit:

> Spontaneous laughter is a motor reflex produced by the co-ordinated contraction of 15 facial muscles in a stereotyped pattern and accompanied by altered breathing. Electrical stimulation of the main lifting muscle of the upper lip, the zygomatic major, with currents of varying intensity produces facial expressions ranging from the faint smile through the broad grin to the contortions typical of explosive laughter.

Contain your uproarious mirth. This monstrous paragraph is hardly at all representative of the article, which turns out to have been written by none other than the late Arthur Koestler.

Twenty years ago, this brilliant Hungarian émigré excited all manner of enthusiasm and outrage over his magnum opus *The Act of Creation*, in which Koestler advanced a theory that tried to account in one hit for the essence of art, science and humor. Mystical or artistic experience he puckishly summarized as the

AH...response, science as AHA!, and humor, needless to say, as HAHA! Vividly, this schema catches Koestler's underlying unity, for it's at once cheeky, intellectually stimulating, concise, and droll.

Experts jumped feet first into the fray, finding Koestler's analysis glib, journalistic, nastily reductionist, absurdly holistic, or whatever else they were not personally in favor of that day. I've always been rather attracted by it, and regard Britannica's choice of Koestler as refreshing and courageous. Happily, very little of his article is as mechanical and droning as its lead-in. Consider this charming discussion of tickling.

> Why tickling should produce laughter remained an enigma in all earlier theories of the comic... [A] child will laugh only—and this is the crux of the matter— when it perceives tickling as a mock attack, a caress in mildly aggressive disguise. For the same reason, people laugh only when tickled by others, not when they tickle themselves.

> Experiments at Yale University on babies under one year revealed the not very surprising fact that they laughed 15 times more often when tickled by their mothers than by strangers...for the mock attack must be recognized as being pretence... The rule of the game is "let me be just a little frightened so that I can enjoy the relief."

> Thus the tickler is impersonating an aggressor but is simultaneously known not to be one. This is probably the first situation in life that makes the infant live on two planes at once, a delectable foretaste of being tickled by the horror comic.

What really lifts this out of the dusty realm is Koestler's happy choice of that wonderful word "delectable" for our pleasure in fantasy and horror. Laughter is the bright side of terror. In a volume where we might expect to find only facts and figures, it does us no harm to be reminded of this deep ambiguity.

§

Still, it's a damned sight physically easier to carry a paper-back with you—from room to room, perched on your knee in the toilet, sitting in the bus or plane—than to lug around an *Encyclopaedia Britannica* volume.

It was a real breakthrough the first time I felt like taking a volume back to bed with me when I'd finished my breakfast. The piece I was reading over my muesli was Anthony Burgess's amusing discussion of the NOVEL. In that decision, I was assimilating the massive thing as a book, instead of something cut by a divine force into granite. Burgess's style helped, of course.

For all that, the Britannica remains physically tricky to read, hard to prop up so you can read it while eating a boiled egg and toast. And its monumental form imposes a lofty sense of expec-tation. It started as a series of pamphlets; I wish they'd consider releasing it now as, say, 500 trade paperbacks.

However, we're stuck with its present format. What's it like to use, as a tool for education—in the words of the brochure, "as your private tutor"?

On the largest scale, ASIA has a dramatic and comprehen-sive study of its geography, running across 138 pages—at more than 1,000 words a page, the length of a major book—written by a college of specialists from Moscow, Brussels, California, everywhere, and introduced by Chakravarthi V. Narasimhan, Undersecretary-General of the U.N. Impressively non-chau-vinist.

I find it enchanting to be able to flip open a volume and find a clear map of Berlin, or Moscow, or New York (though only the southern end of Manhattan, oddly enough), and roam in imagination—and for the first time accurately—through streets explored in a hundred books and movies. It certainly helps make sense of Len Deighton spy novels.

And suppose, though you know what you like, you wish to learn something about ART? Nearly a hundred pages of theory is laid out here and there in the Macropaedia, in essays ranging from PHILOSOPHY OF ART (now relocated to PHILOSOPHIES OF THE BRANCHES OF KNOWLEDGE), through CLASSIFICATION, CRITICISM, PRACTICE AND PROFESSION OF (which includes SOCIAL AND ECONOMIC ASPECTS), and STYLE IN.

> The way in which ancient Athenians contrasted the "rational" sound of the stringed cithara and the "irrational" reed-pipe wail of the aulos suggests the distinction between classical and romantic styles that was made in the nineteenth century, and the parodies of the tragic dramatist Euripides by the Athenian comic playwright Aristophanes imply modern conceptions of a personal style.

For the Visual Arts proper, you may turn to Volume Twenty-Five for a huge display of color, ideas, and history in ART OF PAINTING, followed by fifty-seven text pages of HISTORY OF WESTERN PAINTING, illustrated by color plates of the kind children stare at in awed wonder. Together with other long pieces on such topics as HISTORY OF WESTERN SCULPTURE (Vol. 25) and EAST ASIAN ARTS (Vol. 17), there's as much material on everything you ever wanted to know about everything to hang on your wall or goggle at in the Prado as two fat conventional art books. As well, individual greats are detailed under their own names in both Micro and Macropaedias.

§

Have I read all these wonderful articles during the six years they have been perching on my shelves?

By and large, no. But I must instantly qualify that.

Certainly I've consulted these volumes, endlessly. I reach above my desk to where the Britannica sits in the bookshelf I built for it, over the computer, flip out a volume, check a fact, follow a reference to another volume—and find myself seduced, often enough, by something fascinating that's caught my eye.

That's how I chanced on a lovely macabre story about Jeremy Bentham, the Utilitarian philosopher and economist. (As I recall, I got to him somehow by way of Fawn Brodie's exemplary biographical piece on Sir Richard Burton):

> Bentham died in London on June 6, 1832, in his 85th year. In accordance with his directions, his body was dissected in the presence of his friends. The skeleton was then reconstructed, supplied with a wax head to replace the original (which had been mummified), dressed in Bentham's own clothes and set upright in a glass-fronted case. Both this effigy and the head are preserved in University College, London.

I don't believe anyone except Isaac Asimov and the little raggedy man up the back of the public library actually *reads* the Britannica, not like a book, not the way you'd read Barbara Tuchman on the fourteenth century or Paul Davies on quantum mechanics, for the simple intellectual thrill of it.

But that's okay. The Britannica, I've come to realize, is a resource, like Jung's collective unconscious, like an extra lobe to your brain. It sits there quietly waiting for you to access it, and as you get used to the process it gets easier and more taken-for-granted.

I can't stay still at table, I must confess. Sooner or later, usually after the Cabernet Sauvignon, someone raises some point that none of us can settle and I'm off, letting my dinner cool, dashing into the study for a quick delve into the bloody Britannica... Or in the more usual case, reading a novel over the microwaved frozen meat pie, finding some thing or personage or place I've never heard of...up and at it, the way I used to be with a dictionary before I learned all the words off by heart.

If the encyclopedia could be plugged into the back of my head, with access through an electro-neural index, how happy I'd be. I'd have the thing grafted in, take my word for it. Don't laugh. Just because the Britannica is in printed form today, it need not be so in the future.

It takes about 250 million bytes of storage to contain the sum of human knowledge, as represented by the words in Britannica. A quarter of a gigabyte. Suppose we wanted to store that in a computer instead of thirty-two fat volumes. My venerable Kaypro-II computer uses two single-sided diskettes with a combined data capacity of just under 400 kilobytes. A Kaypro 10, which today is just about the same price as my primitive machine three years ago, has hard disk storage built in, which can contain twenty-five times that much information—ten megabytes. That's a lot short of the whole Britannica, admittedly. But wait.

Consider the common or garden laser-read Compact Disk record. A couple of years ago these astonishingly high-fidelity musical recordings were well beyond the financial range of all but demented audio fiends. Today, CD players cost about $500, and the price is still falling. The disks themselves are now about the same price as an old-fashioned LP record, and contain no less than 540 megabytes of information. And the worse-case time to locate and access any particular part of that information (once you've loaded the disk into the machine) is one and a half seconds.

So think of a single mirror-shiny CD disk containing the entire text of the *Encyclopaedia Britannica*, with enough space left over for at least some of the illustrations. (Pictures are data-costly, and there are 24,000 of them, including 1,300 maps.) Use it as a Read-Only Memory mass storage medium for a simple home computer, and you have the ideal Encyclopaedia of Tomorrow. It could cost less in mass production than a home movie videotape.

You'd have an almost instantaneous index, instead of two biggish books to lug off the shelf, an index that would search for any topic you key in, tracing all kinds of possible pathways for you as swiftly as you can respond to the little blinking cursor on the screen.

What's more, a computer could pull out all the relevant bits and pieces from a hundred articles stored throughout the *Encyclopaedia Britannica* and paste them together into a big, custom-tailored piece to fit the information requirements you nominate. In fact, this is just the sort of thing the dreaded Propaedia attempts so unsuccessfully to let you do by hand now.

I'm told that Chicago have decided against retailing a computerized Britannica in the foreseeable future, deeming the 1985 upgraded edition suitable until the twenty-first century, but I wouldn't be at all surprised if the pressure of technology forced them to change their minds.

You see, while CD Random Access might be one way of plugging the Britannica into your computer, there's no reason why it shouldn't be physically built-in. This is what the science writer Nigel Calder has to say in his futurological study *1984 and Beyond*:

> All the words of the *Encyclopaedia Britannica* could be transmitted from New York to Washington DC in one second by the lightwave optical-fiber ecommunications link now in service. The words could also be stored on a wafer of silicon no wider than a saucer.

That's as may be. What about right now? It's a little like the question teasing so many middle-income minds: should I buy a computer now or wait for Utopia?

Yes, you can always go up the road to the public library and use their Britannica set (except at the weekend, and the morning, and at night when they're closed...), just as you can always use public transport when it's running. Public is cheaper and more socially redemptive; you have to wait until it's available, assuming it is; and the truth is, most people have cars and go places in them.

I've found this: having the Britannica around the place is more-ish, like cashews.

The only thing better for comprehensive answers to virtually anything you're likely to wish to know, all in one place, is the Junior Woodchuck's Handbook.

Devotees of Donald Duck comics dream of finding a copy of that fabled vade-mecum. The triplets Huey, Dewey and Louie were never without a copy. It fitted neatly into a back pocket, and was absolutely exhaustive, practical, wise and simple to understand. What a shame it doesn't exist.

Emerging technology might make the Junior Woodchuck's Britannica possible inside ten years, and then all the disadvantages of bulk and eye-testing print will be forgotten. The entire 250 megabytes will be there in the palm of your hand, ready to be consulted on a flat screen (or maybe projected in hologram, as the dashboard instrument panel is already in some flashy new-model cars). With any luck its cover will say, in large friendly letters, like *The Hitch-hiker's Guide to the Galaxy*: DON'T PANIC.

Until that day, here's what I found in my six-year road test:

Fifteen hundred dollars is a lot of money. But you get a lot of bang, as the nuclear weapons-designers say, for your buck.

If you bought the contents of Britannica in individual standard-issue books at the same total price, you'd be getting them for three bucks a piece, fully indexed and cross-referenced. Considering that the usual run of paperbacks these days costs between $5.95 and $19.95, with hardcovers two or three times as much, this is spectacular value.

I haven't stinted myself in pointing out some of the drawbacks, errors and omissions. The *Encyclopaedia Britannica* will not be found at the barricades, it lags behind the calendar, it was built by a team of experts in an age when expertise itself is under question, and the architect was the last of the Aristotelians. But the fact remains that I have looked into it just about every day. Each time I get the 'flu I check hopefully to learn how long I'll be sick, and this is what I read (sadly it never changes):

> Influenza...is generally more frequent during the colder months of the year. The infection is transmitted from person to person through the respiratory tract, by such means as inhalation of infected droplets resulting from coughing and sneezing. The onset...with its characteristic symptoms tends to be sudden, and the acute phase of the infection is ordinarily over in three to four days...
> There is no specific treatment...; drugs such as aspirin and codeine sulphate are used to relieve discomfort and to control the fever.

Britannica hasn't replaced the rest of my non-fiction reading—I still get through a book a week on computers, physics, information theory, genetics, economics, relativity for the grunt in the street, all that stuff. (Which adds up every decade to about the same total wordage as the Britannica.) But those books are now enhanced because I can duck into the study and dig in the Britannica for any detail I'm unsure of. Sometimes it's not there, or at least I haven't been able to track it down. Usually it is, though, and I'm the richer for it.

So the bottom line is this: if you can afford to buy a set, indulge yourself with a clear conscience. How often do you get a chance to buy a spare, pre-programmed brain lobe?

1995 Update: BRITANNICA CD Version 2.0

The following mini-review was written for the Computer Pages of the Australian newspaper *The Age*, and due to a catastrophe of software it appeared in a heinously mangled form. For posterity, I posted it on the internet, with the comment that if EB feel obliged to sue me, they will find very little in of my meager piggy-bank.

A decade ago, I road-tested the *Encyclopaedia Britannica* for the late, lamented *Age Monthly Review*. No-one would have the gall to *review* the EB, that hallowed compendium of all human knowledge. It had taken me seven years, by which time the whole damned thing had been redesigned and I had to start again. To everyone's disbelief, I declared that the end of hard-copy encyclopedias was nigh. See, these new-fangled compact thingees were just around the corner. A single optical disk could gulp the vast text of those twenty-nine volumes, two crowded indexes, and a free dictionary, with room to spare for illustrations. EB denied this prediction vehemently: there would be no CD-ROM Britannica before the year 2000.

Well, in a sense, they were right. Although Britannica CD 2.0 is now available, for $A1,998, it's a dog.

Most people hate reading on monitors, especially if they've been doing it all day at work. But I looked forward eagerly to the instant access of computer search and hypertext links on my 486-DX2.

Alas, we're caught between past and future. One CD-ROM can't yet hold enough data to store the thousands of photos and maps that make the print EB such a rich visual source of knowledge—let alone the multimedia bells and whistles we expect today from a CD-ROM product.

Unlike Microsoft's child-oriented *Encarta*, brilliantly adapted from the rudimentary Funk and Wagnall's that sell for a few bucks apiece at K-Mart, EB has no audiovisuals. You can't hear a sound-bite of Nelson Mandela's victory speech, or watch a cheetah hurtle through the grass. At best, there's a batch of crudely tinted diagrams and charts—and its maps even lack lines of longitude and latitude. True, there's an endless gray cascade of facts-as-words, forty-four million of them, but that's why God gave us paper.

Worse than the technical limitations, Britannica CD reeks of laziness and inattention. Running under Windows 3.1, it installs an early version of Netscape, the browser designed for the Internet. The ergonomics are awful. Displays are typically cut into chunks a screen or three long. You advance with Page Down or the scroll bar at extreme right. Getting to the subsequent chunk, though, involves hauling the cursor to a "next section" button on the left of the screen, then back again for more scrolling. Why not place the button near the scroll bar? Early Netscape code restriction, I'm told. Sloppy. Indeed, the Home Page didn't even fit until I reset my screen resolution parameters, then an .INI file, not skills your average out-of-the-box buyer is likely to be at ease with. (There are probably smarter and simpler ways to do it, but I'm a writer not a computer expert.)

Worse is the brainless "hit list" of best-guesses glopping on your screen when you lodge your inquiry. It looks easy: a Query Box allows you to pose questions in ordinary English, even to sharpen those requests using Boolean operators such as ADJ, AND, NOT and so on. (So "citizen ADJ kane' whips you straight to "Citizen Kane," bypassing scads of stray citizens and all those other folks called Kane.) In practice, it's either hilarious or a nightmare, depending how rushed you are.

I asked after Sir John Kerr, Australia's former Governor General, notable for dismissing the lawfully elected government and for his tendency to lurch at the racetrack. The first hit posted was Shakespeare's Sir John Falstaff, described as "a fat, dishonest, cowardly knight who is given to drinking..." Sardonic wit is not what you expect from a machine. Alas, just a failure of the WAIS search engine. Kerr simply failed to appear. What about "Bill Hayden," a more recent incumbent? No luck. The first hit was BIRDS (they have bills, you see), followed by Hayden, Ferdinand Vandiveer. "William Hayden" didn't help.

Let's try for the world's best science fiction writer, Ursula K. Le Guin. No entry, not even a passing mention. I couldn't believe it. I tried again, by mistake typing "LeGuin," no space. It found this incorrect version, as EB's authority had made the same mistake. Logical, Captain. How about American logician

Charles Sanders Peirce? I erroneously typed "Pierce," and up it came, fearlessly taking me to the one entry where his name was misspelled. Entering "Peirce," I did find what I wanted—but a more lateral system might have put me straight to begin with.

Weirder things awaited. Consulting "History and Kinds of Logic" in the sub-section "immediate inference," I was told several times to "[see print Britannica for tabular display]." Gee, thanks.

As a fairly swift method of searching the index—fifteen or twenty seconds is typical—the disk is preferable to thumbing through three or four heavy print volumes. I'd prefer the relevant tables to pop up reliably on the monitor. Granted, there are indeed tabular displays on view. One listing Nobel Prize winners is current to 1994, but it disappears off the right-hand edge of the screen. Running the scroll-bar all the way didn't help me; the Physiology winners were left hacked in half. Maybe it's my clumsy upgraded system, but you'd hope an expensive product like this would be free of such blatant bugs.

To be fair, I've stumbled upon some cute updates. I found "ectrodactyly" which isn't in my 1985 print version; presumably, since then, it's become a sexier genetic disorder. On the other hand, using the wild card option to check out "sci* fi*" I got zip. How about "sci* fiction," then, to make it easier? Not really: it suggested (1) drum, 160 species of fishes of the family Sciaenidae, (2) gymnosperms, (3) Pratolini, Vasco, (4) Sciacca... Go figure.

Worse than technical oddities is Britannica's self-destructive meanness. Each CD comes with a manual, a brief video, plus, aargh, a dongle that you must first insert into your printer port. This odious security key is designed, I guess, to stop people pirating the database by downloading it to cheap gigabyte storage. A much better method would be to lower the CD's price to match competitors—under $100, say—and make up the difference by sheer stupendous numbers of sales. They'd sell hundreds of millions, instead of thousands. Maybe in 2001.

In 1985, I concluded: "If you can afford to buy a set, indulge yourself with a clear conscience. How often do you get a chance to buy a spare, pre-programmed brain lobe?' Today, I still feel the same way—about the print version. Forget the bogus CD-ROM. Wait a few years until EB wake up and provide decent software. Meanwhile, buy a second-hand copy of the print version, from a tenth to a quarter the price.

LIFE BEFORE WIKI: LOOKING BACK FROM NOW

Reading the Britannica.

Of all the vast changes reflected in this book, I suspect one of the largest is almost invisible to us: our ability to get answers (whether reliable or not) in an instant from the collectively created and endlessly mutated Wikipedia, and resources of knowledge, opinion, gossip, visual gallery and pornography via Google and other search engines—on your computer or smartphone, and *all of it without charge.*

In August, 2010, it was announced that the third edition of the venerable Oxford English Dictionary, in the works since 1989, would appear as a web-searchable resource. Never again those unwieldy, magisterial volumes, readable only with the enclosed magnifying glass. (And not a moment too soon!)

By much the same token, there is still an E.B., an *Encyclopedia Britannica,* but these days you access it via the web (although some of its treasures remain locked behind a paywall). I loved my desk-wide set of Britannica, had delved into it for years, as testified above in my anatomy of the back-breaking tower of paper and sturdy covers, but when I had my worldly possessions packed up to be shipped from Australia to the United States, my Britannica was consigned to the dumpster (I surmise) along with the custom-made bookshelf I'd built for it thirty years ago, because who needs to haul an enormous trove of dead knowledge halfway around the world? Who needs to waste the space to keep it handy by the desk? That's why we have computers with large monitors that can display a million colors and just about all the knowledge ever compiled, as well as (alas) all the gibberish and weirdness ever dreamed up by crackpots and the unscrupulous.

Up here in the twenty-first century, that is, where we do things differently. Let's meet in another forty or fifty years, employing whatever transcendental mode of archive and communication is then fashionable (a biochip in the brain, finally? dark energy modulations straight to the soul? immersion in the core of some Singularity god?), and do it again, shall we?

SELECTED READING

Because most of the essays in this book were written decades ago, and for popular magazines, few citations were footnoted or even sourced with anything approaching academic rigor. Rather than attempting the impossible by trying to trace all the sources (still out of the question even with marvelous search aids such as Google and Google Scholar), I offer here only a select list of the books or articles that underpin those essays.

Ardrey, Robert, *The Social Contract: a personal inquiry into the evolutionary sources of order and disorder.* New York: Atheneum Publishers, 1970.

Blackford, Russell, and Udo Schüklenk, *50 Voices of Disbelief: Why We are Atheists.* Wiley-Blackwell, 2009.

Brizendine, Louann, *The Female Brain.* Broadway, 2007.

—— *The Male Brain.* Broadway, 2010.

Broderick, Damien, "Reading the Britannica," *The Age Monthly Review*, Vol. 5, No. 8, December 1985.

—— *The Architecture Of Babel: Discourses of Literature and Science*, Melbourne University Press, 1994.

—— *Theory and Its Discontents*, Deakin University Press, 1997.

—— *The Last Mortal Generation: How Science Will Alter our Lives in the 21st Century.* Sydney, Australia: New Holland, 1999.

—— *The Spike: How Our Lives are being Transformed by Rapidly Advancing Technologies.* New York: Tor/Forge,

2001.

—— *Ferocious Minds: Polymathy and the New Enlightenment.* Borgo Press, 2005.

Bronowski, Jacob, *Science and Human Values.* Harmondsworth: Penguin, by arrangement with Hutchinson, 1964.

Carson, Rachel, *The Silent Spring.* New York: Houghton Mifflin, 1962.

Cathie, Bruce L., *The Pulse of the Universe: Harmonic 288.* New Zealand: Reed, 1978.

Colapinto, John, *As Nature Made Him: The Boy Who Was Raised As A Girl.* HarperCollins, 2000.

Comfort, Alex, *Sex in Society.* Harmondsworth: Penguin, 1964.

—— *Darwin and the Naked Lady: Discursive essays on biology and art.* New York: Braziller, 1962.

Commoner, Barry, *Science and Survival.* New York: Viking, 1966.

Conway, Ronald, *The Great Australian Stupor.* Sun Books, 1971.

Dawkins, Richard, *The God Delusion.* Mariner Books, 2008.

Dennett, Daniel, *Breaking the Spell: Religion as a Natural Phenomenon.* Viking, 2006.

Dickinson, Emily, in "Emily Dickinson's Letters" by Thomas Wentworth Higginson, *Atlantic Monthly,* October, 1891, cited http://www.earlywomenmasters.net/essays/authors/higginson/twh_dickinson6.html.

Dobson, Geoffrey P., *A Chaos of Delight: Science, Religion and Myth and the Shaping of Western Thought,* Equinox, 2005.

Dooley, Thomas, *The Night They Burned The Mountain.* New York: Farrar Straus & Giroux, 1960.

Eliot, Lise, *Pink Brain, Blue Brain: How Small Differences Grow into Troublesome Gaps and What We Can Do About It.* New York: Houghton Mifflin Harcourt, 2009.

Ellis, John M., *Against Deconstruction,* Princeton University Press, 1990.

Fine, Cordelia, *Delusions of Gender: How Our Minds, Society, and Neurosexism Create Difference.* W. W. Norton & Company, 2010.

Hart, Kevin, *The Trespass of the Sign: Deconstruction, Theology and Philosophy.* Cambridge University Press, 1989.

Harris, Sam, *Letter to a Christian Nation.* New York: Knopf, 2006.

Hartley, L. P., *The Go-Between.* London: Hamish Hamilton, 1953.

Hawking, Stephen, and Leonard Mlodinow, *The Grand Design.* New York: Bantam Books/Random House, 2010.

Holroyd, Stuart, *Psi and the Consciousness Explosion.* The Bodley Head, 1977.

Hutt, Corinne, *Males and Females*, Harmondsworth: Penguin, 1972.

Huxley, Aldous, *Brave New World.* Chatto&Windus, 1932.

—— *Island.* [1962] Harmondsworth: Penguin, 1964.

Hynek, J. Allen, *The Hynek UFO Report.* New York: Dell, 1977.

Isaacs, Alan, *The Survival of God in the Scientific Age.* Harmondsworth: Penguin, 1966.

Jacobs, David M., *The UFO Controversy in America.* Indiana University Press, 1975.

Kean, Leslie, *UFOs: Generals, Pilots and Government Officials Go On the Record.* Crown, 2010.

Klass, Philip J., *UFOs Explained.* New York: Vintage Books, 1976.

Koestler, Arthur, *Darkness at Noon.* London: Cape, 1940.

—— *The Sleepwalkers: A History of Man's Changing Vision of the Universe.* New York : Macmillan, 1959.

—— *The Lotus and the Robot.* Hutchinson: London, 1960.

—— *The Act of Creation.* Hutchinson: London, 1964.

—— *The Ghost in the Machine.* Hutchinson: London, 1967.

Laing, R. D., *The Divided Self.* Harmondsworth: Penguin, 1965.

—— *The Politics of Experience and the Bird of Paradise.* Harmondsworth: Penguin, 1967.

—— *Knots.* Harmondsworth: Penguin, 1970.

—— *Wisdom, madness, and folly: the making of a psychiatrist.* New York : McGraw-Hill, 1985.

Levy, David, *Love and Sex With Robots: The Evolution of Human-Robot Relationships.* New York: Harper Perennial, 2008.

Livingston, Paisely, *Literary Knowledge: Humanistic Inquiry and the Philosophy of Science.* Ithaca and London: Cornell University Press, 1988.

Mailer, Norman, *The Presidential Papers.* New York: Putnam, 1963.

Marcuse, Herbert, *Eros and Civilization: A Philosophical Inquiry into Freud.* Boston, Beacon Press, 1955.

—— *Soviet Marxism.* Columbia University Press, 1958.

—— *One Dimensional Man.* Boston, Beacon Press, 1964.

Mead, Margaret, *Male and Female.* [1949] Harmondsworth: Penguin, 1964.

Pirsig, Robert, *Zen and the Art of Motorcycle Maintenance.* New York: Morrow, 1974.

Pohl, Frederik, "Day Million." *Rogue,* Feb-Mar, 1966.

Pustay, John S., *Counterinsurgency Warfare.* The Free Press: MacMillan Inc, 1965.

Robinson, Bishop John A. T., *Honest to God.* SCM Press, 1963.

Skinner, B. F., *Walden II.* Hackett, 1948.

Stenger, Victor J., *The Comprehensible Cosmos: Where Do the Laws of Physics Come From?* Prometheus, 2006.

—— *God: The Failed Hypothesis: How Science Shows That God Does Not Exist,* Prometheus, 2007.

Sullerot, Evelyne, *Woman, Society and Change.* London: Weidenfeld and Nicolson, 1971.

Targ, Russell, and Harold Puthoff, *Mind Reach.* London: Jonathan Cape, 1977.

Taylor, John G., *The Shape of Minds to Come.* London: Michael Joseph, 1971.

Toffler, Alvin, *Future Shock.* New York: Random House, 1970.

Warner, Denis, *The Last Confucian: Vietnam, South-East Asia, and the West.* Harmondsworth: Penguin, 1964.

Watts, Alan, *Psychotherapy East and West.* New York: New American Library, 1963.

Wilson, John, *Logic and sexual morality,* Harmondsworth: Penguin, 1965.

ABOUT THE AUTHOR

DAMIEN BRODERICK, Ph.D., always wanted to be Isaac Asimov, but so far has only got about a fifth of the way. A former journalist and critical theorist, he has published numerous science fiction novels and short stories, books about literary theory and postmodernism, polymathy, the science versus humanities gulf, the impending technological singularity, prospects for radical life extension, and research parapsychology, and has edited anthologies of science fiction and its criticism, and about the Year One Million. He has won prizes ranging from the Ditmar and Aurealis to the 2005 Distinguished Scholarship Award from the International Association for the Fantastic in the Arts, and the A. Bertram Chandler Award in 2010. To match the late Dr. Asimov's record, however, he will have to keep publishing books for at least the next 200 years.